Researching Creative Learning

It is a common ambition in society and government to make young people more creative. These aspirations are motivated by two key concerns: to make experience at school more exciting, relevant, challenging and dynamic; and to ensure that young people are fit and able to leave education and contribute to the creative economy that will underpin growth in the twenty-first century.

Transforming these common aspirations into informed practice is not easy. It can mean making many changes:

- turning classrooms into more exciting places;
- introducing more thoughtful challenges into the curriculum;
- making teachers into different kinds of instructors;
- finding more authentic assessment processes;
- putting young people's voices at the heart of learning.

There are programmes, projects and initiatives that have consistently attempted to offer such change and transformation. The UK programme Creative Partnerships is the largest of these, but there are significant initiatives in many other parts of the world today, including France, Norway, Canada and the US. This book not only draws on this body of expertise but also consolidates it, making it the first methodological text to explore creativity.

Creative teaching and learning is often used as a site for research and action research, and this volume is intended to act as a textbook for this range of courses and initiatives. The book will be a key text for research in creative teaching and learning and is specifically directed at ITE, CPD, Masters and doctoral students.

Pat Thomson is Professor of Education at the University of Nottingham, UK, an Adjunct Professor at the University of South Australia and a Visiting Professor at Deakin University, Australia.

Julian Sefton-Green is an independent consultant and researcher working in education and the cultural and creative industries. He is Special Professor of Education at the University of Nottingham, UK.

Researching Creative Learning

Methods and issues

Edited by Pat Thomson
and Julian Sefton-Green

Routledge
Taylor & Francis Group

LONDON AND NEW YORK

First edition published 2011
by Routledge
2 Park Square, Milton Park, Abingdon, Oxon, OX14 4RN

Simultaneously published in the USA and Canada
by Routledge
270 Madison Avenue, New York, NY 10016

Routledge is an imprint of the Taylor & Francis Group, an informa business

Typeset in Galliard
by Keystroke, Station Road, Codsall, Wolverhampton
Printed and bound in Great Britain
by TJ International Ltd, Padstow, Cornwall

British Library Cataloguing in Publication Data
A catalogue record for this book is available from the British Library

Library of Congress Cataloging-in-Publication Data
Thomson, Pat, 1948–
Researching creative learning : methods and issues / Pat Thomson and
Julian Sefton-Green.
p. cm.
Includes bibliographical references.
1. Creative teaching–Research. 2. Creative ability–Research.
I. Sefton-Green, Julian. II. Title.
LB1025.3T535 2011
370.15′7072–dc22
2010021480

ISBN13: 978–0–415–54884–7 (hbk)
ISBN13: 978–0–415–54885–4 (pbk)
ISBN13: 978–0–203–83894–5 (ebk)

Contents

Contributors

Selçuk Acar received his BA from Bogaziçi University and MA from Istanbul University, Turkey. He is currently a doctoral student at the University of Georgia, studying the measurement of creativity and specifically divergent thinking. He has contributed several chapters to the revised edition of the *Encyclopedia of Creativity* (Academic Press), which is due to appear in late 2010.

Sara Bragg is a Research Councils UK Academic Fellow in Child and Youth Studies at the Open University, UK, and previously worked at the University of Sussex and the Centre for the Study of Children, Youth and Media at the Institute of Education, London. Her research and publications address sexualization, youth media cultures and consumption, education and participation, and 'creative' research methods.

Nur Çayırdağ received her BA and MA degree in counselling psychology in Turkey. Her most recent article appears in the revised edition of the *Encyclopedia of Creativity*. She is a member of American Counseling Association and is working towards her Masters at the University of Georgia, Athens.

John Churchley is an Assistant Superintendent for the Kamloops/Thompson school district in British Columbia, Canada. He has taught elementary and high school music, conducted community and university choirs, and has worked as a fine arts curriculum consultant and as a school and district administrator. He was the founding principal of Beattie School of the Arts in Kamloops, British Columbia.

Tony Cotton is Head of Initial Teacher Education and Assessment, Learning and Teaching at Leeds Metropolitan University, UK. His professional background is as a mathematics teacher. He has carried out a range of evaluative projects in the past ten years, ranging from a large Department for Education and Skills-funded evaluation of the Intensified Support Programme in 'underachieving' primary schools to evaluations of specific projects at local authority level.

Shane Dawson is the Director of Instructional Support and Information Technology with the Faculty of Arts, University of British Columbia, Canada. His research activities centre on the application of interaction data derived from student online engagements to inform teaching and learning practice. He is currently investigating real-time social network visualization tools.

Christine Hall is a Professor in the School of Education at the University of Nottingham, UK. A former English teacher in schools, she has been involved in initial teacher education and the professional development of teachers for many years. She has written on issues concerning English teaching, literacy, children's literature and children's reading choices. Currently, her research is into the teaching of the arts, and the pedagogies and policies that promote inclusion and creativity.

Bob Jeffrey is a Senior Research Fellow at The Open University in the UK. Since 1992, he has researched, with Professors Peter Woods and Geoff Troman, the work of primary teachers. Bob is co-founder of the journal *Ethnography and Education* and now edits it, co-organizes an annual ethnography conference in Oxford, and co-edits a book series with Tufnell Press. He is Link Co-ordinator of the ECER Ethnography Network (www.ethnographyandeducation.org).

Ken Jones is Professor of Education at Goldsmiths, University of London. His research focuses on two areas: the first is policy, and its contestation (*Schooling in Western Europe: the new order and its adversaries*, 2008); the second is the (re)emergence and development of 'creativity' as a theme in educational and cultural policy. Recent work includes the literature review *Culture and creative learning* (Arts Council England, 2009).

Erica McWilliam is an Education Futurist at the Brisbane Girls Grammar School, and is also an Adjunct Professor and co-leader of the Creative Workforce Program in the Australian Research Council Centre of Excellence for Creative Industries and Innovation, based at the Queensland University of Technology, Australia. Her most recent book is *The creative workforce: How to launch young people into high-flying futures* (UNSW Press, Sydney, 2008).

David Parker is strategic lead on research and evaluation for Creativity, Culture & Education (CCE), a national organization in the UK which aims to transform the lives of children and families by harnessing the potential of creative learning and cultural opportunity to enhance their aspirations, achievements and skills, and is responsible for generating key learning from its programmes by managing a series of externally led, objective research and evaluation programmes. Previously, David was Head of Research at the British Film Institute, where he took a particular interest in the uses of moving image media in the teaching and learning of literacy.

Emily Pringle trained originally as a painter. She has worked for several years in the field of creative and cultural learning as an artist educator, a gallery curator and, more recently, as a researcher and writer. Her particular interest (and the focus for her PhD) is in the relationship between artistic practice and pedagogy and the potential for artist-led creative learning. She is currently Head of Learning Practice, Research and Policy at the Tate Gallery, London.

Mark A. Runco is the Torrance Professor of Creative Studies and the Director of the Torrance Creativity Center at the University of Georgia at Athens. He has been Senior Editor of the *Creativity Research Journal* since its founding in 1989 and is currently co-editing the second edition of the *Encyclopedia of creativity* (Academic Press). He received a Lifetime Achievement Award from the National Association for Gifted Children and is a Fellow in the American Psychological Association.

Naranee Ruthra-Rajan is the Research Manager for Creativity, Culture & Education. She has worked on the monitoring, evaluation and research of the Creative Partnerships initiative and the CCE Literature Review Series since 2004.

Julian Sefton-Green is an independent consultant and researcher working in education and the cultural and creative industries. He is a Special Professor of Education at the University of Nottingham, UK, and an Adjunct Associate Research Professor at the University of South Australia. He has researched and written widely on many aspects of media education, new technologies and informal learning.

Elisabeth 'Lissa' Soep is Research Director and Senior Producer at Youth Radio–Youth Media International, a youth-driven production company based in Oakland, CA, with bureaux and partners in every region of the United States and around the world. Her new book, *Drop that knowledge: Youth radio stories* (with Vivian Chávez), examines how youth media production can reorganize literacy, pedagogy and justice work.

Malcolm Swan is Professor of Mathematics Education and Director of the Centre for Research in Mathematics Education in the School of Education at the University of Nottingham, UK. Malcolm has been particularly concerned with the design of classroom experiences that impact the beliefs and practices of mathematics teachers. This has led to the development of resources that have been distributed to schools and post-16 colleges nationally and internationally. Malcolm is on the executive committee of the International Society for Design and Development in Education (www.isdde.org).

Jennifer Pei-Ling Tan is a Global Research Manager at the International Baccalaureate. Previously, she was a Research Fellow at the ARC Centre of Excellence for Creative Industries and Innovation (CCI) at Queensland University of Technology, Australia. Her research focuses on creative literacies and the adoption and diffusion of innovative learning technologies in formal and informal learning environments.

Pat Thomson is Professor of Education in the School of Education at the University of Nottingham, UK, an Adjunct Professor at the University of South Australia and Special Professor at Deakin University (Australia). She is an editor of the international journal *Education Action Research* (Taylor & Francis). She is a former headteacher in disadvantaged schools in South Australia. Her research now focuses on the arts, creativity and school change, the work of school leaders, and doctoral education.

Geoff Troman is Professor of Education at Froebel College, School of Education, Roehampton University, UK. He is also Visiting Professor at the University of Boras, Sweden. He was Director of the Economic and Social Research Council-funded project Primary Teacher Identity, Commitment and Career in Performative Cultures (PTICC) from 2005 to 2007. Geoff is foundation editor (with Bob Jeffrey, The Open University; Geoffrey Walford, University of Oxford; and Tuula Gordon, University of Helsinki) of the international journal *Ethnography and Education* (Taylor & Francis).

Acknowledgements

We need to thank some people for their support and assistance during the production of this book. Our editor, Philip Mudd, was enthusiastic and helpful – as always – and efficiently supported by the Routledge editorial and production team.

Uta Feinstein provided secretarial support as we solicited material from prospective authors. We want to extend our thanks to the authors in the book, who generally dealt with our naggings and requests for changes promptly and generously. We thank the following for their kind permission to use their photographs: 'Surprised boy with tube' – Lillian De Lissa Nursery and Belgravia Children's Centre, Birmingham; 'Tree-house and upside-down girl' – Leighswood Primary School, Walsall; 'Feet in yellow ribbons' – MUF architecture, art, London. We also want to put on record our regard for the English arts initiative Creative Partnerships (CP), without which we would not have had the impetus and context for the book, and our gratitude for the support by Creativity, Culture & Education for Julian to work on this project. We think English schools have been the better for the singular emphasis CP has placed on creative learning.

Chapter 1

Introduction

Pat Thomson and Julian Sefton-Green

It would appear we live in creative times. As political aspiration, as economic driver, as a manifesto for school reform and curriculum change, the desire for creativity can be found across the developed world in policy pronouncements and academic research. But creativity – in an educational context – can mean many things: turning classrooms into more exciting experiences, curriculum into more thoughtful challenges, teachers into different kinds of instructors, assessment into more authentic processes and putting young people's voice at the heart of learning. In general, these aspirations are motivated by two key concerns: to make experience at school more exciting, relevant, challenging and dynamic; and ensuring that young people are able and fit to leave education able to contribute to the creative economy which will underpin growth in the twenty-first century.

Transforming these common aspirations into informed practice is not easy. Yet there are programmes, projects and initiatives that have consistently attempted to offer change and transformation. We have both been involved with the English programme Creative Partnerships (www.creative-partnerships.com), which is the largest of these projects, but there are significant initiatives in other parts of the world including France, Norway, Canada, Australia and the US.

This geographical eclecticism is matched by the wide range of people who are interested in forms of creative learning, from teachers and other educationalists to policy advisers and politicians. As we will discuss, the ambivalence of the concept of creative learning makes it seem 'polyvalent' and thus useful to all of these different constituencies. But what counts as evidence of creative learning, how effective initiatives might be and what difference the concept makes both in practice and in terms of what it makes possible in education are also questions addressed in this book.

All creativity initiatives struggle to understand what they do, and how they might become more informed and effective. Traditionally, creativity has been the domain of psychology, but research in that field builds on its own disciplinary paradigms and methods – some of which do not quite capture how these initiatives have impacted in real schools and classrooms around the world. For this reason, Creative Partnerships has made a significant investment in research and has funded and supported schools, teachers and academics to grapple with the practices of inquiry into creative learning and school change. As a result of this initiative, and smaller programmes with similar aims, there is a growing body of expertise in researching creativity, as well as a significant number of new and experienced educators who wish to investigate it.

Creative teaching and learning is often used as a site for research and action research, and this volume is intended to act as a textbook for a range of courses and initiatives exploring these issues. Additionally, in the current climate, creative learning research often offers itself as a form of advocacy and frequently engages with understanding the new and the innovative or different practices. This book aims to offer researchers with aspirations to work in this field access to both a range of methods and ways of making sense of findings in order to help cement the integrity of creative learning as a research field. This isn't the same thing as 'creative research'; it would be hubris to suggest that some methods or theories are in and of themselves more (or less) creative than others. However, we do suggest that the kinds of approaches outlined in this book and the methods they draw on offer a productive, confident and disciplined way of researching creative learning. We also hope that the kinds of findings described here act as a way of drawing a 'line in the sand' to enable the field to develop maturity and sophistication, rather than reinventing itself repetitively with each initiative – a common lament around the world.

One peculiarity of our location within developments in the UK means that, unlike our colleagues in some other countries, we do not solely equate creative learning with the arts. While it is the case that creative learning can and does occur in the arts, there can equally be a preponderance of routine and transmission learning in arts 'subjects'. Our view is that there are aspects of all domains of knowledge that can be constructed creatively.

We therefore begin by canvassing what is meant by the term 'creative learning' and then go on to consider what might be distinctive about researching it. We then introduce the chapters in the book, showing how they each build a corpus of knowledge not only about creative learning but also about associated research practices.

What is creative learning?

When educators talk about creative learning, they generally mean teaching that allows students to use their imaginations, have ideas, generate multiple possible solutions to problems, communicate in a variety of media and in general 'think outside the box'. They may also mean practices in which children and young people show that they have the capacities to assess and improve work, sustain effort on a project for a long period of time, exceed what they thought was possible and work well with others to combine ideas and approaches. Some may extend the notion to include projects and approaches that allow young people to apply their creativity through making choices about what and how they will learn, negotiating about curriculum and involvement in generating possibilities for and making decisions about school priorities and directions.

But while there may be commonalities about what creative learning looks like as, and in, students' behaviours, there may also be profound differences. The notion of creativity may be associated with particular subjects, such as those that go under the umbrella term of the arts, in which generating new, odd and interesting perspectives on familiar topics is valued and rewarded. Or it may be seen as integral to science, where habits of transforming curiosity into hypotheses have a long history. Or it may be connected to business and the goal of schooling students to have strongly entrepreneurial dispositions and capacities. These interpretations – and many more – are all possible and legitimate understandings of creativity and creative learning.

Generating lists of potential meanings is not merely a rhetorical exercise, and we suggest that it is an essential part of researching creative learning. But before we elaborate on this point, we want to address some of the histories that underpin the various notions of creative learning and the views of the child and the teacher, classroom and school that they imply.

As we will argue, although the term 'creative learning' may be new and fashionable, it draws on older and more entrenched sets of values that have helped give it legitimacy and that frame its current meaning (see *The Routledge International Handbook of Creative Learning*). Here we trace the origins of the concept in progressive education, through a contemporary interest in creativity, ending with a notion of a particular type of learner and learning.

Childhood, progressivism and creativity

At the same time as children in Western nation-states were progressively removed from workplaces and expected instead to be formally educated, a body of theories about children was constructed (Aries, 1962). These ways of understanding children were, up to World War II, predominantly developed through the emergent disciplines of psychology and educational psychology and pedagogy, and in philosophy. Theories of child development posited linear progressions from a totally sensory state of knowing nothing to an adult state of responsibility and complete comprehension. Competing views of learning, notably behaviourist approaches (e.g. Skinner, 1968), vied with play-based approaches as the most effective means of children learning to become mature and educated/learn-ed. Education was variously seen as: (1) needing to be highly child-centred and led by child interests (Dewey, 1897, 1934; Dewey & Dewey, 1915); (2) as a process through which children could construct knowledge under adult guidance (Vygotsky, 1978); or (3) as a system in which children's capacities and accomplishments could be measured and therefore rationally developed over time through various levels and phases (Roid, 2003; Tyler, 1949).

In Britain, the twentieth century saw the gradual development of a collection of ways of thinking about and doing school. These began as isolated experiments – 'free' schools (e.g. Neill, 1918), the introduction of methods influenced by Maria Montessori (www. montessori.edu), the Dalton plan (www.daltoninternational.org/daltoneducation.html), eurhythmics (see www.dalcroze.org.au/eurythmics.html) – but over time these coalesced into a constellation of practices that we now call 'progressivism' (Grosvenor & Myers, 2006; Labaree, 2005; Sliwka, 2008). Educational historian Peter Cunningham (1988, p. 13) suggests that this was not so much a theory as a set of

> shared common themes; a reduction in the traditional authoritarianism of the teacher, alternatives to the dominant pedagogical forms of the class lesson, removal of harsh punishments and unnecessary drill and discipline, with a preference for self-government by pupils, dissolution of the formal timetable, and a shift in curriculum emphasis from the routine of the 3Rs to more creative and expressive activities.

Progressive early childhood and primary schooling drew on child-centred and constructivist knowledge traditions and focused on the provision of learning environments in which children were able to explore material and imaginative worlds (e.g. de Lissa, 1949); this was, however, accompanied by highly structured instruction such as reading schemes intended to move children through predetermined stages. There was an attempt to ensure 'balance' between more open and more structured approaches. Creativity was to be exercised and developed through play-based and investigation-based activities but also through a new emphasis on curriculum that was deemed 'creative', most often as the subjects of art, movement, music and creative writing. From the 1920s onwards, children were seen as 'naïve' artists in their own right, and their work exhibited (White, 2005).

The ways in which various threads of thinking about children, their learning and their creative capacities came together as a progressive pedagogical approach can be seen in the extended passage in the following box, from Christian Schiller, a pioneering British progressive primary educator.

Christian Schiller discusses creative learning

During the past twenty-odd years the pathetic imitations in chalk or paint of 'an orange', 'a whip', 'teacher's bag', have become in so many infant schools vivid pictures, where the sure use of colour and pattern is only less remarkable than the radiant imagination which has conceived the whole. How has this change come about in a single generation?

In those schools known to me where the paintings are most remarkable as expressions of the individual imagination of each child, it happens that the children come from poor homes. In no case have the teachers much, if any, skill in painting. But in every case there is in every classroom a certain climate, which may be found in all schools where painting flourishes.

It is a climate in which painting is an interesting thing to do. You paint what you want to paint, how you want to paint it: on the floor, in the passage, on a small or very large piece of paper, with a large or fine brush, or both, and with many colours or few. It is a climate in which teacher is interested in you painting, rather than in how or what you paint, and knows how to come without being called when you need help, but not otherwise.

It is a climate in which painting is a delightful but serious business. There are no school painting rules, but paint has its own rules; dirty brushes spoil the colours, colours run if they touch when wet, and so on. It is a climate in which experience reveals the way of using paint; in which each child sees his birth-gift of good taste to accept this or reject that; in which each child assumes the discipline of dealing well with the material.

This is the climate in which the imagination thrives; in which it thrives like a flower and not like a weed. The imagination borders with phantasy, and is kept within its rightful territory only by that discipline which distinguishes the artist from the lunatic.

In this climate Mary's imagination grows, and at the same time she assumes the discipline of respect for the material which is the nature of creative work. . . .

I have described the climate in which painting thrived. The imagination will thrive in such a climate not only when dealing with paint, but with words, with movement, and also with people, with living beings.

Young children deal with all their material, living as well as still, not as technicians but in the mode of the artist. In a climate in which the imagination thrives young children see their world of living beings as a number of individual persons, each interesting to explore, to experience, to understand, to use with the imagination. And with persons, as with paint, they assume the discipline of respect for the material. For young children, living is not a technique: it is an art.

Christian Schiller, June 1948 (Griffin-Beale, 1979, pp. 26–27)

This description of creative learning is one that would not be unfamiliar to many educators today. We have the child exhibiting instinctive curiosity and natural talent, a desire for self-expression and the capacity to learn not only the craft skills associated with artistic traditions, but also at the same time the practice of self-discipline. The teacher has provided the necessary materials, opportunities and encouragement, and thereafter, through close observation, is able to support and intervene at the appropriate times. The teacher and the schools in which this pedagogical approach is used are cast as pioneers, models from whom other schools might learn. But we might also note that this is a highly individualized mode of creative learning. Schiller and others of his ilk have been criticized for their unproblematic assumptions about social contexts, teachers' capacities and institutional constraints. Later, progressive educators noted that the tendency to teach about creative learning/teaching through anecdote also meant that there was little theorization about pedagogy, and a reliance on normative dogma delivered charismatically (Cunningham, 1988).

Progressive pedagogies also penetrated other areas of the school curriculum besides the arts, notably through a nature study-based approach to science, a 'real-world' take on social science, 'process' approaches to writing, and the development of integrated approaches to 'topics', 'themes' and 'projects'.

In Britain, the progressive view of education, with its naturally curious child exploring her or his world and engaging in creatively expressing themselves in a range of media and genres, was consolidated in the Plowden Report of the mid-1960s (see www.education england.org.ukdocuments/plowden). Critics saw progressivism as a somewhat flabby peda-gogical approach. It was ridiculed by conservatives for its lack of attention to tradition and the teaching of the canon; neglect of 'the basics'; alleged excesses of libertarianism in which teachers allowed children to do what they pleased when they pleased; lack of standards; and an inequitable distribution of equal opportunity to succeed in a meritocratic system. Some of these views were shared by those from the political left, who noted that pro-gressivism failed to deliver socially just outcomes and, through its individualized approach, prevented children from learning the ways in which the world was economically, socially and politically inequitable (Jones, 2003). But despite the introduction in the 1980s of tighter measures to control schools – a national curriculum, decentralized school management, centrally developed standards for teaching and inspection, and performance management systems (see Ball, 2008; Gewirtz, 2002; Tomlinson, 2001; Whitty, Power, & Halpin, 1998) – and regulation of the kinds of pedagogies in use in British primary schools, a recognizable set of progressive practices have remained both in practice and as espoused school vision or mission statements (Jeffrey & Woods, 2009; Vulliamy & Webb, 2006).

New times, new creativities

While some of reasons for the survival of these older sets of values may derive from the formation of teachers themselves, the current era has introduced a new set of values for creativity and their role in education. We identify two key drivers: an attention to applied or instrumental uses of the arts, and a focus on the creative (or knowledge) economy. The 1982 Gulbenkian Report into the arts (Robinson, 1982) began the process of rationalizing the study of the arts not so much from a cultural perspective or even from an interest in aesthetics, but as a site for the learning of a wider skill set including team work, negotiating, risk-taking and self-presentation through performance. Harland's series of studies of the arts in schools (Harland, Kinder, & Hartley, 1995; Harland et al., 2000, 2005) explored the impacts of learning in and through the arts in terms of wider learning, and although neither of these benchmark studies or sets of studies was motivated by the idea of justifying the arts from wider social and pedagogic perspectives, they point to the ways in which the arts start becoming a site for the investigation of more generic forms of 'authentic' learning.

Creativity thus emerges out of the perspective as an outcome of arts education, and one that is explicitly developed by the practices which comprise good arts education.

At the same time, the 1990s saw a socio-political interest in the production of non-material goods, especially the commodification of knowledge (Poster, 1990) and the valorization of the intellectual property derived from technological growth – especially the internet – in both private and public spheres (Benkler, 2007; Castells, 1996, 1997, 1998). Creativity became fetishized in the Zeitgeist (Buckingham & Jones, 2001) as the driver for the economy (Department for Culture, Media and Sport [DCMS], 1998). Emblematic texts such as *The creative age* (Bentley & Seltzer, 1999) argue that the education system needs to reform so as to generate productive citizens who are flexible, creative and can operate entrepreneurially and imaginatively in the new weightless economy (Banaji & Burn, 2007).

In England, these two trends – a concern with instrumental outcomes from arts learning processes and a fascination with changing needs of Britain's economy – came together in a high-status, highly publicized report chaired by Ken Robinson, known as the NACCCE Report (National Advisory Committee on Creative and Cultural Education [NACCCE], 1999). It was supported by the Ministries of both Culture and Education, itself emblematic of a shift in attitudes, and argued that creativity should be made central to learning as part of a wider reform of schooling (Jones, 2009). Creativity, in this report, was given a democratic and individualistic capability slant: it was something to be realized in all of us rather than as the property of an exceptional few (Craft, Jeffrey, & Leibling, 2001; Cropley, 2001; Grainger, Gooch, & Lambirth, 2005).

In institutional terms, the NACCCE Report gave birth to the initiative Creative Partnerships (CP). Unusual in terms of international comparison, on account of its scale and profile, CP brokered partnerships with artists and schools to support a wider range of creativity learning initiatives at all levels of the curriculum, from one-off arts projects to whole-school change programmes. While this model of working can be found in many parts of the world, CP developed opportunities for creative learning in an effort to programmatize this turn towards the creative as a distinctively contemporary set of values for schools.

Recent research (Thomson, Jones, & Hall, 2009) which examined the ways in which English schools were taking up the offer made through Creative Partnerships suggested that

[h]eads and their staffs generally reported:

- a rejection of many of the elements of the technicist and rational mode of curriculum in which the teacher is 'deliverer', the students are passive learners divided on the basis of ability/performance and there are absolute, permanently boundaried subjects, and
- the adoption of elements of a 'practical' approach to curriculum where the strongest students are encouraged to go beyond the basics, but where there is a strong emphasis on vocational and life 'skills' and 'self esteem', and/or
- the adoption of elements of a 'progressive' approach in which the teacher is a facilitator and students are unique individuals who are encouraged to learn through problem solving, collaborative work and extensions of their own experiences and interests.

(after Cooper & White, 2004, p. 21)

Related progressive trajectories and trends can be observed in other parts of the world, for example in the moves in Australia to middle schooling (Carrington, 2006) and productive pedagogies (Hayes, Mills, Christie, & Lingard, 2005; Lingard, Christie, Hayes, & Mills, 2003) and in the Coalition of Essential Schools (Sizer, 1985, 1996; Wasley, 1994; Wasley, Hampel, & Clark, 1997) and arts-initiated reform (Noblit, Dickson, Wilson, & McKinney, 2009) in the US.

Creative subjects

The final piece in this jigsaw derives from studies of changing subjectivities and analysis of how the person of the learner is constructed through discourses, especially those deriving from institutional power relations. Developing in some respects out of the child-centredness of progressivism, a different view of children emerged in the last half of the twentieth century. Associated with the children's rights movement and with the body of knowledge dubbed 'the new sociology of childhood' (James, Jenks, & Prout, 1998), previous views of children as 'becomings' were replaced with the notion of children as 'beings' in their own right (Qvortrup, Bardy, Sigritta, & Wintersberger, 1994). Rather than as immature adults needing guidance, children are seen as able to speak for themselves, to have particular perspectives that they are capable of articulating for themselves. Importantly, this view of the child as an actor capable of being witness to his or her own life encompasses the notion that children have a right to have their views heard, taken seriously and acted on – including in research projects. Childhood itself is also seen to have changed, with the social, political, cultural and technological conditions that are commonly lumped together as 'globalization', being seen as making a profound difference in the way children and young people can live their lives (Buckingham, 2000; Holloway & Valentine, 2000; Sefton-Green, 1998; Steinberg & Kincheloe, 1997).

We suggest that the idea of the creative learner meshes well with this changing attitude towards the child-subject. This view of the child is highly complementary with progressive pedagogical methods. In contemporary versions of creative learning in schools, there is often a blend of aspects of progressive pedagogy combined with practices that allow students not only to explore and express their concerns but also to have a say in the way in which learning occurs (Bragg, Manchester, & Faulkner, 2009). Indeed, some argue that one of the major contributions of creative learning, apart from allowing more opportunities for pupils to express their views, has been to open up a range of new media and genres through which youthful voice(s) can be expressed and new audiences to whom they can speak (Jones & Hall, 2009).

Creative learning, then, can stand for a type of learner, a mode of pedagogy, a form of institutional organization, an ideological rallying cry or simply as an attempt to be different. We do not suggest that one meaning should dominate, nor do we think that many of the authors who have contributed to this volume are firm believers in a single attribution. Researching creative learning does of course rest on a definition of the object of research, but we suggest that many contributors represented here are equally interested in how the research process plays its part in co-constructing the topic under review. Building on this history of influences, the next section lays out some of these difficulties in more detail.

Researching creative learning

Researching creative learning is clearly a subset of researching learning. But it is also located within the creativity research field. It thus draws on both, and seeks to make a contribution to both fields of inquiry. As well, it must be situated epistemologically – that is, within a tradition of knowledge production.

In general, researchers working on creative learning share some constructivist understandings: they believe, for example, that children and young people construct knowledge through creative activity, and researchers do so as well. They start with the view that there is not a set of 'facts' about creative learning out there waiting to be found and documented. Rather, it is through the research process and engagement with 'data' that they will bring new understandings into being (Crotty, 1998; Freebody, 2003; Pring, 2000). In addition, the vast majority of researchers in the creative learning field operate from a position that is somewhat critical of conventional modes of pedagogy.[1] Furthermore, while it is almost impossible for researchers in education to be unaware of poststructuralism and its concerns for particularity, situatedness and provisionality (Gallagher, 2008; Haraway, 1988; Lather, 2007), the writers in this volume are variously informed by these kinds of understandings, as can be seen in the ways that they describe their projects and their 'findings'.

Despite these epistemological differences, all researchers in this volume shared a common task when they began their research. They had to move from a generalized notion of creative learning as practice, such as those found above, to a more nuanced understanding that could be researched. This is more complex than simply a question of using or developing different methods appropriate to different situations: it is also a question of conceptualizing the object of research in the first place.

If teachers hold that creative learning is about 'thinking outside the box' but also bring to it the view that only a chosen few can be creative (creative genius), and that this is somehow linked to extraordinary abilities (creativity and cognition), they will have an approach to creative learning that is grounded in the identification of particular gifted and talented young people and the subsequent provision for them of specialized separate opportunities and programmes. If, on the other hand, teachers hold to the view that creative learning is about having ideas and sustaining effort over a long period of time, and their point of reference is the changed demands of knowledge economies (creativity as an economic imperative), then they and their schools may well initiate programmes in which students are engaged in projects that foster longer-term relationships with businesses and local leaders and give them opportunities to take on 'real-world' challenges that require business-like initiative and behaviours.

These potential differences in the ways in which creative learning can be understood have major implications for researchers. These stem not only from the different ways in which creativity can be understood but also from the nature of contemporary communities, schools and teachers. Despite the production of single statements of philosophy, schools are organizations that are inherently diverse, and there will be many views of creativity that are held, not just those that are officially endorsed. One or more may be dominant, and some may be very marginalized. Nevertheless, all are important. Because teaching and learning is a co-construction which occurs continually, in all of the formal and informal locations that a school has to offer, there will be many enacted and articulated approaches to creative learning. These versions of creative learning may not be consistent, or congruent. Indeed, individuals themselves may hold several views of learning and pedagogies which they suture together as a repertoire of professional practice. The kinds of creative learning that a teacher might offer may well shift depending on the situation in which they seek to apply it. It may also change over time in the light of experience, events or changed contexts.

This lack of homogeneity means that researchers have to do more than think about the organization of their fieldwork in community, schools and classrooms, the techniques they will apply, the tools they will use and the ethical dilemmas they may face. Some who study contemporary research fieldwork (Law, 2004; Rabinow, 2008) suggest that it is now imperative for researchers to focus on their own naming and framing practices – categorizations – at the same time as they focus on how participants in their studies name and frame their everyday worlds. This is more than reflexivity as a simple act that occurs before fieldwork begins: it is a continual process of self-interrogation throughout the research process and all of its messiness.

However, just like communities, schools and classrooms, the research community is also multiple and diverse, situated in particular disciplinary traditions and conventions as well as locations, is continually changing and has multiple ways in which its purposes and practices can be understood. The chapters in this book are deliberately reflective of some of these differences. As editors, we think it is helpful therefore to read the chapters not simply for what they might tell us about creative learning but also for what they might tell us about the extant and emergent practices of researching creative learning. We suggest that readers might like to consider some of the following questions when approaching the chapters in this book:

- How have the researchers named and framed the creative learning they are researching?
- What does it mean to think about creative learning in this way? What practices does it encourage and what kinds of practices are backgrounded/ignored? What other ways of thinking about creative learning might be possible in this situation?
- What set of cultural practices, relationships, events, things and systems are brought to this research? How has this 'assemblage' worked to produce this way of thinking about creative learning as 'findings'? How much of this 'thinking apparatus' is represented as reflexively interrogated and modified/adapted/changed?
- How is the site represented? How is it temporalized or set in networks of relations? How are these relationships and trajectories understood and named? What are the implications for knowing about creative learning that are constructed through these rationalities?

About this book

There is already a pantechnicon of research methods books on the market and one might be forgiven for wondering why another is needed. We agree that more of the same is not going to be helpful, and we have therefore seen this book as offering something complementary to those usually prescribed in research methods courses.

Our experience in teaching about research is that there is often a silence between the question and the method. New researchers are told that they should fit the method to the question but then are mystified about how to make this crucial connection and decision. In the absence of reference material about how to put the question and the choice of method together, new researchers often turn to the more conventional research tools: surveys, interviews and case studies. We have nothing against these methods and use them ourselves.

But we do think that more might be on offer to help researchers think through the reasons for their choices.

We have put this concern together with our experience in researching creative learning. We have organized the book around three broad issues that we know are of concern to many in the field, and we solicited writings and thinkings about some of the kinds of methods that have the capacity to address them. These are of course not the only methods on offer, but we hope that they are illustrative of the thinking the researchers do about how methodological choices are made. The three issues that are addressed in the book in three separate parts are as follows:

Part 1: What are the practices of creative learning?

Many of those who are interested in creative learning are also engaged in its production. There are particular complexities that arise from researching something about which one has strong views and, often, emotional commitments. Practitioner researchers and those who aim to change practice must focus on the robustness of their methods and continually interrogate their own beliefs and taken-for-granted assumptions.

Part 1 focuses on both practitioner research in creative learning and also on how research might change learning practices so that they become more creative. John Churchley, a headteacher, writes about the dilemmas and difficulties of researching his own practice, and Tony Lyng reflects on his experiences as headteacher of a school being researched. Emily Pringle reflects on researching the practices of artists and how and whether artists can offer distinctive types of pedagogy. Pat Cochrane and Pete McGuigan (CapeUK) talk about how they support teachers to research their own practice. Malcolm Swan explores design research in mathematics education, showing us not only how creative learning is not an exclusively arts-based concept but also how creative research can be used as a way of transforming teaching practices.

Part 2: Can researchers 'see' creative learning and can their research help others to 'see' it?

A number of researchers are concerned to document the processes that together constitute creative learning. This is important not only to ascertain whether what is being advocated does have particular forms and practices, but also to codify what is happening in order to mobilize it in professional education.

This part of the book focuses on observation, the visual and questions of representation. Kathleen Gallagher talks about her work as an ethnographer of young people's drama, and Geoff Troman and Bob Jeffrey offer a succinct analysis of the principles of ethnography and how they have used it in researching creative learning. Sara Bragg writes about visual research and its applications in creative learning research, and Pat Thomson offers an example of visual research. Erica McWilliam, Shane Dawson and Jennifer Pei-Ling Tan show how digital tools allow new ways of capturing data relevant to the design of pedagogical processes and processes of inquiry and thus 'seeing' creative capacity as socially constituted thinking and doing. This chapter segues into an extended essay on questions of written representation: Christine Hall, Ken Jones and Pat Thomson trace the various ways in which research findings can be presented as cases, as cross case analysis and as portraits.

Part 3: Can creative learning be measured and evaluated?

The more creative learning has been taken up in policy and the more it is funded and marked off as an 'initiative', the more pressure there is to say what happens as a result. Do creative learners learn more? Do they learn different things? Or do they just learn the same things differently?

Part 3 of the book focuses on research methods through which these questions might be answered. John Harland, a veteran arts and creativity researcher, talks about how understandings about the effects of creative learning grow over time and through various projects. Mark Runco, Nur Çayırdağ and Selçuk Acar outline the relative merits of various kinds of quantitative and statistical approaches to the measurement of creative learning. Tony Cotton addresses programme evaluation and how sometimes numbers just won't do. Elisabeth Soep alerts us to the problem of timing – when does the research actually finish? – and place – what happens when research participants move around? David Parker and Naranee Ruthra-Rajan discuss how issues of measurement and the evaluation of creative learning appear from a national programme perspective.

Notes

1 This does not necessarily mean that their research sits within a critical tradition. Critical researchers make explicit that the purpose of their research is to contribute knowledge that might make a difference to groups that are currently socially marginalized and de-powered (Alvesson & Deetz, 2000; Carspecken & Apple, 1992; Thomson & Wellard, 1999). Critical researchers reject the notion that research can 'sit on the fence' about social issues (Gitlin, 1994; Griffiths, 1998).

References

Alvesson, M., & Deetz, S. (2000). *Doing critical management research*. Thousand Oaks, CA: Sage.

Aries, P. (1962). *Centuries of childhood*. New York: Vintage Books.

Ball, S. (2008). *The education debate*. Bristol: Policy Press.

Banaji, S., & Burn, A. (2007). *Rhetorics of creativity: A review of the literature*. London: Arts Council England.

Benkler, Y. (2007). *The wealth of networks: How social production transforms markets and freedoms*. New Haven, CT: Yale University Press.

Bentley, T., & Seltzer, K. (1999). *The creative age: knowledge and skills for the new economy*. London: Demos.

Bragg, S., Manchester, H., & Faulkner, D. (2009). *Youth voice in the work of Creative Partnerships*. London: Creativity Culture and Education. Retrieved from www.creativitycultureeducation.org/data/files/cp-youth-voice-report-146.pdf.

Buckingham, D. (2000). *After the death of childhood: Growing up the age of electronic media*. Cambridge: Polity Press.

Buckingham, D., & Jones, K. (2001). New Labour's cultural turn: Some tensions in contemporary educational and cultural policy. *Journal of Education Policy, 16*(1), 1–14.

Carrington, V. (2006). *Rethinking middle years: Early adolescents, schooling and digital culture*. Sydney: Allen & Unwin.

Carspecken, P., & Apple, M. (1992). Critical qualitative research: Theory, methodology, and practice. In M. Le Compte, W. Millroy, & J. Preissle (Eds.), *The handbook of qualitative research in education* (pp. 507–553). San Diego, CA: Academic Press, Harcourt Brace.

Castells, M. (1996). *The information age: Economy, society and culture*. Vol. 1, *The rise of the network society*. Oxford: Blackwell.

Castells, M. (1997). *The information age: Economy, society and culture.* Vol. 2, *The power of identity.* Oxford: Blackwell.

Castells, M. (1998). *The information age: Economy, society and culture.* Vol. 3, *End of millennium.* Oxford: Blackwell.

Cooper, K., & White, R. (2004). *Burning issues: Foundations of education.* Lanham, MD: Scarecrow Education.

Craft, A., Jeffrey, B., & Leibling, M. (Eds.). (2001). *Creativity in education.* London: Continuum.

Cropley, A. J. (2001). *Creativity in education and learning.* London: RoutledgeFalmer.

Crotty, M. (1998). *The foundations of social research: Meaning and perspective in the research process.* Sydney: Allen & Unwin.

Cunningham, P. (1988). *Curriculum change in the primary school since 1945: Dissemination of the progressive ideal.* London: Falmer Press.

de Lissa, L. (1949). *Life in the nursery school and in early babyhood.* London: Longmans.

Department for Culture, Media and Sport (DCMS). (1998). *Creative Industries mapping document* (2001 ed.). London: DCMS.

Dewey, J. (1897). My pedagogic creed. *School Journal, 54*(3), 77–80.

Dewey, J. (1934). *Art as experience* (1980 ed.). New York: Perigee.

Dewey, J., & Dewey, E. (1915). *Schools of tomorrow.* New York: Dutton.

Freebody, P. (2003). *Qualitative research in education: Interaction and practice.* Thousand Oaks, CA: Sage.

Gallagher, K. (Ed.). (2008). *The methodological dilemma: Creative, critical and collaborative approaches to qualitative research.* New York: Routledge.

Gewirtz, S. (2002). *The managerial school: Post-welfarism and social justice in education.* London: Routledge.

Gitlin, A. (1994). *Power and method: Political activism and educational research.* London: Routledge.

Grainger, T., Gooch, K., & Lambirth, A. (2005). *Creativity and writing: Developing voice and verve in the classroom.* London: Routledge.

Griffin-Beale, C. (Ed.). (1979). *Christian Schiller: In his own words.* London: by private subscription through A&C Black.

Griffiths, M. (1998). *Educational research for social justice: Getting off the fence.* Buckingham, UK: Open University Press.

Grosvenor, I., & Myers, K. (2006). Progressivism, control and correction: Local education authorities and educational policy in twentieth-century England. *Pedagogica Historica, 42*(1&2), 225–247.

Haraway, D. (1988). Situated knowledges: The science question in feminism and the privilege of partial perspective. *Feminist Studies, 14*(3), 575–599.

Harland, J., Kinder, K., & Hartley, K. (1995). *Arts in their view: A study of youth participation in the arts.* Slough, UK: National Foundation for Educational Research.

Harland, J., Kinder, K., Lord, P., Stott, A., Schagen, I., & Haynes, J. (2000). *Arts education in secondary schools: Effects and effectiveness.* Slough, UK: National Foundation for Educational Research.

Harland, J., Lord, P., Stott, A., Kinder, K., Lamont, E., & Ashworth, M. (2005). *The arts–education interface: A mutual learning triangle?* Slough, UK: National Foundation for Educational Research.

Hayes, D., Mills, M., Christie, P., & Lingard, B. (2005). *Teachers and schooling making a difference: Productive pedagogies, assessment and performance.* Sydney: Allen & Unwin.

Holloway, S., & Valentine, G. (Eds.). (2000). *Children's geographies: Playing, living, learning.* London: Routledge.

James, A., Jenks, C., & Prout, A. (1998). *Theorizing childhood.* New York: Teachers College Press.

Jeffrey, B., & Woods, P. (2009). *Creative learning in the primary school.* London: Routledge.

Jones, K. (2003). *Education in Britain: 1944 to the present.* Cambridge: Polity Press.

Jones, K. (2009). *Culture and creative learning: A literature review.* London: Creativity, Culture and Education.

Jones, S., & Hall, C. (2009). Creative partners: Arts practice and the potential for pupil voice. *Power and Education, 1*(2), 178–188.

Labaree, D. (2005). Progressivism, schools and schools of education. *Pedagogica Historica, 41*(1&2), 275–288.

Lather, P. (2007). *Getting lost: Feminist efforts toward a double(d) science.* New York: State University of New York Press.

Law, J. (2004). *After method: Mess in social science research.* London: Routledge.

Lingard, B., Christie, P., Hayes, D., & Mills, M. (2003). *Leading learning: Making hope practical in schools.* Buckingham, UK: Open University Press.

National Advisory Committee on Creative and Cultural Education (NACCCE). (1999). *All our futures: Creativity, culture and education.* London: The Stationery Press.

Neill, A. S. (1918). *A dominie's log.* London: H. Jenkins.

Noblit, G., Dickson, C. H., Wilson, B. A., & McKinney, M. B. (2009). *Creating and sustaining arts-based school reform: The A+ schools program.* New York: Routledge.

Poster, M. (1990). *The mode of information: Poststructuralism and social contexts.* Cambridge: Polity Press.

Pring, R. (2000). *Philosophy of educational research.* London: Continuum.

Qvortrup, J., Bardy, M., Sigritta, G., & Wintersberger, E. (Eds.). (1994). *Childhood matters: Social theory, practice and policy.* Aldershot, UK: Avebury.

Rabinow, P. (2008). *Marking time: On the anthropology of the contemporary.* Princeton, NJ: Princeton University Press.

Robinson, K. (1982). *The arts in schools: Principles, practice and provision.* London: Calouste Gulbenkian Foundation.

Roid, G. H. (2003). *Stanford–Binet intelligence scales* (5th ed.). *Examiners manual.* Itaska, IL: Riverside Publishing.

Sefton-Green, J. (Ed.). (1998). *Digital diversions: Youth culture in the age of multimedia.* London: UCL Press.

Sefton-Green, J., Thomson, P., Bresla, L., & Jones, K. (2011). *The Routledge International Handbook of Creative Learning.* London: Routledge.

Sizer, T. (1985). *Horace's compromise: The dilemma of the American high school.* Boston: Houghton Mifflin.

Sizer, T. (1996). *Horace's hope: What works for the American high school.* Boston: Houghton Mifflin.

Skinner, B. F. (1968). *The technology of teaching.* Englewood Cliffs, NJ: Prentice Hall.

Sliwka, A. (2008). The contribution of alternative education. In Centre for Educational Research and Innovation (Ed.), *Innovating to learn, learning to innovate.* Paris: OECD.

Steinberg, S., & Kincheloe, J. (Eds.). (1997). *Kinder-culture: The corporate construction of childhood.* Boulder, CO: Westview Press.

Thomson, P., Jones, K., & Hall, C. (2009). *Creative whole school change.* Final report. London: Creativity, Culture and Education; Arts Council England. See also www.artsandcreativity research.org.uk.

Thomson, P., & Wellard, S. (1999). *Get a grip on research: Critical and postcritical approaches.* Geelong, Victoria: Deakin University Press.

Tomlinson, S. (2001). *Education in post-welfare society.* Buckingham, UK: Open University Press.

Tyler, R. (1949). *Basic principles of curriculum and instruction.* Chicago: University of Chicago Press.

Vulliamy, G., & Webb, R. (2006). *Coming full circle? The impact of New Labour's education policies on primary school teachers' work.* London: Association of Teachers and Lecturers.

Vygotsky, L. (1978). *Mind in society: The development of higher psychological processes.* Cambridge, MA: Harvard University Press.

Wasley, P. (1994). *Stirring the chalk dust: Tales of teachers changing classroom practice.* New York: Teachers College Press.

Wasley, P., Hampel, R., & Clark, R. (1997). *Kids and school reform.* San Francisco: Jossey-Bass.

White, M. (2005). Exhibiting practices: Paper as a site of communication and contested practice. In M. Lawn & I. Grosvenor (Eds.), *Materialities of schooling: Design, technology, objects, routines* (pp. 177–200). Oxford: Symposium Books.

Whitty, G., Power, S., & Halpin, D. (1998). *Devolution and choice in education: The school, the state and the market*. Buckingham, UK: Open University Press.

Part 1

What are the practices of creative learning?

Chapter 2

Capturing the 'plaid' moment

The use of practitioner research and student researchers in researching experiences with the arts

John Churchley

In educational research, it is often difficult to document incidents of a behaviour or an experience such as creative learning when its occurrence is unpredictable (Cziko, 1989; Taylor, 1996). It is difficult for the researcher to plan to be there, field book or camcorder in hand, when a child finds a new use for a toy or tool, makes a discovery about mixing colours to create an effect in a painting, works out a novel solution to a mathematical problem, or creates a spontaneous dance. I had this difficulty in a research study of my own school – a specialized arts school. I was trying to collect and document the aesthetic experiences of students and teachers. However, aesthetic experiences in classroom situations are not necessarily predictable and therefore I wasn't always able to observe (or video) them when they happened.

This chapter is about my experience as a practitioner researcher, trying to collect those elusive moments in arts education classrooms that I consider to be aesthetic experiences. It deals with the challenge of trying to predict (or at least capture) the unpredictable.

I will first attempt to explain what I mean by aesthetic experiences and then describe how I intended to study them using a 'practitioner research' approach. I will explore this approach in greater detail, particularly reflecting on my context as a headteacher-researcher, describing how I attempted to collect aesthetic moments, both expected and unexpected. I also developed an additional methodology involving the use of students as co-researchers. Finally, I will share a glimpse of my findings, which were the result of this practitioner researcher/student co-researcher project.

Aesthetic principles

Aesthetic experiences have always been important to me. As an audience member, I have sought them for myself; as a musician, I have sought to create them for my audience; and as an arts educator, I have sought to understand how children experience them and how they can learn to create them. I have always had a fascination with these 'magic' moments that happened in my music classroom and on the stage. These experiences were both inspirational and memorable for me, my students and our audiences. They were also a regular occurrence for teachers, students, parents and me at an arts-focus school where I was headteacher (principal). Therefore, when it came time to choose a topic for my doctoral thesis, the choice for me was easy: I needed to explore the nature of aesthetic experiences at school for students and teachers. However, I found that the types of experience that I was seeking to explore tended to be unpredictable.

In my former role as a music teacher, I spent countless hours working with children to create music in classrooms and in other performance contexts. However, experiences with music that were inspiring or aesthetically satisfying, while predictable at times, often came unexpectedly. The students and I hoped that these powerful responses would happen at our public performances, and indeed, part of our preparation for these performances was the explicit planning to create an aesthetic response for ourselves and for the audience. However, sometimes these experiences just happened spontaneously during a music class. The same proved true during my time as headteacher of Beattie School of the Arts, a publicly funded kindergarten-to-grade-8 school in Kamloops, British Columbia, that has a focus on learning through the arts (integrated with other subjects). I had these experiences myself at Beattie's performances. However, the teachers also came to me quite regularly to tell me of special moments that had happened in their arts classrooms. The teachers described the experiences as exciting, inspiring, and sometimes moving to the point of tears. Unfortunately, when I would visit the class the next day, the moment would be gone and wouldn't necessarily be repeated. While the teachers and I could not necessarily predict when these moments would happen, we did agree that they could be described as aesthetic experiences.

I started my research about these elusive moments at Beattie through an exploration of the literature of aesthetic experience and aesthetic theory. I found that my initial understanding of these experiences had been too limited. I had thought them simply to be an intense emotional response to a performance. While this assumption might be true for some aesthetic theories, it is not for others. In fact, I found that there is no generally accepted definition of aesthetic experience:

> There are many aesthetic theories that define art – some of which describe the nature of the aesthetic experience. What does it mean to say that someone is having an aesthetic experience? Strangely enough, in all the literature on aesthetic experience, I cannot find a direct and concise answer to this question.
>
> (Beardsley, 1982, p. 81)

I needed a starting point for a definition of aesthetic experience that would be open to a variety of interpretations that I might find. In fact, from my experiences at Beattie, I expected the students and teachers to have a variety of aesthetic responses – some individual, some in common. That is, I was assuming that their aesthetic experiences were defined, created and experienced both individually and socially. This assumption comes from pragmatist aesthetic theory – primarily that of John Dewey (1934), but also of more recent pragmatists such as Richard Shusterman (1992). Dewey's aesthetic theory, outlined in *Art as experience* (1934), gives a very broad definition of art and gives the aesthetic experience a central place in this definition. His description of an aesthetic experience is focused on the 'experience' itself. This applies to experiences extending beyond just those with 'high' art espoused by traditional analytic (formalist) aesthetic theorists, to include interactions with all art forms (such as commercial art and crafts), as well as nature and life itself (Shusterman, 1992).

Dewey does not claim that all experiences in life are aesthetic experiences. First, he distinguishes between mundane experiences and having *an* experience:

> [W]e have *an* experience when the material experienced runs its course to fulfillment. Then and then only is it integrated within and demarcated in the general stream of

experience from other experiences. A piece of work is finished in a way that is satisfactory; a problem receives its solution; a game is played through; a situation . . . is so rounded out that its close is a consummation and not a cessation.

(Dewey, 1934, p. 35)

He further suggests that an intense consummated experience of life is aesthetic by describing it as having 'a satisfying emotional quality because it possesses internal integration and fulfillment reached through ordered and organized movement' (p. 38). This is not to say that all emotional experiences are aesthetic, but that there is a subjective satisfying quality that is part of the experience that makes it aesthetic. According to Dewey and other pragmatists, the aesthetic experience happens temporally inside a person, as a result of that person's construction of meaning from *an* experience, rather than happening *to* a person by a piece of art. This does not mean that the art has no place in the experience. It means that the experience happens in and because of an individually and socially constructed interaction between the art and the person experiencing it.

With this broad view of aesthetic experiences, I set out with my two-part research question: to define and describe what aesthetic experiences might be for students and teachers at Beattie; and to analyse these experiences in the context of the school-wide arts integration pedagogy.

Researching the aesthetic experience

As I planned my research approach, I struggled to find a method with which to study aesthetic experiences, given the fact that there was no guarantee that these experiences would happen when I was present. I was drawn to ethnographic methods, which offered a partial answer to this problem. Hammersley and Atkinson (1989, p. 2) describe ethnography in this way:

> The ethnographer participates, overtly or covertly, in people's daily lives for an extended period of time, watching what happens, listening to what is said, asking questions; in fact, collecting whatever data are available to shed light on the issues with which he or she is concerned.

This approach seemed appropriate; as headteacher of the school, I was 'participating' in the daily life of the school. However, as I was a part-time graduate student and full-time headteacher, a practitioner research approach to ethnography was the most realistic choice for my study. I could not 'live' among the subjects for an extended period of time, totally devoted to my research role, as would a traditional ethnographer. I also chose to include student co-researchers to help me to be 'on the spot' as participant observers using video ethnographic methods to collect the data. My plan was that as participant observers, the student co-researchers and I were more likely to be directly involved in the aesthetic experiences wherever and whenever they happened.

Before I describe this project, I need to clarify what I mean by practitioner research. I rely on the definition by Anderson and Herr (1999, p. 20):

> By practitioner research we refer to a broad-based movement among school professionals to legitimate knowledge produced out of their own lived realities as

professionals. This includes an ongoing struggle to articulate an epistemology of practice that includes experiences with reflective practice, action research, teacher study groups, and teacher narratives.

While practitioner research is often equated with action research, this broader definition includes other methods. These include various types of inquiry undertaken by a practitioner to document, reflect upon and theorize his or her lived professional experience.

Practitioner research has several important benefits. A primary benefit is to the research context itself. Practitioner research brings an awareness of the research topic directly to those practitioners who should (in a perfect world) be accessing and applying the results of research in their field. It involves the researcher in the practical application of research in the environment in which it was conducted. Biesta and Burbles insist on this benefit of practitioner research for teachers: 'It is, after all, only when teachers approach their own educational practices in an experimental and investigative way, and not simply as a site for the application of educational laws and rules, that intelligent educational action becomes possible' (2003, pp. 80–81). Practitioner research focuses on the local knowledge that resides inside the mind and experience of the practitioner. However, the individual's history which provides the inside knowledge is still socially constructed and, as such, is not necessarily more 'true' than that of an outside researcher (Anderson & Herr, 1999). Nevertheless, practitioner research recognizes and honours this 'tacit' knowledge (Cochran-Smith & Lytle, 1993). This approach is not unlike the heuristic research approach suggested by Moustakas (1990). He defines the heuristic inquiry as a question that 'has been a personal challenge and puzzlement in the search to understand one's self and the world in which one lives' (p. 15). While this could be said of the motivation for many different research paradigms, what makes the heuristic inquiry different is the pursuit of this question through direct personal experience. This double approach – a focus on a personal quest and the answer lying in the experience of the researcher – mirrors the epistemological position of practitioner research. It is appropriate for practitioner research, as the reflection that it provides contributes to the professional development of practice (Anderson, Herr, & Nihlen, 1994). It also describes my own stance, as the research question about aesthetic experiences in my study has been a lifelong personal quest.

My own experience as a musician and arts educator was therefore a 'source of knowledge' that informed my interpretation of data, as well as being data itself. I documented my experience in two forms: a research journal that consisted of field notes and reflections upon these notes, as well as an autobiographical narrative about my personal experiences with the arts as a performer, audience member and arts educator. However, the primary data source was transcribed video that had been recorded by the students and me in our search for aesthetic moments in the classrooms (and on the stage) of Beattie.

Given the nature of the localized and contextual knowledge generated by practitioner research, there is concern about the validity of the methodology. As practitioner research is not always accepted as rigorous in the academic world, the question of validity is of particular concern (Cochran-Smith & Lytle, 1993; Anderson et al., 1994). However, there are several criteria for validity (or trustworthiness) which can be useful for practitioner researchers: process validity (the continual looping back to initial assumptions to reflect on the data to inform further data collection); democratic validity (the collaboration of all parties involved in the research); and catalytic validity (the transformation of the researcher's and participants' perspectives on reality as a result of the research) (Anderson et al., 1994).

The contextual nature of practitioner research also does not necessarily lend itself to theoretical generalizability. However, practitioner researchers can make use of naturalistic generalization (Stake, 1986) where research is presented as contextualized stories that teachers can vicariously experience and from which they can create meaning.

Besides the academic concerns with the nature of practitioner research, there were other issues with this methodology that arose because of my position as headteacher.

The headteacher as researcher

Entering into my research project, I was aware that my tripartite role as school leader (supervisor), arts educator (participant) and researcher (observer) would require some careful negotiation. I tried to ensure that I didn't use my authority to influence the participation or the actions or words of the subjects or co-researchers. I also tried to ensure that I didn't let my role as the school leader influence the positive or negative nature of any of the data collection or analysis. Negative results could potentially reflect poorly on my leadership or the school itself. Despite my best attempts to limit these influences, there is an inherent power relationship between headteacher and teacher, and headteacher and student.

Another potential issue for me to deal with was the micro-politics, which could have affected my ability or confidence to ask difficult questions or effect significant change (Anderson *et al.*, 1994). This political landscape included the micro-politics within the school (teachers, parents and students) and the broader community, and the institutional politics of the public school system. As I was the founding headteacher of the school, this practitioner research also gave me the challenge of being too close, and hence not being able to see taken-for-granted aspects of the school that might be noticed by an outside researcher (Cochran-Smith & Lytle, 1993; Anderson *et al.*, 1994).

Despite these challenges, there are advantages in a headteacher researching his or her school. The role of the headteacher as researcher is also one of participant-observer. It is an excellent position from which to conduct an ethnographic study, as the headteacher plays an important role in the community and culture that he or she is observing. He or she is more connected with this community and culture than would be an outside researcher. However, as the school ethnography is often about life in classrooms (and arts studios in this case), the headteacher is also one step removed from the teachers' and students' roles as active participants in this part of school life. This allows him or her to have a slightly more objective approach than might the teachers and/or students as researchers.

A headteacher also typically has excellent access to his or her school as a research site. While still busy doing my work as a headteacher, I was more or less available to move about the school as a 'free agent' during the day to wherever an aesthetic moment might be happening. I was not tied to one class, as a teacher-researcher might be, nor did I have any access restrictions, as might an outside researcher.

Being headteacher at Beattie also gave me access to ongoing discussions about the arts and arts education practice: these inspired me to pursue my inquiry and also informed my research question.

Capturing 'plaid moments'

Prior to embarking on my research, I had many conversations about aesthetic moments in classrooms with teachers – who were very excited about these experiences. One of the goals for my research was to collect these experiences on video. I wanted to capture the context and the reactions of the students and teachers during these special classroom moments. However, the difficulty I faced was anticipating when and where these experiences might happen. Therefore, I came up with a system to try to react to emerging experiences on the spot.

Each teacher in the school was given a laminated card with a plaid design. This card was intended to serve the same function as red or yellow cards often do in schools – where a student runner is sent to the school office with the card to signal that help is needed for a severe behavioural incident. However, the plaid card was to signal that a potential aesthetic experience was happening in the classroom, and that a student co-researcher or I should be sent to video the happening.[1] To facilitate this data collection, a camcorder and tripod were made available in each co-researcher's classroom.

Unfortunately, while the plaid card plan was discussed and agreed to by the staff, in reality it was used on only a few occasions. In some cases, the teachers reported that they got so engaged in the moment that they forgot about the cards. In other cases they felt that the moment had already passed. The teachers did tell me about 'plaid moments' on a regular basis prior to, during and after the data collection. However, they often didn't make use of the plaid cards to allow the moments to be recorded. In these cases, I documented their comments about the moment in my research journal.

Rather than using plaid cards, a different pattern developed for video data collection. The students videoed various performance events at the school and conducted post-event student interviews. They also recorded their own post-event video journals. These events included performances by outside arts groups in the school, an extra-curricular student performance of a scripted play, and sharing evenings where classroom arts activities were shared with (performed for) parents. The bulk of the data came from these sharing evenings.

The co-researchers tried in the first couple of sharing evenings to record three types of video: the performance happening on stage; the simultaneous audience reactions to the performance; and post-performance interviews of students and teachers who were involved in the performance and/or audience reaction videos. The purpose of this strategy was to clarify each subject's response to the performance as an audience member or performer that the co-researchers had noticed through his or her body language as they collected the video. This strategy was designed by the co-researchers, and worked well technically. However, the students were inexperienced interviewers, which unfortunately limited the responses that they obtained.

I asked the teachers as well as the student co-researchers to complete video journals – particularly after major performance events. Video journals are video clips of the subject speaking to the camcorder alone in a private setting. These are currently popular, owing to their use in reality television. However, the use of video journals in reality television is of course a staged and edited representation of reality. Despite this, Noyes (2008) points out that video diaries can still serve a useful purpose, particularly when used as only one method within a broader set of ethnographic methods. The video journals at Beattie were more structured than those in reality television and were based on sets of questions that were developed by myself and the co-researchers. The questions were different for each event. The use of video journals generated some emotional responses from the teachers that might not have happened in an interview with another person present. The student video journals also had interesting responses, but weren't as probing as those of the teachers. The advantage of students doing the video journals alone was that there was less fooling around than there was when they interviewed each other.

While the plaid card system of collecting aesthetic experiences did not work especially well, its use together with the other strategies meant that we did collect an adequate amount of data documenting aesthetic experiences in process or those that had just happened. We managed to collect some live plaid moments on video that happened during performances and a few that happened on the spot in classrooms. The remainder of the data was post-plaid moment reporting of the experiences in video journals, interviews and discussions.

The student co-researchers were able to collect much of this data by being in several places at once during and after performances. I could not have accomplished the same strategies without their help. The student co-researchers also provided insight about their aesthetic experiences (and what aesthetic experiences might be) through the video journals and our group discussions. While not directly connected with the practitioner research methodology, the use of student co-researchers assisted me in my research project, while also creating some challenges.

The rise and fall of student co-researchers

One of the major challenges in my study arose from my use of an additional methodology: the use of student co-researchers. The intent of this part of the research design was to get right to the source of the experience – to get as close as possible to those experiencing aesthetic moments. However, the challenge associated with this was the fact that the research question was my own. *I* was the one who wanted to learn about aesthetic experiences. The students were only helpers – willing ones, but not heavily invested in the actual research question. As a result, they spent a great deal of time trying to understand what they were to research.

The participation of students as researchers or co-researchers is an approach that is based in critical theory. It gives children their own voice in research, rather than being interpreted by an adult researcher, and in principle can empower students. This empowerment should include their choice to participate in a research project and how they wish to take part (Johnson, 2000; Fraser, Henderson, & Price, 2005). In theory, it also has the potential to give children power to make changes within an adult-controlled system – in this case with me as the headteacher (Grover, 2004; Johnson, 2004). However, in order for these changes to take place, there needs to be a cultural shift to allow for greater (or any) student voice.

There are a number of complex issues that arise around the issue of voice with student co-researchers (Thomson, 2008). One of these issues that we dealt with at Beattie was the difference between (1) the student co-researchers acting as *representatives* of the researched voice, and (2) being the researchers collecting the voice of the group being studied. While their voice was collected as part of their research, the student co-researchers were only a small part of the school, and not necessarily representative of the collective student voice. I made it clear to them that it was important that they did not just collect research data from themselves and their friends. For the most part, they were able to collect data from all types of students, including those who gave responses with which they disagreed. Finally, there is the socially constructed nature of the student voice, which includes what is asked of students, when it is asked and how it is asked (which, again, can be influenced by adult power) (Thomson, 2008).

However, having student co-researchers conduct many of the interviews meant that there was an opportunity for a more natural context to elicit responses devoid of the adult–child subject power differential (Eder & Fingerson, 2002). I was more confident of the representativeness of the student voice in the student responses to questions from their peers as against responses to questions from me as their headteacher. If I had been conducting these interviews, students might have been influenced by my adult headteacher position of power. In that situation, they might have given responses that they thought I wanted to hear, rather than what they really wanted to say.

The term 'co-researchers' also requires clarification. Fielding differentiates between students as co-researchers and students as researchers. In both methods, students are engaged as 'researchers, enquirers, and makers of meaning' (2004: 307). They are involved in the design of the research project, the collection of data, the analysis of the data and the presentation of the data. The primary difference is that when students are the primary researchers, they learn the skills necessary to initiate and complete a research topic of their own choosing. As co-researchers, the children rely on the principal researcher for direction concerning the overall inquiry, the design and the completion of the research. At Beattie, the students acted as co-researchers working under my direction.

The creation of a pedagogy of research methodology is important for explicitly teaching students to be co-researchers in visual research methods (Johnson, 2008; Thomson & Hall, 2008). In order to prepare the students as co-researchers, I started a research club to discuss with them the research questions, the research design and their role in the project. The meetings for this club were held over the course of the data collection and were used to discuss our preliminary findings, and the methods that we might use to get at more data. Most of the meetings were videoed as part of the data collection, as the co-researchers came up with many perceptive observations. One of the most difficult issues to explain at the beginning was the concept of aesthetic experience to the co-researchers, and exploring this concept together without biasing our perspective about what we might find as aesthetic experience. This search for an explanation became the primary question for the study: 'What is an aesthetic experience?'

The students did appear to enjoy doing their data collection using video cameras. Only a few of them had any experience using the camcorders, so the use of them was quite novel. The joint role of researcher and videographer may also have given the students a sense of power in the representation of their peers' voices. One of the student co-researchers commented at the beginning of the data collection that the use of video made research fun:

Student co-researcher: It makes the . . . word *research* sound funner.
Churchley: Why?
Student co-researcher: Because . . . we get to videotape people and interview them at the same time that we're doing research. So, when you interview, it's fun, because it has a bit of drama and stuff, and then you get to videotape, which is fun and at the same time you're researching, so it's fun.

The novelty of using the camcorders did create some difficulty, as on several occasions the students acted with them in a manner that I found 'silly'. In these cases, they play-acted while on camera, trying to make each other laugh. They also had difficulty remembering to conduct interviews in a quiet place where the voice of the subject could be heard. However, the students became quite adept at using the camcorders, and were able to record a significant amount of data with little or no supervision. We met regularly as a research group and collected the video over the course of four months.

Besides the use of camcorders, the post-performance interviews conducted by the student researchers involved formulating questions and employing interviewing techniques. Interviewing requires a great deal of skill in order to follow up the subject's responses. However, at times the student researchers found that it was difficult to elicit information from the other students. They unsuccessfully tried using leading questions to generate responses, as they were not satisfied with the responses that they got to their initial questions. This lack of interviewing skill influenced the data, both by the bias introduced through the leading question and through the loss of 'deep' responses from the interview subject.

There are critical issues with the choice of students as co-researchers, rather than as primary researchers. This was particularly the case in my study. While the students may have felt important in being a part of the research team, they were still somewhat marginalized members of that team. They had no say in the research question and had little or no control over the resources available to them in terms of time, equipment or methods. In short, while they were consulted extensively, they essentially did what they were told. This lack of empowerment was evident when some of the co-researchers responded to my question about researching the aesthetic experience:

Churchley: So, why are we interested in investigating it?
Student 1: 'Cause then we know if we can make the school better.
Churchley: What else?
Student 2: Uh, you're collecting research to get your PhD? (students laugh)
Churchley: Well, yeah. That's my . . . selfish little reason.
Student 3: No, it's because you want to, not us. (some giggles)
Student 1: I want to.

Student 1 appears interested in being directly involved in the research; students 2 and 3 clearly understand that they are involved as helpers (albeit willing helpers) for my research project.

Unfortunately, at the end of the data collection the role of the student co-researchers ceased. This was for several reasons. The transcription and analysis of the video took a great deal of time over the summer and outside of school hours. The students were not available at this time, and once this process was started, it would have been too difficult to develop the pedagogy to teach them about the process of analysis. In addition, at the end of the data transcription I left the school to take a different job. This essentially cut me off from access to the student co-researchers and silenced the student voice in the latter stages of my research.

While they did not participate through to the end of the study, the student co-researchers were invaluable to me in our initial discussions of the research topic. They helped to determine the research question and the data collection strategies. The students were also crucial in doing the video ethnography. They were 'on-the-spot' data collectors and together we were able to collect enough video data for me to generate a preliminary definition of aesthetic experience.

Findings

The focus of this chapter is on methods, not findings. However, I suggest that by using a practitioner research approach I was able to establish some interesting results: a pluralistic definition of aesthetic experience; and a pedagogical model for arts education with this definition at the centre. Without going into detail, I can say that my definition can be summarized as twelve distinct types and sub-types of aesthetic experience which are layered together to create an overall experience. These include different types of response to the arts such as comic, tragic, somatic (physical), sentimental (emotional), as well as eight others. Not all of these types are new to various aesthetic theories, but the pluralistic typology is a new way to look at the distinct layers found within an experience with the arts (Churchley, 2009).

I also made some preliminary connections between these types of aesthetic experience and the types of pedagogical practice that we observed teachers using at Beattie in all four of the arts disciplines (dance, drama, music and visual art). These practices included rehearsal (adult-led performance practice), studio (student-focused creative work), and theory/analysis (often referred to as art 'appreciation'). These pedagogical types were incorporated into an arts education framework that has aesthetic experience (the pluralistic definition) at the centre, in addition to the curricula for the four arts disciplines. The framework represents a complete arts education programme that focuses on aesthetic experiences, which, I suggest, are common to all disciplines.

The connections between aesthetic experience and pedagogy imply that different pedagogical traditions found between and within each of the arts disciplines affect the nature of aesthetic experiences produced in the teaching and learning moment. The sharing of this discovery helped the teachers at Beattie to understand the pedagogical tensions at the school that were the result of these differences. As a result, the school has adopted a more pluralistic approach to pedagogy and aesthetic experience which in turn has deepened these experiences for staff and students.

Summary

The impetus for the research (my quest to understand the aesthetic experience), the research question (a definition of aesthetic experiences), the results (the pluralistic definition, the connections with pedagogy, and the arts education framework), and the implementation of the results (a new approach to arts education by the teachers) all happened at and because of Beattie School of the Arts. The practitioner research methodology allowed this research process to happen. The student co-researcher methodology helped me as a headteacher-researcher to collect and discuss data that I would not otherwise have been able to access. The students gave me many extra eyes and ears as well as a connection to the student voice.

At the end of the day, the question remains: is practitioner research useful for the academic community to research aesthetic experience (or other topics such as creative learning)? The results are highly contextual and as such can have limited generalizability for broader research goals. However, practitioner research is invaluable for teaching research skills to professionals involved in part-time graduate studies. It also improves awareness into practice at the research site. It can be argued that this in and of itself provides more than enough justification for the methodology.

At Beattie, the practitioner research process increased the awareness of teachers to aesthetic experience and how their own experiences and pedagogical choices can influence the experiences of students. Although the plaid card system didn't really work, the notion of 'plaid moments' became a shared understanding for the teachers. They still use this term when speaking of aesthetic experience.

My results included a preliminary theoretical construct – a framework for arts education with a central pluralistic typology of aesthetic experiences connected to pedagogical practices. As I used practitioner research to develop this preliminary framework, I cannot claim that I have identified a definitive set of aesthetic experience that applies universally, or universal connections with pedagogical practices. Further research would be necessary to make such claims. I can only claim that they apply to the site researched and in the limited time in which it was researched.

However, without the student co-researchers and my own reflective journal on the research process I would not have had any place to start my investigation into aesthetic experiences, let alone any theorization. In this way, practitioner research has been for me a part of a journey in professional inquiry, rather than a final destination.

Note

1 I chose plaid as it was entirely different from the yellow card/red card behaviour system, and because it was a creative option that was appealing to me. This creative choice got a laugh from the teachers, which helped to highlight the cards. However, I also explained to the staff that plaid has many different colours woven together to make a whole (implying that aesthetic experiences might be the same).

References

Anderson, G. L., & Herr, K. (1999). The new paradigm wars: Is there room for rigorous practitioner knowledge in schools and universities? *Educational Researcher*, *28*(5), 12–21, 40.

Anderson, G. L., Herr, K., & Nihlen, A. S. (1994). *Studying your own school: An educator's guide to qualitative practitioner research*. Thousand Oaks, CA: Corwin Press.

Beardsley, M. (1982). Aesthetic experience regained. In M. J. Wreen & D. M. Callen (Eds.), *The aesthetic point of view* (pp. 77–92). Ithaca, NY: Cornell University Press.

Biesta, G. J. J., & Burbles, N. C. (2003). *Pragmatism and educational research*. Toronto: Rowan & Littlefield.

Churchley, J. F. (2009). Aesthetic experiences at an arts school: A practitioner research inquiry. Unpublished doctoral thesis, University of Nottingham, Nottingham, UK.

Cochran-Smith, M., & Lytle, S. L. (1993). *Inside/outside: Teacher research and knowledge*. New York: Teachers College Press.

Cziko, G. A. (1989). Unpredictability and indeterminism in human behavior: Arguments and implications for educational research. *Educational Researcher*, *18*(3), 17–25.

Dewey, J. (1934). *Art as experience*. New York: Minton, Balch.

Eder, D., & Fingerson, L. (2002). Interviewing children and adolescents. In J. F. Gubrium & J. A. Holstein (Eds.), *Handbook of interview research: Context and method* (pp. 181–202). Thousand Oaks, CA: Sage.

Fielding, M. (2004). Transformative approaches to student voice: Theoretical underpinnings, recalcitrant realities. *British Educational Research Journal, 30*(2), 295–311.

Fraser, D., Henderson, C., & Price, G. J. (2005). The art of the matter: Researching children's learning in art, music, drama, and dance. 3rd International Conference on Imagination and Education, Vancouver, BC.

Grover, S. (2004). Why won't they listen to us? On giving power and voice to children in social research. *Childhood, 11*(1): 81–93.

Hammersley, M., & Atkinson, P. (1989). *Ethnography: Principles in practice.* London: Routledge.

Johnson, K. (2000). Research ethics and children. *Curriculum Perspectives, 20*(4): 6–7.

Johnson, K. (2004). Researching with children: Children's perspectives of their place(s) in primary schools. Paper presented at the Australian Association for Research in Education, International Education Conference, Melbourne, November 29–December 2.

Johnson, K. (2008). Teaching children to use visual research methods. In P. Thomson (Ed.), *Doing visual research with children and young people* (pp. 77–94). London: Routledge.

Moustakas, C. (1990). *Heuristic research: Design, methodology, and applications.* Newbury Park, CA: Sage.

Noyes, A. (2008). Using video diaries to investigate learner trajectories. In P. Thomson (Ed.), *Doing visual research with children and young people* (pp. 132–145). London: Routledge.

Shusterman, R. (1992). *Pragmatist aesthetics: Living beauty, rethinking art.* Cambridge, MA: Blackwell.

Stake, R. (1986). An evolutionary view of educational improvement. In E. R. House (Ed.), *New directions in educational evaluation* (pp. 89–102). London: Falmer Press.

Taylor, P. (1996). Doing reflective practitioner research in arts education. In P. Taylor (Ed.), *Researching drama and arts education: Paradigms and possibilities* (pp. 25–58). London: Falmer Press.

Thomson, P. (2008). Children and young people: Voices in visual research. In P. Thomson (Ed.), *Doing visual research with children and young people* (pp. 1–19). London: Routledge.

Thomson, P., & Hall, C. (2008). Dialogues with artists: Analysing children's self-portraits. In P. Thomson (Ed.), *Doing visual research with children and young people* (pp. 146–163). London: Routledge.

Chapter 3

From the other side of the fence

The experience of being researched from a headteacher's point of view

Interview with Tony Lyng

Tony Lyng was headteacher for fifteen years at Brockhill Park School, Hythe, Kent. During that time, the school gained prominence in the creativity field, beginning in 2002 with the onset of Creative Partnerships (CP) in Kent and leading to several publications about its work (www.creativitycultureeducation.org/data/files/made-for-each-other-heath-boehncke-wolf-2007-129.pdf; accessed 15 March 2010). As Tony explains, the school supported a wide range of research from 2002 onwards. This was a challenging experience in a number of ways: it created a number of logistical burdens and was potentially disruptive for staff and students. And of course it isn't always clear whether a school being researched will benefit from any findings – or if it does, what form these benefits might take.

To explore these questions, Julian Sefton-Green interviewed Tony in January 2010 about his experiences of being the head who made all of this happen.

Getting into research

JSG: The school has a reputation for dance, but did this become a topic of research prior to 2002?

TL: We had some outside interest but it would be from either teachers or local-authority-based people in Kent who wanted to come and see how it worked. So, in terms of research it was probably more informal than maybe some of the stuff that happened after that; there was some interest from Christchurch, Canterbury, at the time and they were interested in the fact that we did dance for boys right the way through. Again that was for a very short term and on an informal level rather than any kind of longitudinal study.

It involved people coming in and talking to key practitioners; talking to some staff but not actually talking to students. The staff were quite buoyed up by the fact that somebody was interested in their practice and so it had a very positive effect.

JSG: And then from 2002 you became a Creative Partnerships school.

TL: We had moved the school on from a fairly desperate performance in many areas in about '93 to being quite a reasonable school in terms of performance but we couldn't actually break some barriers. These were related to elements of motivating students; elements of classroom practice and standards of achievement where we seemed to have plateaued out. So we, at that time, were looking for something different to be able to move the school on to another level because there was a feeling that we (although, against the performance indicators that people would have applied to us, we were doing well) personally felt that we were doing badly.

JSG: And was that a whole-staff thing?

TL: Yes, there'd been a process from about the end of 2001 where we'd undertaken a lot of reviews and brainstorming around processes with our staff, governors and students really looking at what we did well and what we didn't do well.

JSG: So things started happening in the school from when?

TL: The real impact I think began in 2003, and in that first year, 2002/3, there was a lot of reflection in the school but with this additional level now of being able to look at things with I think the first level, if you like, of creative response. We were doing projects with the students and, in terms of whole-school shift, the first level was to really look at how we were structured ourselves and also how we actually organized the children. That gave us a platform to be able to develop all sorts of things that didn't exist before that.

The student research project

TL: In 2003, CP activity became very substantial. There were several projects that we were involved in with other schools but there are aspects of our practice that CP invested in heavily, and the student research project was one example of this. The student research project started in early 2004 and ran through then for eighteen months. That's when we were linked up with a team from the States. They put a research worker into the school.

Shirley Brice Heath oversaw the whole project with Shelby Wolf. But it was actually Elka Paul-Boehncke who worked in the school. The project essentially involved two all-age, all-ability tutor groups with their teachers – one was a scientist and one was a dance teacher – and the initial question was: was there any difference in the way that the arts and sciences use language or work in school? And that was the stimulus.

We had an ongoing project where the students were trained as researchers by Elka and she was obviously researching it as well, so it was a kind of action research. The two staff involved were heavily involved in the research and one of them was a physics PhD, and so she had some good research skills in her own right. The other was a dance teacher, and that was quite interesting because dance was our flagship area for teaching and learning in the school. Their whole group widened; they started off focusing on that particular question but it actually went into the substance of what we were doing in terms of curriculum, teaching and learning structures, social reconstruction, etc. It became quite a massive project. It involved Elka being in the school as an observer for days at a time.

We were also involved in a project around emotional intelligence – I think, again, because some of the work came from people who'd been into the school because of CP. They believed that the school was emotionally intelligent and so they wanted to come and look at why that was. That, again, was very much based around questionnaires and discussion groups with staff and students, and it was that kind of instrument that was used. We were also involved with a project from the University of Nottingham and we were one of ten schools that were looked at for our overall practice, and that was very interesting. We had a researcher from Nottingham who, I think, spent a total amount of three days in the school. And then, of course, around all of that we tended to get a lot of people interested in what we were doing and all wanting to find out how we did things, particularly vertical tutoring, and what the impact of that was. At one stage, the whole place was sort of a hive of activity with different people coming in and out. So it was a very interesting situation to be in.

Pain or pleasure?

JSG: So, from 2002 onwards you had researchers coming in and people living with you and being part of your establishment; you had people doing surveys. Did you have any special meetings with either parents or governors or teachers?

TL: Yes, certainly at all three levels there was involvement either in forum discussions around key questions related to what was going on by a number of different groups of researchers, so it was quite encompassing. And also we created a forum with the village and they were involved too, and so we brought in people who had technically nothing to do with the school other than being neighbours.

JSG: All of this was obviously an extra burden in practical terms; was it annoying or difficult?

TL: Well, I think much of it was not really a burden because we had very good systems for communicating with staff, and it was staff in the end who carried the burden, and we kept them apprised all the way through the process about who was doing what. I think the burdens, occasionally, were apparently silly things like having a conversation, and where can this take place? And just occasionally servicing needs around that. But, to be honest, in terms of the actual process I think there was little or no feedback – that people found it too intrusive. I think that's because we've developed a culture where it was kind of assumed that whatever was going on in the classroom had a wider audience, if that makes sense.

JSG: Did it disrupt teaching and learning?

TL: No, I don't think it did. Again, the view that was taken by some of the leadership team was that the benefits of what we got out of being involved in the research at all levels – staff and students, because we were very keen to engage students and student voice – outweighed any loss of time. We were also trying to shift staff away from being time dependent anyway, so in a sense it served an aim. Where people who previously might have been very worried about losing five minutes or ten minutes, we were saying to them that it's not about that but about how you organize the learning and how the students take responsibility for their learning. We said to them that you'll be surprised by what you used to think took six weeks before; you could probably do in three or four. So, to an extent, a part of what we were doing with that, and embedded in the research, was the use of time-out cards. This was where students who had got ahead in their work and their work was of a good quality were actually given time to go and do something that they wanted to do. It had to be something that wasn't frivolous but linked to their learning so they could follow a project of their choice.

The research facilitated that because sometimes we had to pull students out of lessons, and this goes back to the original point about the inconvenience, but the agreement that we had was that any crucial work would be caught up with and there was a contract there.

We had a feeling from some previous work that we'd done before about this that rewarding students with time-outs was a much better thing to do than to give them another page of the same work in terms of their motivation. But I think that we didn't really see the real benefits of it until after the event when we could analyse it.

JSG: And was there any opposition to this?

TL: Some. There are about eighty-four teachers and seventy other staff at the school and so there would have been a small percentage of teachers who found this personally threatening, and the reason for that was their view of how accountable they were. They weren't objecting in principle to it but they were worried about the fact that if something did go wrong, they would take the blame for it.

JSG: Did people come to you with concerns?

TL: Yes. And through talking them through the benefits and also the systems that would be in place to make sure that the students wouldn't be at a disadvantage and also that it was very clearly the case that this was not the teacher's responsibility, so most people were able to live with that.

They did trust me, but, in the end, where perhaps they'd spoken to another member of the leadership team and been quite difficult about it, I intervened.

The value of research

JSG: So, were there some people in the school who were very interested in research?

TL: Yes. We'd encouraged people to undertake various research through bursary systems that we brought in to encourage people to try things out. But there was also a good programme of getting people involved in what were, in a sense, action-based research MAs at Kent.

JSG: Do you know whether your staff were better qualified or less qualified than [those in] other schools?

TL: I think if you're looking at Kent non-selective schools then overall we had better-qualified teachers, I would say. And at any one moment in time, about 10–15 per cent of staff would have been studying.

JSG: And was research used as a way of theorizing changes?

TL: I think we've developed a system around using research action models just to do school development planning. So that was our kind of focus, and it was articulated in that way because if you're seeking to promote any kind of development for improvement, you really need to determine what your starting points are; the research questions are a really good way of framing how you're going to think about your planning, and because it was reflective practice that we were looking at, you had your kind of feedback in there so that you could continually adjust where you were going.

I was doing a doctorate at Lincoln in educational leadership, which I am about to complete – the great thing about that particular doctorate was it was all embedded in your own practice.

To be honest, all the way through the time I was teaching I was certainly committed to the view that if you approach things through an action research model and you are reflecting on your practice, it would get better.

JSG: So tell us about the experience of having Shirley Brice Heath and Shelby Wolf in school and the impact of published outcomes.

TL: That was really enriching in every possible way. They came in just to talk to us and after we'd spoken to them for about an hour or so, they said could they come and do this, and I think there was no point of the contact that we had with them which was in any way disabling in any sense. In the end, the people we were involved with did really become like members of our staff.

I think some of the shorter papers were probably quite widely disseminated. The book, I've no idea, to be honest. I know it's been passed around Kent and we gave all of the students a copy and any parents who wanted it. The messages in it are very valuable for anyone going down that road but it kind of moved on to another stage.

JSG: So in one sense you weren't terribly interested in the formal outputs?

TL: No, not really. The book didn't matter either way; it was the process that mattered. I think research is one of the best forms of ongoing feedback you can possibly get.

JSG: And were you interested at all in any of the status outputs – the reputational value of all this?

TL: I think that was very, very good for the staff and their morale to go to places and have a bit of renown. It's nice to be part of an organization that is well respected, but probably one of the things that we really didn't do too much of was trying to make anything of it other than what other people made of it. We just kind of got on with what we were doing but freely shared any outcomes.

Governors and other stakeholders in the school were very proud of the research. The location of the school makes it a bit of a backwater and it became clear, post-2005, that there were all sorts of amazing things happening on our campus and we suddenly became a popular destination.

JSG: And were you at all calculating about that or did you just realize that it would be a dividend?

TL: Not at all calculating. It was a very busy place and I think one of the good things about it was staff actually embraced change as their normal activity.

JSG: Do you think that you or any staff learned anything that was troubling or difficult from the research?

TL: No, although there were negatives and challenges around some of the ideas. The thing is, if you are doing a lot of research, you get asked questions that you don't particularly want to live with, but if you're true to it then you can live with them. I think we had issues around student ownership of the buildings and spaces and things like that, and we got some answers from the students which didn't match with what we thought. But they were right and so we undertook the changes, but there was a financial cost to that. And things to do with the staff in terms of saying, this is how we are going to do it in the future and you've got to accommodate, which required some extra work.

We did a huge survey on teaching and learning and aspects of personalized learning and we were really surprised to find at one point how, in certain areas that we thought had certainly changed their practice, they hadn't. We just hadn't seen that and the kids told us indirectly, and when we checked up on it, again the children were right.

JSG: As a result of the research, the school now has a particular flag around pupil voice and pupil ownership, so which do you think came first: the research interest or the reshaping of power relations?

TL: The research interest, probably, because we'd formed the new learning communities based on a totally different way but, in fact, through the student involvement in the research we realized what a powerful way that could be to engage with students. And there would be, at one stage, around four to five hundred students involved in research on a whole variety of levels – and that was real engagement.

JSG: Some of what you're describing – the knowledge that is produced and circulated by the research process – is, in a sense, generated by people reflecting and seeing things from different perspectives; it's not introduced by different philosophical or academic perspectives, so were there any key readings or was the knowledge generated by yourselves?

TL: We certainly imported some knowledge. I suppose we did initially rely heavily on the kind of philosophical and methodological approaches that Shirley Brice Heath, Shelby Wolf and Elka brought into the school. Some staff went away and read *Ways with words* (by Shirley Brice Heath), and some of the questions she got people to think about were very interesting. In terms of the training of the student researchers, a key issue around that was having a firm ethical base so nobody would be damaged by the process.

We referred staff to BERA guidelines because that was quite a good common-sense basis for moving forward. But in terms of linking it directly to one particular school of thought, no, I don't think that was the case.

In the end, I would just say that any school that goes down this path of having active student research projects with outside researchers coming in to support it will not regret doing so.

Chapter 4

What's with the artist?

Researching practice with visual arts practitioners

Emily Pringle

Introduction

Artists are increasingly recognized as making a significant contribution to young people's creative learning.[1] Yet claims for what artists achieve in education contexts can be based on untested assumptions regarding what artists are: artists are inherently and uniquely creative, artists are experts in making and doing, artists bring something new and different, for example. Arguably, these assumptions regarding practitioner-led creative learning stem from specific constructions – in the case of the visual artist, informed by art history and cultural theory. Each construction ascribes particular knowledge and skills to the artist, which has implications for what these practitioners are expected to 'teach' or share with learners, and the forms of engagement they engender with others. It stands to reason, therefore, that interrogating these constructions and how they translate into pedagogy can contribute to our understanding of how artists enhance creative learning.

However, issues arise in terms of researching creative learning practice since historically there has been a relative lack of work addressing the artist as educator, and even less that investigates artists' perspectives. Too often the artist's voice is absent in evaluation reports, where the focus can be on the impacts on young people exclusively. Yet a fuller understanding of why such impacts are generated is more likely to be achieved through interrogating the creative learning process and the forms of pedagogic and creative engagement occurring between participants, artists and others from a range of perspectives.

This chapter starts by examining three constructions of the artist that have emerged over the past hundred years (although they are themselves informed by earlier models). For the purposes of this chapter, the interrogation focuses primarily on visual artists, although the three models examined here can be seen to resonate with other creative practitioners, including musicians, writers, dancers and those working in theatre. An examination of selected research into creative learning then demonstrates how these constructions frame the visual artist in education contexts, while highlighting the implications of identifying artists as special or unique. Recognizing the complexity of the artist's role leads to an analysis of methodological approaches to working with arts practitioners which gain understanding of their motivations, working processes and perceived outcomes. The chapter seeks to make clear why it is important to involve arts practitioners in the research process; however, it also outlines some of the risks, challenges and limitations of these methods of investigating creative teaching and learning.

Three constructions of the artist

The idea that creative practitioners make a special contribution appears regularly in arts in education publications. An example can be found in a 1998 report from the UK Office for Standards in Education (Ofsted) which extols the virtues of artists in schools. Indeed, as the authors conclude:

> There is a growing body of evidence and testimony to indicate that the work of artists in schools and colleges enhances the quality of teaching and learning in the classroom and makes a significant contribution to the quality of school life.
>
> (Oddie & Allen, 1998, p. 18)

The implication here is that artists bring something extra to schools and add value to the existing pedagogic relations taking place. This in turn assumes that it is possible to understand 'the artist' in the same way that we comprehend other professionals (including teachers, for example) who are acknowledged as having specific expertise and function in particular ways. In other words, artists can be defined according to certain skills and knowledge that differentiate them from others and which, in this instance, enable them to contribute in 'significant' ways in learning scenarios. But how do we understand or define the artist?

Artist as uniquely inspired individual

One dominant model of visual artists portrays them as uniquely inspired and original individuals who, by drawing on their own wellspring of innate gifts and engaging exclusively with their chosen medium, imbue art with particular meaning (Greenberg, [1940] 1993). This theoretical construction, which is informed by ideas associated with eighteenth- and nineteenth-century Romanticism, locates artists as exclusive authors or creators of work. Thus, within this particular construction, artists struggle with self-expression by engaging with their imagination and chosen medium, in order to 'create' entirely original, aesthetically autonomous works of art with a unique signature style.

Here, artists are deemed to possess 'special' creative gifts and to operate in an exemplary creative realm.

The model of the uniquely creative individual taps into the notion of the artist as 'avant-garde', particularly as the latter frames artists as existing beyond or outside of conventional society (within a bohemian sphere). It also suggests that their work, through exhibiting radical and advanced ideas, has the potential to stretch and challenge current structures and ways of thinking. Artists here operate as individuals who have sole responsibility for their development and destiny. Yet as Suzy Gablik identifies, this construction contains 'the subtle and far-reaching message concerning the loneliness and isolation of the self' (1995, p. 17). In turn, the emphasis on the articulation of individual and innovative ideas encourages an esotericism that can preclude the sharing of ideas and communal forms of reflection and meaning making (Kester, 2004) (criticisms that can equally be made of more individualistic pedagogic models). At the same time, the focus on the exceptional creative genius has implications in terms of how we understand creativity (Banerji & Burn with Buckingham, 2006) and the potential to develop it in others.

As a result, since the late 1960s in particular, this understanding of the artist as a uniquely inspired genius who operates autonomously, beyond the realm of society and theory, has undergone reassessment. Cultural theorists, feminist art historians and artists themselves have critiqued the concept of the lone (typically male) creative genius and provided alternative considerations of artistic production and reception and, as is examined below, broader, more inclusive views of creativity. Yet the construction is seductive in many ways and continues to shape our understanding of the visual artist.

Artist as craftsperson or designer

An alternative model locates the artist as craftsperson or technician producing objects primarily for functional or decorative purpose rather than their aesthetic quality. Associated on one level with the pre-Renaissance, the artist as artisan maker is defined not by his or her unique vision or individual creativity, but rather by his or her technical prowess. At its most reductive, this model confines artistic expertise to craft knowledge and technical skills.

However, during the twentieth century, and specifically emerging from the Bauhaus school of art and design in Germany in the 1930s, a more nuanced model of the artist as craftsperson emerges. Indeed, the Bauhaus merits attention here not least because of its continuing influence on art education and perceptions of what and how art should be taught. Unlike in previous European art academies, where students were expected to learn through imitating historical examples, at the Bauhaus emphasis was on learning through making in order to become skilled in the manipulation of materials. Therefore, in Bauhaus workshops the division between 'artist' and craftsperson was blurred since teachers such as Johannes Itten instilled in students the importance of combining rigorous knowledge of form, colour and materials while acknowledging the significance of singular expression in defining the individual's visual language.

Echoes of the previous model of the uniquely inspired individual surface here, but whereas inspiration alone is foregrounded in that case, here individual expression is linked to art-form skill with knowledge acquired through experience of making. As the artist Josef Albers describes:

> First we seek contact with material. . . . Instead of pasting it, we will put paper together by sewing, buttoning, riveting, typing, and pinning it; in other words we fasten it in a multitude of ways. We will test the possibilities of its tensile and compression-resistant strength. In doing so we do not always create 'works of art,' but rather experiments; it is not our ambition to fill museums: we are gathering experience.
>
> (Quoted in Bergdoll & Dickerman, 2009, p. 17)

Arguably, this focus on experiential learning shapes our understanding of what artists know (artists possess knowledge of practical art making, and this tacit or craft knowledge enables them to express their ideas), but also of how we should 'learn' art (art can only be learned through doing). Thus, the artist is inextricably linked to making and the meaning of a work of art is 'a result of craft knowledge' (Dormer, 1994, p. 26).

Artist as collaborator or facilitator

The third construction considered here locates artists in terms of their relations with, and responsibility towards, others. While the lone, avant-garde protagonist is familiar through-out the twentieth and twenty-first centuries, an alternative construction of the socially engaged artist is also present during this period. As early as the 1930s, Marxist intellectuals and artists were questioning the function of art and the role of the avant-garde, and arguing for more politically motivated and collaborative artistic practice (Harrison & Wood, 1993). Furthermore, from the 1950s onwards the model of the artist as collaborator or facilitator and social activist can be found in the work of feminist and leftist-leaning artists, whose interests lay in social activism, redefining the role of art and the audience and in developing a collaborative methodology (Lacy, 1995).

Within the UK, practitioners working as part of the so-called community arts movement exemplified one manifestation of this model. Emerging in the late 1960s, community arts was stimulated by artists' unease with the political, social and cultural situation at that time. In practice, community arts embraced a range of artists and activities broadly sharing a belief in empowerment through participation in a creative process, a dislike of cultural hierarchies (specifically, the distinctions between high art practice and other forms of creativity located outside the discourses and physical locations of fine art) and a belief in the creative potential of all sections of society (Morgan, 1995). A more democratic view of creativity is thus espoused, wherein creativity is seen to be the preserve of the many, not the exceptional few.

So how is artistic expertise framed within this construction? Insights are provided by Walter Benjamin's seminal text 'The author as producer' (1934), in which he argues for a radical, innovative, socially engaged practice wherein artists (in this instance writers) have an overall responsibility to educate. According to Benjamin, the artist/intellectual is 'an engineer' (p. 102) in the service of others. As a collaborator/facilitator and potentially social activist, the artist has as his or her purpose to operate within society, and the artist's value lies not so much in terms of what he or she knows, but more how the artist uses his or her knowledge and skills to facilitate and enable others' creativity. This suggests that artists' expertise is manifested in their modes of engagement or, conceivably, in education contexts, their pedagogic relations.

Framing the artist in creative learning research

The significance of the three models outlined in the previous section becomes apparent when one looks at how artists are located within existing research into creative learning. If we return to the Ofsted report cited earlier, for example, we see that artists are deemed to be especially effective in schools. This conclusion comes at the end of a report that 'seeks to provide a picture of practice from a practitioner's perspective' (Oddie & Allen, 1998, p. 1) and is informed by the testimonies of over a hundred artists, as well as a survey of literature and historical overview. Arts practitioners are placed at the centre of this study, and the authors provide a broad overview of artists' work.

It is illuminating, therefore, that the report outlines the relationship between artists, teachers and learners and provides a typology of artistic roles which include 'artist as role model' and 'artist as outsider'. This latter category frames the artist as alien and different, seeing it as positive in a classroom scenario. Appearing to stem directly from the construction of the artist as uniquely inspired individual, here the creative professional is valued for bringing something alternative from 'outside'. Similarly, the discourse around artists in schools tends to imply that artists can be more liberated and challenging. For example, in a text that draws on ten years of research projects with artists in museums, Veronica Sekules argues that

[i]n absolute contrast to the clarity of objectives necessary in school, artists work with enigma and uncertainty, and are not bound to explain anything about what they do. Artists are expected to push forward new boundaries, they are predisposed to innovate, try the untested and challenge authority. They can range freely into controversial subjects without moral judgements or clear right or wrong answers.

(2003, p. 139)

This suggests strongly that an artist contributes through being the charismatic creative genius who inspires through being an outsider, beyond the bounds of convention. Whereas teachers, in Sekules's view, have to 'set clear aims, to follow clear and lucid paths to learning, to quantify results and aim for close targeting of achievements' (p. 139), artists do not work within such constraints.

At the same time, artists working in education can be portrayed as technicians or crafts-people whose role is to support the curriculum by 'teaching' specific skills (Sharp & Dust, 1997). Here the role appears to echo that of the craftsperson/designer since artists do not introduce an alternative, more radical practice, but instead work within existing pedagogic structures and processes. Another of Oddie and Allen's categories, for example, designates the artist as 'teacher/facilitator' who provides 'specialist, professional arts skills not usually available to the classroom teacher . . . [and] in-service support and experience for hard-pressed teachers' (1998, p. 38). It is notable that 'facilitator' is associated in the first instance with the teaching of skills. At the same time, the authors recognize that 'the artist as co-artist can motivate and encourage students to reach beyond apparent capabilities' (p. 38), which suggests that the more collaborative role outlined above is also present.

The multiplicity of artists' roles is borne out by research that examines the particular forms of engagement between artists and participants in a range of learning environments (Pringle, 2002). This study found that artists occupy different roles (including those of educator, collaborator, role model, activist and researcher) and perform a variety of func-tions, frequently at the same time. In doing so, they do not conform to the constructions identified above exclusively, but incorporate all within a more complex identity. This research differed from Oddie and Allen's study in its methodology. Rather than conducting a survey of a larger number of practitioners, here a selection of artist-educators were interviewed at length not only about what they perceived they did in schools, but also about the ways they went about it. This more in-depth study of a smaller group yielded detailed insights into the specifics of the creative learning process, which is harder to achieve in a broader-scale, but necessarily shallower, study.

Further productive insights can be found within research that seeks to pinpoint whether there is a specific artistic pedagogy (which takes us back to the artist as collaborator/ facilitator construction), perhaps deriving from and informed by art practice. Harland *et al.* (2005) appear to think so. Drawing on a detailed examination of a range of arts-based interventions in schools, their research indicates that 'artists' pedagogy' embraced several different elements, which included 'the quality of explanation and the nature of feedback; the use of resources; the provision of opportunities for creativity; the extent to which pupils were allowed ownership of activities and the artist's flexibility to pupil needs' (p. 130). Again a case-study methodology was used, but here space was given to teachers, pupils, school managers and significant others (including parents) as well as artists. It is significant that artists' pedagogy was identified by teachers and pupils as having the strongest influence (more so than project content, relevance and curriculum enhancement) on the outcomes of the project. These outcomes included enhanced knowledge, greater thinking and developments in creativity, which suggests that the approach artists adopt (which is in turn informed by their practice) plays a critical role in facilitating creative learning.

Additional support for the formulation of an artistic pedagogy is indicated by those writers who draw parallels between art practice and teaching, in some cases arguing that the former can provide a basis for good practice in the latter. For example, in an article exploring artistic behaviour as a model for teaching, Parks (1992) identified six characteristics of 'artistry' that provide models for effective teaching. Similarly, the concept of 'reflective practice' in art and design can be considered as a basis for the professional development of specialist teachers of that subject (Prentice, 1995) – in particular, the creative and reflective/responsive capacities that are required to be an artist, as well as the artist's need to remain open, take risks and make radical changes where necessary. The artist is identified here as a reflexive practitioner, a position that Prentice argues is preferable to that of the 'infallible expert' which teachers can too easily adopt.

However, Parks's and Prentice's differentiation between artist and teacher (and Sekules's portrayal of the artist as radical outsider) highlights one danger of research focusing on artists alone – for by looking at artists exclusively and attributing to them a uniquely innovative practice, we run the risk of polarizing art making and teaching, thereby potentially disempowering the teacher and placing unreasonable expectations on the artist. It hardly needs stating here that the boundaries between artists and teachers can be blurred, most notably in secondary schools, where art teachers frequently maintain their own art practice. Furthermore, as was noted earlier, the construction of the fine artist as uniquely creative has been challenged by more democratic notions of creativity. Thus, the National Advisory Committee on Creative and Cultural Education (NACCCE) report *All our futures* (1999), for example, identifies creativity as rooted more in the potential for everyone to engage in imaginative and original activity, and argues that not just artists but a range of professionals, including scientists, can enhance others' creative learning.

The current picture appears mixed, and this complexity seems to extend to how artists' practice is constructed within projects such as Creative Partnerships. On the one hand, Creative Partnerships 'in general espouses an eclectic notion of creativity' (Banaji & Burn with Buckingham, 2006, p. 3) and draws on the NACCCE definition. Yet at the same time it appears at times to privilege the creative practitioner:

> We understand that creativity is not simply about 'doing the arts' – it is about questioning, making connections, inventing and reinventing, about flexing the imaginative muscles. We do believe, however, that working with creative professionals from many different artforms and disciplines helps develop creative thinking, as these processes are central to the work of such practitioners.
>
> (Collard, 2007, p. 1)

This description of a 'creative' way of working is valuable in drawing attention to particular aptitudes that creative professionals may possess. However, the subsequent observation that 'creative practitioners bring a new approach . . . they bring a different language and a different practice, which stretches and challenges the teaching staff and young people' (p. 2) appears to return again to the model of artist as uniquely inspired individual, while reinforcing the potentially damaging binary between artists and teachers.

Given the recurrence of this construction of the artist as something special in terms of creative learning, it is crucial to clarify the ways in which these practitioners operate, not least to ensure that artistic expertise is appropriately acknowledged, while avoiding undermining and underestimating teachers. So how can we gain a greater understanding of the practice from the artist's perspective in a way that can usefully inform creative learning in different contexts? One must be aware of the dangers of focusing on artists alone, but one solution lies in exploring research methodologies that enable artists to make explicit the way they work and foreground collaboration. By working with artists to interrogate their perceptions of knowledge and practice we can start to address some of these many questions.

What research has been done? Methodologies and approaches

Similar methodological approaches have been taken in two recent studies that examine arts practitioners in education contexts. Chappell's study of three dance professionals working on projects under the auspices of the Laban dance centre in south-east London took a qualitative interpretive stance and used a multi-case educational case-study approach to consider how creative learning was facilitated in dance education (Chappell, 2008). Similarly, Pringle's qualitative research was designed as interlocking, tiered case studies. This study examined relationships between art practice and pedagogy through focusing on five artist-educators operating within the community education programme at Tate Modern, London (Pringle, 2008). Data collection in both instances was done through semi-structured interviews and participant observation, although Chappell also involved video, photography, documentation and reflective diaries. By adopting these methods, both researchers were able to gain insights into the practitioners' perceptions of how they worked with participants and what it was that they were 'teaching'. The studies reveal the process these artists underwent with learners and what outcomes they aspired to generate. In neither study are teachers or learners involved.

In each study, the framing of knowledge is highlighted, and in particular the concept of what knowledge is intrinsic to practice is significant. In Chappell's work, the practitioners place 'very high value on aesthetic and embodied knowing' (2008, p. 85). Seeing these forms of knowing as central to the practice of dance, the dancers aspired to facilitate their development in the pupils: 'The teachers worked to achieve aesthetic and embodied knowing by encouraging children to intertwine their personal and collective voice with their craft and compositional knowledge' (p. 86). The dancers perceived aesthetic and embodied knowing to be central to their own epistemology and sought to engender the development of such expertise in learners. In doing so, they aimed to help children understand how dance can creatively communicate the young people's ideas.

Similar findings emerge in Pringle's study. Here the artist-educators saw their knowledge as largely experiential and embodied; it enabled them to embark on the creative process and realize their ideas. Others have described this expertise as 'aesthetic intelligence . . . [which is] about judgements and . . . a form of intelligence that can know what to do when making' (Pollock interviewed in Raney, 2003, p. 149). Recognizing that this expertise (which encompasses skills such as active questioning, risk taking, accommodating the unexpected and tolerating uncertainty alongside critically reflecting) is intrinsic to art making, these artist-educators aspired to facilitate its development in the learners they worked alongside. Furthermore, these visual art practitioners' aspirations mirrored those of the dancers; they aimed to enable learners to use art making as a means to articulate their thoughts and ideas.

So if both dancers and artists work to develop specific knowledge in learners related to their own practices, how do they set about doing so and what are the implications for creative learning? Chappell (2008, p. 87) describes how the dancers used strategies from three core 'pedagogical spectra'. The first spectrum identifies how a balance was achieved between 'working inside out', where the creative source for dance ideas was prioritized within the children, and 'working outside in', where knowledge that was typically manifested within the teacher was transmitted to learners. The second spectrum articulates how the dancers variously intervened: either directly, at close range, through, for example, focused criticism, or through more reactive, praise-based comments. The final spectrum concerns how responsibility for sharing creative activities accommodated both freedom to explore and play and more structured scaffolding of tasks linked more closely to the teacher's own knowledge. In developing these spectra, Chappell makes explicit the complex modes of engagement between all the participants. Creative learning is facilitated through a collaborative process wherein learners play an active role and dance-educators share their own knowledge using a variety of pedagogic devices.

While Pringle does not devise a formal categorization of the artist-led teaching and learning process, a similarly complicated and sophisticated picture emerges. The artist-educators describe, for instance, how they engage students in a process of learning by acknowledging learners' existing knowledge while providing opportunities to experiment, take risks and play, within a supportive, yet critically rigorous, environment. Artist-educators impart knowledge to learners through dialogic exchange, and learners are constructed as active generators of their own knowledge. Thus, as within the dance study, experiential and collaborative (and hence creative) learning by artists and young people takes place, not because the practitioners embody a particular 'artistic' role but because they draw on particular expertise and interact in multiple ways with learners.

The learning context is also addressed in these studies, as both the Laban and the Tate Modern have long-standing education programmes with established pedagogic frameworks. Situated outside of formal education criteria, these frameworks privilege specific knowledge development and teaching methodologies that arguably differ from those found in the school context. For example, the Tate's methodology foregrounds learners' existing knowledge and skills, encourages an attitude of questioning and experimentation, and highlights plural reading of works of art, thereby fostering multiple responses (Pringle, 2008). All of this suggests that these artists were working within epistemological contexts highly conducive to creative learning.

Through using methodologies that foreground the artist-educators' perspectives and allow for detailed investigation of process and context, these two studies provide useful insights into a number of issues relevant to creative learning. In the first instance, they illuminate how certain artists construct an 'artistic' epistemology. In doing so, potentially these findings provide a basis for making realistic comparisons with teachers; for instance, are artists equipped with specific 'creative' knowledge and skills that teachers lack? The studies also enhance understanding of the artist-led learning process and how this supports creative learning. Chappell's study explicitly addresses this issue, but even within Pringle's research (which did not), evidence is widespread of how the practice under investigation corresponds with many of the criteria for developing creativity. Finally, the studies touch on the learning outcomes: what types of knowledge have been developed in participants. In doing so, the studies provide robust evidence to support the use of artists in scenarios aspiring to develop creative learning.

Yet the focus on the learning context also draws attention to the at times privileged position artists can occupy in schools and elsewhere. The arts practitioners in both these studies were working outside of the constraints of the National Curriculum for England and Wales, and beyond the pressures of the assessment culture. Within the context of schools, therefore, while examining the valuable contribution artists can make to creative learning, research with arts practitioners also needs to recognize that teachers are too rarely afforded the same freedom to experiment and take risks. Otherwise, there is a danger, as Addison and Burgess (2006) argue, that normative relations will be reinforced. Artists act as a 'one-off bubble' while teachers' practice remains unrecognized and therefore potentially unchanged.

There are further risks and limitations inherent in adopting Chappell's and Pringle's research methodology. Both studies focus on an investigation of specific individuals' perceptions of their practice within a given context, hence the logic of adopting a qualitative case-study approach seems inescapable. As Cohen, Manion, and Morrison (2002, p. 181) acknowledge, the case study 'provides a unique example of real people in real situations, enabling readers to understand ideas more clearly than simply presenting them with abstract theories or principles'. However, a criticism levelled at case studies (see, for example, Cohen et al., 2002; Denzin & Lincoln, 1998) is the hazard of generalizing more widely from findings. In the case of these two studies, for example, can we justifiably conclude that other artists think and behave in the way the case-study interviewees do? This question would appear particularly relevant in relation to a field as heterogeneous and complex as artistic practice. Realistically, it would require a far greater number of studies, focusing on a wider range of practitioners, to be able to make any form of acceptably reliable generalizations, certainly from a positivist perspective. Yet this does not invalidate the contribution these studies make, since they assist our understanding of artist-led practice by drilling down to the details, something that remains difficult if alternative research approaches are adopted.

Another limitation in the approaches adopted in these studies is the lack of multiple perspectives: in both cases, the focus is on artists exclusively. Although there can be a focus on outcomes within research and evaluation relating to creative learning, there also exists a tendency for claims to be made regarding the impact of the arts on learners which are not sufficiently supported by rigorous or long-term empirical evidence gathered from those participants. Therefore, although it is artists' perceptions of themselves and their pedagogic activities that are under investigation, arguably, exploring the extent to which others (in particular learners) share these perceptions could avoid accusations of selectivity and bias.

Conclusion

The positive contribution arts practitioners can make in terms of creative learning is increasingly recognized and supported by research, but studies can at times appear to reinforce existing conceptions of 'the artist' without unpicking the implications of such constructions or interrogating the details of artistic epistemology and process. Given the added value that artists are seen to provide, it is important to move beyond designating the artist as 'special' or uniquely creative, and it is potentially damaging to the practice of artists and other professionals they work with (including teachers) to assume a specific 'artistic' expertise without having a fuller understanding of what that might be. However, employing research methodologies that uncover artists' skills, expertise and preferred pedagogies can yield insights not only into what artists do but also into how and, perhaps most crucially, why they operate as they do. Although research that focuses exclusively on creative practitioners has limitations, existing studies suggest that there is real value and much to be learned from including artists' perspectives in studies of creative learning.

Note

1   A variety of definitions of creative learning are currently in circulation and it remains to some degree a nebulous concept. Those that resonate with the concerns of this chapter focus on the development and use of imagination and experience to develop original thinking and new knowledge, and emphasize the importance of a collaborative pedagogic process (Spendlove & Wyse, 2008).

References

Addison, N., & Burgess, L. (2006). London cluster research report. In B. Taylor (Ed.), *Inspiring learning in galleries: Enquire about learning in galleries*. London: engage.

Banaji, S., & Burn, A., with Buckingham, D. (2006). *The rhetorics of creativity: A review of the literature*. London: Arts Council England.

Benjamin, W. ([1934] 1993) The author as producer. In C. Harrison & P. Wood (Eds.), *Art in theory, 1900–1990: An anthology of changing ideas*. Oxford: Blackwell.

Bergdoll, B., & Dickerman, L. (Eds.) (2009). *Bauhaus: Workshops for modernity 1919–1933*. New York: Museum of Modern Art.

Chappell, K. (2008). Facilitating creative learning in dance education. In A. Craft, T. Cremin, & P. Burnard (Eds.), *Creative learning 3–11 and how we document it*. Stoke-on-Trent, UK: Trentham Books.

Cohen, L., Manion, M., & Morrison, K. (2002). *Research methods in education* (5th edn.). London: Routledge.

Collard, P. (2007). This much we know . . . Creative Partnerships: Approach and impact. Available at www.creative-partnerships.com/data/files/cp-approach-and-impact-17.pdf (last accessed 12 October 2009).

Denzin, N., & Lincoln, Y. (Eds.). (1998). *Collecting and interpreting qualitative materials*. London: Sage.

Dormer, P. (1994). *The art of the maker: Skill and its meaning in art*. London: Thames & Hudson.

Gablik, S. (1995). *Conversations before the end of time*. London: Thames & Hudson.

Greenberg, C. ([1940] 1993). Towards a newer Laocoon. In C. Harrison & P. Wood (Eds.), *Art in theory 1900–1990: An anthology of changing ideas*. Oxford: Blackwell.

Harland, J., Lord, P., Stott, A., Kinder, K., Lamont, E., & Ashworth, M. (2005). *The arts–education interface: A mutual learning triangle?* Slough, UK: National Foundation for Educational Research.

Harrison, C., & Wood, P. (Eds.). (1993). *Art in theory 1900–1990: An anthology of changing ideas*. Oxford: Blackwell.

Kester, G. (2004). *Conversation pieces: Community + communication in modern art*. London: University of California Press.

Lacy, S. (1995). *Mapping the terrain: New genre public art*. Seattle: Bay Press.

Morgan, S. (1995). Looking back over 25 years. In M. Dickson (Ed.), *Art with People*. Sunderland, UK: AN Publications.

National Advisory Committee on Creative and Cultural Education (NACCCE) (1999). *All our futures: Creativity, culture and education*. London: DfEE/DCMS.

Oddie, D., & Allen, G. (1998). *Artists in schools: A review*. London: The Stationery Office.

Parks, M. (1992). The art of pedagogy: Artistic behavior as a model for teaching. *Art Education, 45*(5) (September), 51–57.

Prentice, R. (1995) Learning to teach: A conversational exchange. In R. Prentice (Ed.), *Teaching art and design: Addressing issues, identifying directions.* London: Cassell Education.

Pringle, E. (2002). *'We did stir things up': The role of artists in sites for learning.* London: Arts Council of England.

Pringle, E. (2008). The practitioner as educator: An examination of the relationship between artistic practice and pedagogy within contemporary gallery education. PhD thesis, Institute of Education, University of London.

Raney, K. (2003). *Art in question.* London: Continuum and the Arts Council of England.

Sekules, V. (2003). The celebrity performer and the creative facilitator: The artist, the school and the art museum. In M. Xanthoudaki, L. Tickle, & V. Sekules (Eds.), *Researching visual arts education in museums and galleries.* London: Kluwer Academic Publishers.

Sharp, C., & Dust, K. (1997). *Artists in schools.* Slough, UK: National Foundation for Educational Research.

Spendlove, D., & Wyse, D. (2008). Creative learning: Definitions and barriers. In A. Craft, T. Cremin, & P. Burnard (Eds.), *Creative learning 3–11 and how we document it.* Stoke-on-Trent, UK: Trentham Books.

Chapter 5

Supporting schools to do action research into creative learning

Interview with Pat Cochrane and Pete McGuigan

CapeUK is an independent agency that focuses on creativity and learning, linking practice with theory, research and professional development. Its overall purpose is to develop approaches that support children and young people to face an increasingly complex and challenging future. Partnerships between schools and creative practitioners have been key to CapeUK's work since its beginnings in 1997; it has worked with hundreds of schools, teachers and creative organizations and individuals. Between 2005 and 2008, Cape developed and led the national Creativity Action Research Awards (CARA) programme in England on behalf of Creative Partnerships.

Pat Cochrane is the CEO of CapeUK and Pete McGuigan the Learning Director. Both have extensive backgrounds in education leadership and professional learning. Pat Thomson interviewed them in February 2010.

Action research: what's in a name?

PM: One of the things that came out very clearly in the action research part of the Creativity Action Research Awards (CARA) was that action research can be problematic as a term. It was like throwing a pebble in a pond – for some people it felt like proper research because it was called action research. But the feedback we got after the first tranche of people went through was that many people were put off by the word 'research'. It was too much for them and they didn't really want that kind of language used. We took that on board and when we designed materials we tried to head off using the 'research' word; it got softened to 'inquiry'.

Getting started on inquiry

PM: One of the things that we have done with schools is to highlight different positions that they can take in working with creative practitioners. One of them is straightforward: 'putting artists into school'. The second position is more like a 'teacher apprenticeship', where we have teachers working alongside practitioners and they would be trying to learn and glean some of the skills of the practitioner. This is fine but it's not enough. The next step along the continuum we've called 'reflective practice', which is very much about designing and doing a good project which is probably driven by an initial inquiry and then at the end you reflect carefully on what has come out of it.

We describe a fourth position on that continuum, the 'action research' position: doing good work and reflecting on it but not waiting until the end for the reflection, so that it is an ongoing iterative process – a thoughtful inquiry that is acted out and tested in practice. So, on a very short turnaround you're reflecting on what it means. At the end of the session you'd be saying, 'What is that telling us about learning, what's working and not working?', 'What shall we do in the next session to try and push this a bit further?'

The importance of questions

PM: I keep coming back to a key thing – that an inquiry needs to be led by a question. An essential part of this is thinking through how it is going to be answered, and as well as doing the project they really need a research plan.

PC: I worked with Cathy Burke, who is now at Cambridge University but was at Leeds at the time, and we did a workshop about finding the right question and reflecting on what a good question is, and I think that really has informed a lot of our work since. I think that the finding of the good question and understanding that it is appropriate to have quite a focused-in question has been quite significant for us . . . you try to get teachers to focus their observation in on a small group of children so that they can really explore something, but they almost can't do that because they've always got their eye, quite rightly, on every single child in the group, and so actually shifting them to a slightly more research-ful practice is sometimes quite challenging . . . One of the ways in which we worked with people around their questions was to start to help them think about why they had chosen a particular area to focus on and we tried out an introductory process . . . they each wrote a question and they would pass it round the room in quite a structured way and you'd analyse the question from different angles and each person would put a comment on the question.

In the CARA workshops, we did this with the school question, and so each partnership would put their inquiry question on a big flip chart and then we would walk around the room in small groups and each time they moved to a new question, people would be encouraged to interrogate the inquiry question from different perspectives.

. . . We'd ask, 'Why are you making this assumption about boys' learning? What evidence have you got in the school? So each group came back to their original inquiry question and had a series of different perspectives on it that they were then encouraged to take on board . . . repeatedly asking 'Why' questions: 'Why did you make that assumption?' 'Why are you focusing on that area?' 'Why have you thought that?' It's just a structured way of asking 'why?' over and over again that sometimes gets the participants to a very different place.

It's about evidence

PC: What we also try and do is stimulate people to bring some evidence into their reflection. It's not that you are saying to people that this isn't valid unless you've done this piece of analysis and you've done this research and so on, but we're trying to say to people, 'How can you tell that – what kind of evidence have you got for that?' I'm trying to move people away from making assertions which have absolutely no real evidence base to them. So we wouldn't go so far as to say that you need a full bank of evidence for this, but we would try to say that if that's what you are trying to find out, what evidence would be helpful? . . .

I remember mentoring one partnership where it was a professional in the visual arts and a teacher in primary school and they were talking about doing work in science and trying to get the children to be more creative in science. They wanted to find out if you got the children engaged in the selection of the creative practitioner, what impact would that have on children's relationships and on their thinking skills and self-confidence? Would it make them more creative? And when I said to them, 'How would we seek to find that out?', they said we would look at science test scores. So I said, 'But how does that relate to your question?' So it's gently getting them to be a bit more rigorous in the evidence that they use for their reflection and relating it back to their original question.

And then the next challenge that we found was this kind of obsession with documentation. . . . People collect endless images of children doing things but are then not giving themselves the time to reflect with others about what that actually tells us or how it informs us about how we now work with those children.

I remember one of the schools that I mentored ended up with this huge box full of stuff: children's reflections, notes, images, and so on, and actually the research question kept shifting. . . . We'd got quite a focused research question at the start and they moved way away from that, and it was like a digital camera going in and out of focus regularly and every time you thought it was focused – whoops, it came back out of focus again! But there was a question that emerged at one point in the process . . . they were working with a ballet company and it was about would children's writing improve if they worked through a very structured process of thinking through a story through a dance process. But there was one particular moment where they were doing a production for the parents and I happened to go in that day and it was dreadful because the teachers were putting so much pressure on the children to get the performance right that I just questioned whether going for a performance at that point had been productive. But they had all this data and they'd done work with children at different phases about how they felt after different activities. So when we analysed that, it turned out that actually although I, as the external observer, feared that the process was going to have a negative impact on the children, when the children were given time to reflect on it afterwards they'd all actually experienced it positively. But that wasn't what they'd chosen as their research focus in the first place. We got knotted up and there was just too much data, but there was good evidence for certain things, but it did get quite messy because of the complexity of the project – that's what I'm saying!

But I worked in a PRU [pupil referral unit] with a group that were working on radio stuff and neither of the two practitioners were experienced teachers – that was quite interesting – and they engaged in the process very, very positively and did collect data, but they were working with very small groups of children. I think it's that dilemma that teachers face of working with thirty-five children and trying to actually collect data that they can then analyse with regard to that number of children and can they feel that that is a valid way of spending their time . . . I think they feel that it's usually not!

PM: We were very aware of that in the materials we developed – if people interview every child in the class, have questionnaires and video, etc., it panics them. I think that's what we found in the first round of the CARA programme: that they ended up with so much data that they actually didn't know what to do with it; they'd just look at it and say, 'Oh, I can't cope with it!' And what we were saying was 'Think big to start with but actually start very small and if you've got six children that you're trying to track through three processes so that you can triangulate it a bit, that is probably more data than you are going to manage anyway. So keep it simple and if things begin to develop, then that's something else.'

But also this notion that the individual children that will be tracked don't delineate the project; the project itself will be more than that, and actually what is being tracked is a through-line and we've tried very hard to help people keep their eye on that but not to be limited by it: otherwise it's an expensive piece of work. If the school is spending four or five thousand pounds to really track the impact on three children, they wouldn't see that as a good use of money. But, on the other hand, if what comes out of it is a really clear indication about the learning and progress of the small group, then that may well be supported by broader observations and thinking about what happens in the class or the year group or whatever it is that they are working with, then that is seen as good value. So we try to keep that balance. I think there is a really key thing in this as well: the relationship – that business about what goes on in school seems to be so determined by the individual circumstances and it all comes down to people, and if it's the right person in the right place at the right time, then it's got the potential to have a really big impact.

But inquiry has to start where teachers are at

PM: I guess for me it really has to tie in with where people are in their own careers; if they're looking to do a Masters, there's probably quite a slice of their inquiry which is fairly organized and with rigorous research going on. But if teachers are not in that position, then often they want to talk about it; they might want to think about it and talk about it with colleagues . . . if we can get people into that position where they are having professional discussions about learning and teaching and how they relate to each other and how you facilitate that – that's where we seem to get the biggest impact rather than just the paperwork side of it. And it's something about people getting passionate about learning, which often seems to echo something about why people initially went into teaching, and certainly the early days of being idealistic about teaching and learning. But for a lot of teachers they've moved out of that place and it's now much more about the delivery of curriculum.

I remember one teacher, in a moment of reflection, saying, 'What I've really learned from this is that I've got to listen to children', and I remember at the time thinking, 'Well, you've been teaching for twenty years, what do you mean you should listen to children?' But actually for twenty years that teacher hadn't been listening to children; she'd been delivering a syllabus. So, in a way, that's quite a profound place to get to: that sense of knowing that the input of learners into the mix is a really key part of it and you can't just override it.

It's getting to that level where people are genuinely thinking about their own practice and thinking about real learners in real-life situations, then it began to make sense – that the action research/reflective practice stance is actually a good place to be.

I think we got quite a good hit rate on that in CARA, partly because we were coming with this sort of open-minded view of what action research could look like and partly because the mentors that were involved in the project, by and large, understood not just the mechanics of research but actually the philosophical positioning of action research and could really work with people in that way.

Action research and teachers' learning

PC: Just getting people to reflect on what this thing creativity actually is was quite powerful, and we had done that in a number of projects before CARA. . . . In the CARA project, we had two structured days with the teachers and practitioners: one initial session and one review session. So in the initial session, what we did was to introduce the concept of reflective practice and encourage people to start thinking, 'If our programme is essentially about generating creativity in young people, what does that actually mean? How can I do that and what should I be attending to?' We were trying to get people to shift their thinking from 'I am now planning a project' to 'I am now planning a learning process where I would like the children to be developing these skills'. So I suppose it's a curriculum planning process, which I think many teachers have been disempowered from through some of the centrally determined approaches to curriculum and professional development that we've experienced over the last ten years.

After the initial session they were all matched with a mentor. And those mentors came from essentially three broad backgrounds: some were academic, some were people with experience of reflective practice in Creative Partnerships or cultural learning-type practice and some had come from a teaching background. When the mentor role worked well, it was very helpful, but it had to be a process where the mentor really did actively engage with the teacher and the practitioner. In some cases, mentors tended to sit back and wait for the teachers to approach them, which didn't work very well. But overall we did find that the external mentor role was important.

The point of action research

PM: I think there's a danger that if the purpose of action research is too utilitarian, it can get down to tiny little bits of practice which actually don't add up to very much in the longer term. I think there is a real danger of that and it's something to do with the paradigm that people are working in. I think there has been a sense in education – certainly for the past fifteen years – that those 'above' schools know best and they tell schools what they ought to be doing. And in that model, the INSET [in-service training] and cascade model of professional learning is probably the most effective one: someone comes along and tells you what to do, and you go back to school and you tell other people, and then you do it. But there is not much questioning or reflection on learning that goes on, and I think teachers have really struggled with the action research model because, in a sense, it's working from a different paradigm:

as a teacher, you ought to have a professional stance which includes having ideas and thoughts about learning.

That isn't really what teachers have been told over decades. I think it's begun to shift in the past few years so that it's more a sense of teachers being empowered to be truly professional, I think. But my fear is that this might be just a blip. . . . In a sense, in terms of professional learning, the action research model ought to have been the most popular and most effective model of professional learning in the country and yet it's not . . . and I'm not quite sure why it's not. Most teachers don't do action research unless they do it as part of a structured course, and they're often doing it to get it marked, but most teachers don't do it as part of their practice. I think there is something about teachers and that perceived underlying purpose which is to do with implementing the pedagogy that is handed down from further up the hierarchy. I think the action research model has had to fight against that.

I think there is something about the action research model – it feels like helping people to go along a line: from carrying out the work of others and just simply doing, to trying to prove that what you're doing works. With much of the work that we've done, that's often the starting place for people – 'What's the impact of X on Y?' – and what they are actually trying to show is that doing X makes Y better. So it's being able to prove effectiveness: everyone is so much in that mindset . . . I think there's a step that goes beyond that which is actually to explore – moving the question from 'Does doing dance improve boys' writing?', for instance (a common inquiry question), to a question such as 'What's the relationship between an arts process and a cognitive process? What's the relationship between divergent and convergent thinking?' So it moves it away from that fairly deductive starting place where you've got your hypothesis and you're going to prove it, to a much more inductive place where you are setting up situations, carefully observing what's happening, trying to make sense of it and trying to spot patterns in learning.

The importance of documentation

PC: I think one of the purposes of action research, in the context of creative learning, is to try and make explicit what's implicit in their practice so that it can be shared more widely.

. . . [O]ne of the things that we did was to provide a writing frame – we required people to write a report and we structured that. . . . So that encouraged a process of structuring their thoughts, but the final reports were very variable in quality. The mentors were supposed to be supporting each project to reflect on the data, and it's fair to say that the mentors, because they came from such a different range of backgrounds, had varying skills and expertise in that. I think probably, if you'd read the reports, you wouldn't think, 'This is rigorous reflection on data', but what we were getting people to try and do was to actually – I suppose it's a bit grand to call it grounded theory – but it was trying to get people to really look at what the data was and start to try to make sense of it and to see what emerged from it. But I think mentors will have dealt with it differently. I know some went in and gave a kind of very structured frame for their data analysis.

PM: But this also raises questions about what 'good' action research looks like. I think there is quite a tension in that: from one perspective, good action research looks more academic, with an emphasis on process, validity and reliability. This raises questions about how far teachers really want to go down that road or how much they simply want to be in a more reflective frame of mind about their work. For me it raises some interesting questions: does inquiry end up looking more like an academic research paper? Or does it mean that when you start or finish lessons, you've got a thoughtful frame of mind and you never really write it down but you might talk to colleagues about it? Probably both positions are valid, depending on individual circumstances.

The outcomes of action research

PM: It's felt to me, working with a range of people now over these last six years, that helping people to get to that rather thoughtful, reflective place around their practice is actually more powerful than if they are doing a lot of arts practice to help pupils be better thinkers; helping people to move along a line – from doing, to proving, to exploring – feels like a useful direction for understanding and improving practice.

The second thing is that this is not an individual, solitary pursuit; if you have people working together in a community of inquiry, exploring similar but different things and getting into these rather thoughtful conversations about what learning looks like and how you facilitate it – that's a very powerful place to be.

This tends to lead people to other people's writing on it because it relates specifically to their practice and their thinking at that point in time. In a way, it takes the 'academic' out of the abstract and brings it very close into people's real practice. I think, for many teachers, they won't be exploring the kind of academic world of education just because they are fascinated by it: they'll be exploring it because it absolutely relates to what they are doing now and their current need.

PC: . . . [W]e've tried to pull together what's been coming out of a whole series of small-scale action research reflections. In an article that we've been writing with our colleagues in the US, they called it 'layered research' and worked with a partner academic over a number of years in an iterative process. We hadn't worked in quite such a structured way, but what we've tried to do within CARA is to stand back from the individual action research projects and reports . . . and to pull together an overall analysis of the trends . . . and work with academic partners to achieve that. . . .

I think some kind of process where you regularly bring people together across their separate school-located research and engage in discourse with them and try to develop and share the overall analysis is useful. The second meetings that we had with the CARA schools were often very powerful moments. I can remember one that Pete and I did together in Nottingham where somebody working in an early years setting was saying that what he discovered was the value of silence. He was talking about that space to really observe what children were doing. The whole room really went silent and everybody agreed with the importance of standing back from practice and observing how children were responding to the stimulus. That was a very powerful learning moment, and I think those are things that you do in a group. So that kind of iterative process of the small-scale reflection feeding into the bigger space – the bigger exploration – is quite important.

Resources

Cochrane, P., & Cockett, M. (2007). *Building a creative school: A dynamic approach to school development*. Stoke-on-Trent, UK: Trentham Books.

The following are available for downloading from the CAPE website:

Learning to Enquire series by Pete McGuigan:

Professional development through enquiry based practice
Resources to support enquiry based practice
Case studies and starting places for enquiry based practice
(From www.capeuk.org/capeuk-resources/learning-to-enquire.html)

Creativity Matters series:

Cochrane, P. Are we really serious about creativity?
Cockett, M. What contribution can creativity and creative learning make to social inclusion?
Caulton, T. Making space for teaching creative science?
(From www.capeuk.org/capeuk-resources/creativity-matters-series.html)

Chapter 6

Towards the creative teaching of mathematics

A design research approach

Malcolm Swan

Much educational research is about analysing and explaining an existing state of affairs. Design research is different. It is *transformational* in that it challenges the status quo, through the design and implementation of novel experiences and materials. It is also *impact-focused* in that it goes on to study *how* designs function and mutate in the hands of teachers with contrasting styles, beliefs and commitment. This chapter describes the nature and challenges of this research methodology with reference to a project involving low-attaining 16- to 19-year-old mathematics students undertaking a one-year examination course in further education (FE). The aim here was to transform the experience of students from passive imitation and practice to active, collaborative and creative learning. I hope that, although this chapter uses mathematics as the case study, the reader will begin to see ways of applying a similar methodology to the teaching of any subject.

Introduction

Ten years ago, I began researching the fate of 16-year-old students who, after failing to get their required grades for university or employment, embark on one-year 'repeat GCSE' programmes. I began by observing eight teachers in further education colleges in order to appreciate students' experiences. In most cases, I became increasingly depressed by what I saw. Teaching consisted almost entirely of explanation, example then exercise. Students listened, copied worked examples from the board and repeatedly (and mostly silently) practised routine methods using textbooks and past examination papers. The entire curriculum was rapidly revisited. Students became increasingly passive and many dropped out. In one college, the number of classes dwindled from six at the beginning of the year to two at the end. The teachers appeared to view mathematics as a body of knowledge and procedures that had to be 'delivered', and teaching as a linear progression through the syllabus.

Not every lesson I saw was like this, however. Two of the eight teachers tried to encourage students to discuss and reason, make and test conjectures, create examples and explanations, and apply their mathematics to the world around them. In these classes, at least some students became active, creative participants and found enjoyment in the subject. These two teachers appeared to hold fundamentally different beliefs as compared with the others. They saw mathematics as a non-linear, interconnected network of ideas that they and their students could create and explore together. They expressed frustration, however, that their beliefs were often compromised in practice by the limitations of time, a lack of appropriate resources and the expectations of colleagues and students.

My research therefore became focused on finding ways to transform the experiences of students in further education classes so that they could become more active, creative participants. I could see that this would need a fundamental shift in the beliefs and practices of teachers and that this in turn would require the support of new classroom resources to replace the prevalent over-reliance on textbooks. This led me to adopt a research approach that belongs to an emerging family of related approaches known variously as formative research, engineering research (Burkhardt, 2006), developmental research (Gravemeijer, 1998), design experiments (Schoenfeld, 2006) and design research. Currently there is a proliferating terminology and lack of consensus on definitions, which is perhaps natural in any methodology that is still in its youth (van den Akker, 1999; van den Akker, Graveemeijer, McKenney, & Nieveen, 2006).

In this chapter, I shall begin by outlining some aspects of the research methodology I employed for this ambitious task and briefly illustrate some of the difficulties and outcomes.

Design research

Design research may be distinguished from research that attempts to explain and analyse an existing state of affairs in that its main concern is the *transformation* of educational practices in typical classrooms (Kelly, 2003). It seeks to increase the practical relevance of research by reducing the credibility gap between educational research and classroom practice (Burkhardt & Schoenfeld, 2003; van den Akker *et al.*, 2006).

It is only around the turn of the century that we see design research as an emerging paradigm for the study of learning through the systematic design of teaching strategies and tools. The beginnings of this movement are usually attributed to Brown (1992) and Collins (1992), though, in a sense, design research was an idea simply waiting to be named (Schoenfeld, 2006), and our team at Nottingham have been working in this way for the past thirty years. Brown, in her desire to transform classrooms from 'academic work factories' to learning environments that encourage reflective practice, found her training in traditional experimental psychology of limited value. For her, traditional, rigorous, tightly controlled methods lacked validity in the 'blooming, buzzing confusion of inner-city classrooms' (Brown, 1992, p. 141). Collins (1992) helpfully distinguished analytic sciences, where the goal is to explain phenomena, from design sciences, where the goal is to determine how designed artefacts behave under different conditions. He argued for a design science in education, in order to investigate how learning-environment designs might affect teaching and learning. In education, these designed artefacts might include, for example, new teaching methods, materials, professional development programmes, assessment tasks, or any combination of these. The aim is to produce a robust design, an account of the theory underpinning the design, and evidence that the design is effective in achieving its goals in the hands of teachers who have not been involved in the research.

There have been several recent attempts to characterise design-based research (Barab & Squire, 2004; Bereiter, 2002; Cobb, Confrey, diSessa, Lehrer, & Schauble, 2003; DBRC, 2003, p. 5; Kelly, 2003; van den Akker *et al.*, 2006). These may be summarized as follows:

- *Design research is visionary, empirical and highly interventionist in approach.* The role of the researcher evolves as the research proceeds. During early cycles, the researcher may intervene in order to examine core issues more closely. Later, as the design evolves, the researcher must become a non-participant observer in order to see how the design functions on its own.

- *The research process itself is iterative in nature*, involving cycles of design, enactment, analysis and redesign. Scaling up is built into this process. Early iterations may be conducted in favourable contexts, under the researcher's control. The researcher may, for example, teach early drafts of teaching material in carefully chosen classrooms with amenable classes in order to gain insights into what is possible. Much educational research fails to get past this stage. Later iterations aim to study how the design functions in more realistic circumstances, with teachers who have not been involved in the design process, who have not had the benefit of hours of preparation and with classes that are less motivated. Under these conditions, 'mutations' of the design invariably occur (Collins, Joseph, & Bielaczyc, 2004). Rather than being viewed as negative, interfering factors in the study, the designs and theories must evolve to take account of and explain these mutations. When reporting results, the context in which the design has been studied must be carefully described.

- *Design research is theory driven.* Its outputs include developing theories about situated learning, interventions and tools. The aims are pragmatic and process oriented. Emerging theories are generally *local* (and, as Cobb *et al.*, 2003, note, *humble*), and should be judged not by their claims to 'truth' but by their potential to become *useful* (Dewey, 1938). The research does not simply focus on learning outcomes, but seeks to understand *how* designs function under different conditions and in different classroom contexts. This distinguishes design research from 'black-box' evaluation studies, where only inputs and outputs are reported, such as in randomized controlled trials.

- *Design research employs mixed methods*, both qualitative and quantitative, to develop a rich picture of the way the design works as well as the kinds of learning outcomes that may be expected. This can result in a proliferation of data. Brown (1992, p. 152) noted that she 'did not have room to store all the data, let alone time to score it'. In my own work, I have used written tests and questionnaires, interviews and direct lesson observations in order to study the effects of a design on teachers' evolving beliefs and practices, and students' learning, confidence, motivation, learning behaviours and perceptions of teaching styles. In early iterations, close observation plays a major role. Later, however, more indirect means are needed as the sample sizes grow. It is helpful, even at later stages of the research, to select samples of teachers for close observation. To help me select teachers with a wide range of beliefs and teaching practices, I developed a low-inference questionnaire.

The steps in my own design research project in FE is illustrated in Figure 6.1. These steps are more fully explained in the remainder of this chapter.

It can be seen from this analysis that design research is applicable to any curriculum area. Collins *et al.* (2004), for example, offer two contrasting examples of design research with much younger students. The first is Brown and Campione's design of a learning environment for the teaching of biology and ecology. This involved students using and teaching each other to use reciprocal reading techniques, and students collaborating to produce their own teaching resources. Their second example describes the design of a 'passion curriculum'. This approach used students' own interests to motivate their work towards 'serious learning objectives'. This involved designing learning experiences for

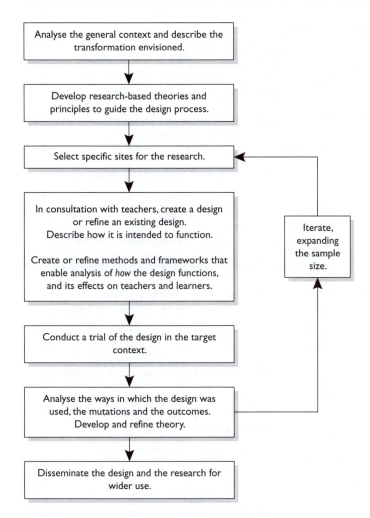

Figure 6.1 Steps in a design research project.

students in which they made videos on topics of interest to them: fables, TV talk shows, sports, dance, singing and street music. The design gradually evolved to include assessment tasks and a student-organized film festival attended by families and friends. In both examples, many iterative cycles of the type shown above were reported and analysed.

Building on prior research

A good design evolves slowly. It should be fit for purpose, be theory-based and use research-based principles. After establishing the context and the need for a design, I therefore review the *purposes* that I want it to serve and the *learning theories* that will underpin the design, and review empirical studies that give insights into the *design principles* that I will try to employ.

Table 6.1 Purposes of learning mathematics

Outcomes	Examples of types of mathematical learning activity implied
Fluency in recalling facts and performing skills	• Memorizing names and notations • Practising algorithms and procedures for fluency and 'mastery'
Conceptual understanding and interpretations for representations	• Discriminating between examples and non-examples of concepts • Generating representations of concepts • Constructing networks of relationships between mathematical concepts • Interpreting and translating between representations of concepts
Strategies for investigation and problem solving	• Formulating situations and problems for investigation • Constructing, sharing, refining, and comparing strategies for exploration and solution • Monitoring one's own progress during problem solving and investigation • Interpreting, evaluating solutions and communicating results
Awareness of the nature and values of the educational system	• Recognizing different purposes of learning mathematics • Developing appropriate strategies for learning/reviewing mathematics • Appreciating aspects of performance valued by the examination system
Appreciation of the power of mathematics in society	• Appreciating mathematics as human creativity (+ historical aspects) • Creating and critiquing 'mathematical models' of situations • Appreciating uses/abuses of mathematics in social contexts • Using mathematics to gain power over problems in one's own life

Sources: Swan (2006a); Swan and Lacey (2008).

Let's consider each of these briefly, using my FE study as an example. First, I attempted to analyse the purpose of my design. Five different purposes may be identified for learning mathematics, and each of these outcomes implies a distinct range of possible learning activities (Table 6.1). These categories are not, of course, mutually exclusive, but there can be problems if the purpose is not clarified. For example, teachers can tie themselves in knots if they simultaneously want students to explore an open-ended task (a divergent activity) and to discover a valued result (a convergent activity) (Jaworski, 1994).

In my own work, in the FE context, it rapidly became clear that I should focus mostly on the development of conceptual understanding, as these students were clearly exhibiting all the symptoms of *instrumental* rather than *relational* learning (Skemp, 1971): they were applying rules for manipulation without showing an understanding of even the most fundamental ideas.

There is only space here to make a few general points about the status of 'grand learning theories'. These theories emerge from different political and philosophical orientations and are often deemed incompatible.[1] When one looks more deeply, however, it becomes clear that they have different domains of interest. Behaviourists define learning in terms of changes in observable performances (e.g. 'fluency' in Table 6.1), and their suggestions for educational design typically emphasize the value of repetitive practice with feedback (Gagné, Briggs, & Wager, 1992). The constructivists focus more on the development of conceptual understanding and emphasize reflection, cognitive conflict (e.g. Piaget) and the role of language (e.g. Vygotsky). Others view learning as a socialization process in which a learner is an apprentice or participant in a community of practice (Lave & Wenger, 1991). While such theories are mostly descriptive rather than prescriptive and do not aim to provide detailed guidance for educational designers, they can offer insights into the conditions under which different forms of learning take place. In my own research, I attempted to summarize some working principles from constructivist and social constructivist theories. Examples of these are offered in Table 6.2.

Table 6.2 Some principles for the design of teaching from a constructivist perspective

Encourage students to become active participants.	Students learn through their active participation in social practices, their reflection on these practices and through the internalization and reorganization of their own experience.
Make students' pre-existing concepts explicit.	Current concepts must be brought to a state of consciousness. If students are not given this opportunity, then 'foreign' methods and concepts may fail to be accommodated and become marginalized.
Expose and discuss misconceptions.	Use learning activities that create 'tension' by confronting learners with inconsistencies and surprises, and allow opportunities for resolution through discussion.
Promote reflection with higher-order questioning.	Use questioning to promote explanation, application and synthesis rather than mere recall.
Make appropriate use of cooperative small-group work.	Interpretations remain mere 'shadows' unless they are articulated through language. Activities are more effective when they encourage critical, constructive discussion, rather than uncritical acceptance or argument for its own sake. Shared goals and group accountability are important.
Offer rich tasks that allow the creation of multiple connections.	Conceptual frameworks do not develop along predetermined linear hierarchies. Activities must be designed so as to provide opportunities for students to create their own multiple connections.
Reduce the level of help and guidance as students develop their own resources.	To mediate learning, the teacher may provide *scaffolding* – conceptual resources necessary for a higher level of cognitive functioning. Through interaction, these resources may be internalized by the child as the scaffolding is progressively removed.
Recognize and give status to students' own constructions.	The teacher should also attempt to foster the *institutionalization* of the concepts and methods generated by students. The teacher must recognize and give status to students' own constructions, reveal their inadequacies, seek generalizations and set them beside socially agreed conventions.

Also underpinning my research were the outcomes of a series of empirical studies carried out in secondary schools (Bell, Swan, Onslow, Pratt, & Purdy, 1985). This work was limited to a series of short-term comparative design experiments on isolated topics occupying a few weeks with committed teachers (often the researchers themselves). In these experiments, we tried to implement some of the above principles and compare them with other approaches (such as the 'guided discovery' approaches found in the better textbooks). We found that a teaching methodology that confronts students with challenging conceptual obstacles, allows interpretations to emerge and be compared, and that creates a 'tension' that is resolved through classroom discussion, was strikingly more effective than the more usual teaching methods, particularly for longer-term retention. It also became clear that such activities demanded a profound shift in students' classroom roles. An orientation to the individual production of 'right answers' had to give way to a recognition that the aim was for teachers and students to work collaboratively in the co-creation of conceptual networks. We explored many ways of making this shift, working in partnership with innovative and enthusiastic secondary teachers. In one such study, we encouraged students to take on more active, creative roles in the classroom, such as those of teacher/explainer, assessor/critic and task designer (Bell, Swan, Crust, & Shannon, 1993). For example, we asked students to:

- *Create mathematical tasks.* They attempted to devise challenging tasks accompanied by worked solutions. These tasks were then offered to other students. In some classes, students went further and created complete worksheets or tests, together with mark schemes. They then used these with their peers and evaluated the outcomes.
- *Create mathematical reviews.* Students compiled dictionaries containing their own definitions for concepts, with accompanying diagrams and worked examples. They created revision aids that summarized important ideas in topics. Some classes analysed the construction of textbooks, reorganized textual explanations and planned textbook outlines showing how the subject fits together. Students also conducted interviews with each other on what had been learned at the end of a topic.

This was a 'brainstorming' project in which teachers were encouraged to explore new classroom possibilities. The outcomes, however, were not developed into a format that could be readily adopted and used by other teachers in perhaps more typical or demanding situations, nor was it possible to systematically analyse the learning effects of some of these interventions on students.

Beginning design research in FE

With this background, I applied for a research grant[2] to see how I could apply what we had learned to the further education context with low-attaining students in mathematics retake classes – those described in the Introduction to this chapter. My plan was to study about eight teachers teaching the same one-year course twice, with comparable groups of students. In the first year, I would observe these teachers working normally, while at the same time I would begin to develop the resources needed for the intervention (in consultation with the teachers). In the second year, I would observe the first drafts of my design in action. I would then be able to compare the effects of the intervention in the second year with the effects of the teachers' normal practices in the first year. These effects would be evaluated using classroom observation and through pre and post interviews and questionnaires with each cohort of students.

The first difficulty came as soon as I began to select my sample. After contacting eight colleges, I found that four were unsuitable because their courses were being restructured, drop-out rates among students were too high and the staffing and groupings of students were too unpredictable. I fortunately found eight teachers from the remaining four colleges who agreed to take part. After a while, four of these teachers withdrew from the research. Two of the withdrawals were due to unforeseeable, external factors: one teacher became seriously ill and one had her classes reorganized when student numbers became unviable. Two more teachers withdrew when they realized the implications of using an intervention that would involve them in using a creative, discussion-based pedagogy for one year. They expressed concern that the intervention would take much more time than their normal approaches and they would be therefore be unable to cover the syllabus before the examination. I was therefore left with four teachers from three different colleges. Fortunately, these teachers represented a range of views and teaching styles. Two were more 'transmission' oriented, in that they tended to view mathematics as a body of knowledge that has to be delivered through optimal sequencing, explanation and then practice until fluency is obtained. The remaining two, I termed 'connectionist' (after Askew, Brown, Rhodes, Johnson, & Wiliam, 1997) because they rather saw mathematics more as a connected network of ideas that have to be co-constructed by the teacher and students through discussion. The connectionist teachers, however, did not consistently put their beliefs into practice, owing to a lack of resources, the time pressure and the expectations of colleagues and students.

A first design iteration

During the first year of the research, I began to compile my ideas into a series of five booklets and a teacher's guide that, I hoped, would encourage discussion and creativity in the mathematics classes (Swan, 2000). I met regularly with the teachers to discuss the feasibility of this approach and they appeared encouraging and enthusiastic. Each booklet was based on one mathematical topic. It contained a series of 'discussion pages' and 'check pages'. 'Discussion pages' were designed to focus on common conceptual obstacles and provide a challenge that would allow students' pre-existing misconceptions to surface. 'Check pages' would revisit the same concepts in a different, more closely guided manner. This involved using a more concrete representation or the use of an alternative method designed to offer meaningful feedback and produce cognitive conflict as students were led to realize the inconsistencies and errors in their own beliefs. In the second year of the research, the four teachers used these booklets regularly. I observed each teacher ten times and recorded, transcribed and analysed sample student–student interactions. In addition, I invited teachers to maintain diaries, complete questionnaires and attend meetings to describe and discuss their impressions of the teaching interventions.

This raises a fundamental concern. Critics sometimes see design research as 'imposing' methods on teachers. When conducting design research, teachers are being asked to give up habitual ways of working, refined over many years, and adopt new methods that often appear 'alien' and 'untested'. However effective the research evidence suggests that the new methods might be, teachers cannot be expected to take risks with the future examination results of their students. In the early iterations of design research, therefore, I had to work very closely with teachers, introducing ideas gradually, expecting teachers to use their professional judgements and to modify the designs. It was not always easy to see whether or not a design was 'working', particularly during small-group classroom discussions. Some of the teachers appeared to measure progress by the productivity of students or by their motivation, rather than the quality of their reasoning. I found that I had to focus very closely on just one or two groups each lesson and audio-record their discussions for later analysis.

The outcomes of this small-scale study were encouraging. In the first year, with teachers using their normal materials and approaches, the students taught by the connectionist teachers achieved significant improvements on only two of the five topics, while the students of the two transmission teachers achieved no improvements at all. In the second year, in which the newly designed materials were used, the students taught by the connectionist teachers achieved statistically significant (but still modest) gains in all five topics. The students taught by the transmission teachers achieved significant gains in just two. Thus, the teaching materials appeared to have potential for improving the learning of mathematical concepts in the hands of teachers who were already predisposed towards creative, discussion-based approaches. I realized that the transmission teachers appeared to need a more profound change in their beliefs and practices before this would be possible.

My classroom observations presented a richer picture of what had happened. All four teachers were extremely enthusiastic about the materials we had developed and all four did try to modify their normal teaching approaches to include much more student–student discussion. There were, however, significant differences. The two transmission teachers rarely attempted to explain the purpose of the booklets to students; they handed them out and used them as if they were just normal classroom textbooks. Students did begin to discuss, but the potential of these discussions were not realized because the teachers continued to dominate classroom exchanges. When talking with groups of students, for example, they did not elicit reasoning through careful questioning; they still preferred to 'launch in' and put students right with their own explanations. They wanted students to 'get through' the materials efficiently and not waste time in rambling discussions.

The connectionist teachers, in contrast, were much less concerned with 'coverage', appeared less hurried, relaxed their control of the classroom interactions and elicited student explanations. They spoke of the resources in terms of 'releasing them' to teach in ways they believed in, but had previously been unable to achieve:

> It has released me with new ideas, like generating discussion, spending more time in groups rather than talking from the front, collecting ideas rather than 'Here's how you do it, go and do 10 or 15 examples' and then reviewing it by churning through worksheets. The new thing it's introduced has been the idea of leading students into errors and concentrating diagnostically on the errors rather than ploughing through the whole syllabus. I don't feel restricted now by the syllabus.
>
> (Interview with a connectionist teacher)

In my evaluation of the project, I realized that my design had not taken sufficient account of the pre-existing beliefs and practices of the teachers themselves. In the next iteration, I would therefore attempt to introduce a professional development element into the design. I also realized that the *form* of my design was as important as its content. By making the design into booklets, I had inadvertently encouraged teachers and students to use them as individual texts rather than as shared resources. In the next iteration, I would try to create resources that were physically large and could be shared, making much more use of cards and posters. On reflection, I had also been over-ambitious in trying to implement the new teaching approach in five different topics. I could have saved myself a lot of work at this stage if I had chosen just one or two.

A second design iteration

For the next iteration, I chose just one topic, algebra, because that had been the one that students had found most difficult during the first iteration. I completely revised the teaching materials, so that there were no student booklets. This time, all the resources were provided in a teacher's guide and were made to be shared between students. I also managed to produce some videos of teachers using these materials in discursive ways, and developed a professional development course around them. The design of the algebra intervention and the professional development resources took most of one year, including time for informally piloting the activities and filming teachers using them. These are briefly illustrated in Table 6.3 and more fully in Swan (2006a, 2008). These types of activity were those that had generated the most intensive discussions during the earlier work. Each type of activity was generic in that it suggested general forms of lesson material that would encourage students to think mathematically and to create examples, counter-examples, arguments and problems.

This time, sixty-three teachers from forty-four different FE colleges were invited to take part in the one-year algebra intervention programme. This involved four full one-day meetings spread through the year, with the intention that teachers would try out the resources in between.[3]

From a research design point of view, my large sample size raised many new problems. How was I going to find out about teachers' existing beliefs and practices? How was I going to monitor the range of ways in which the resources were being used? How could I assess the affective and cognitive effects on students?

In the event, I decided to design a number of new research instruments. These included pre and post questionnaires that invited teachers to list their priorities in teaching GCSE mathematics and describe the different purposes they had in teaching mathematics and their different beliefs about teaching and learning. Using the results from the pre questionnaires, I was able to select a small sample of six teachers for classroom observation. As before, I wanted to observe teachers with a variety of normal practices and beliefs using the teaching materials in order to see how they were interpreted and mutated.

I also developed attitude and learning questionnaires for students. Of particular interest is one questionnaire that asked students to describe their teacher's style of working. Teacher self-reporting can be very biased, so I used student questionnaires to give me a way of relating the effects of the teaching to the teaching styles employed. This gave a less biased way of finding out how teachers were using the resources than if I had depended solely on teacher self-reporting. A full analysis of the construction and reliability testing of the questionnaires is given in Swan (2006b). I analysed the student learning effects by categorizing the classes into three groups, according to how many hours of the teaching interventions had been used ('none', 'few', 'many'), and then subdividing each of these groups into subgroups according to whether the students reported their teachers' styles to be more 'student centred' (connectionist-based practices) or 'teacher centred' (transmission-based practices). I found that students' algebra learning was associated with both the number

Table 6.3 Three types of mathematical activity

Type	Example
Evaluating statements and generalizations These activities are intended to encourage students to focus on common convictions concerning mathematical concepts. A number of statements/solutions are provided and students are asked to decide upon their validity and create examples, counter-examples and explanations to justify their decisions.	*Decide whether the following statements are always, sometimes or never true. Create examples and counter-examples to justify your reasoning.* The square root of a number is less than the number.
Interpreting and creating multiple representations Mathematical concepts have many representations; from conventionally agreed notations to less formal representations. In algebra, these include symbolic formulae, tables, graphs and verbal expressions. Card-sorting activities allow these representations to be shared, interpreted, compared and classified. In noticing the 'sameness' or 'difference' in representations, students begin to create and refine concepts and definitions.	*Match the following cards if they are equivalent. If cards are missing, create them.* Square n then multiply your answer by 3 — Multiply n by 3 then square your answer — Square n then multiply your answer by 9 $(3n)^2$ $3n^2$ $9n^2$
Creating and solving new problems Students create their own problems and examples using given constraints. Other students are then invited to solve them. The originators and the solvers work together to see where difficulties have emerged.	*Create your own equation, beginning with a value for the variable and then building the equation step-by-step. Challenge your partner to solve it and offer advice when she gets stuck.* times 10 $10x = 40$ Add 9 $10x + 9 = 49$ Divide by 8 $\dfrac{10x + 9}{8} = 6.125$ take 7 $\left(\dfrac{10x + 9}{8}\right) - 7 = -0.875$

of tasks that were used and also the manner in which these were used. No learning gains were made in the comparison group that taught their standard algebra curriculum in teacher-centred ways. The greatest gains were made in the group that used 'many' tasks in student-centred ways (approximately one standard deviation). Students' levels of confidence, motivation and algebra anxiety remained largely unchanged, though the group who had used none of the tasks reported a small decline in these affective aspects.

From the pre and post teacher questionnaires, I was able to gain an overview of how teachers thought that their own beliefs and practices had evolved over the year. These showed strong changes towards connectionist beliefs by some teachers, though one can never be completely sure that teachers are not exaggerating their responses because they know that that is what you want to hear. I could, however, do some cross-checking with students' opinions.

By far the richest data came from my own classroom observations. These revealed the nature of the discussions and interactions. Some teachers did 'mutate' the design intentions to fit into their pre-existing belief structures. They anticipated that students would have difficulties and become confused, that progress would be slow and that the scheme of work would not be covered. They therefore simplified tasks in subtle ways (by their questioning), 'took over' explanations and controlled pace. This time, however, these mutations were less severe than in the previous iteration, and students were able to discuss and learn. The tasks themselves exerted a considerable influence and sustained creativity. In particular, they were found to:

- foster sustained collaborative work (the tasks involved shared resources that were sufficiently 'rich' that spending one hour or more per task was typical);
- encourage teachers to use more challenging examples than they would normally have used;
- confront students with specific, conceptual obstacles that were previously unrecognized, and to offer opportunities for learning through 'cognitive conflict';
- influence the nature of questions that teachers and students ask of each other: *What is the same and what is different? What is another way of saying or showing this? When is this true? How can we undo this? What happens when we change . . . ?*

After this iteration, I was able to completely revise and expand the teaching activities, building the outcomes of the research into the next iteration of the design. Recently, a government-funded programme has permitted us to develop a more extensive resource based on the tasks used in this research, and make this freely available to all post-16 providers in England (Swan, 2005).

Closing remarks

I hope in this chapter to have revealed some of the potential of a design research project. I realize that on reading this, one may gain the impression that it is over-ambitious for an individual or beginning researcher. While it may be true that the required combination of research skills and design flair makes this approach more suited to research teams working on funded projects than to individuals, I believe it is possible for an individual to attempt a small-scale design research project if the content focus is restricted and the observed samples are kept manageable. In my early work, I often fell into the trap of spending too long designing an intervention before letting it loose on a classroom. I then became too 'attached' to the design and defensive of it. I now realize that it is much better to collaborate with potential users and experienced designers at even the initial stages and to draft and refine initial ideas quite quickly.

Finally, I do hope that I have shown that design research can have a transformative impact on the beliefs and practices of teachers. Our evidence shows that the designs we have produced have enabled teachers to envision and create new ways of working in classrooms, and have thus enabled students to collaborate in the creation of their own mathematical understanding.

Notes

1 Indeed, most 'theories' of learning are not theories at all, at least in the sense that insists that a theory has to be falsifiable. They are perhaps more akin to *metaphors* or *perspectives* that offer alternative languages for discussing deeper issues of teaching and learning (Sfard, 1994).
2 This was funded by the Esmée Fairbairn Charitable Trust.
3 This multimedia resource and the professional development meetings were funded by the Learning and Skills Development Agency (Swan & Green, 2002).

References

Askew, M., Brown, M., Rhodes, V., Johnson, D., & Wiliam, D. (1997). *Effective teachers of numeracy: Final report.* London: King's College.

Barab, S., & Squire, K. (2004). Design-based research: Putting a stake in the ground. *Journal of the Learning Sciences, 13*(1), 1–14.

Bell, A., Swan, M., Crust, R., & Shannon, A. (1993). *Awareness of learning, reflection and transfer in school mathematics: Report of ESRC Project R000-23-2329.* Nottingham: Shell Centre for Mathematical Education, University of Nottingham.

Bell, A., Swan, M., Onslow, B., Pratt, K., & Purdy, D. (1985). *Diagnostic teaching for long term learning: Report of ESRC Project HR8491/1.* Nottingham: Shell Centre for Mathematical Education, University of Nottingham.

Bereiter, C. (2002). Design research for sustained innovation. *Cognitive Studies, Bulletin of the Japanese Cognitive Science Society, 9*(3), 321–327.

Brown, A. L. (1992). Design experiments: Theoretical and methodological challenges in creating complex interventions in classroom settings. *Journal of the Learning Sciences, 2*(2), 141–178.

Burkhardt, H. (2006). From design research to large scale impact. In J. van den Akker, K. Gravemeijer, S. McKenney, & N. Nieveen (Eds.), *Educational design research* (pp. 121–150). London: Routledge.

Burkhardt, H., & Schoenfeld, A. (2003). Improving educational research: toward a more useful, more influential and better-funded enterprise. *Educational Researcher, 32*(9), 3–14.

Cobb, P., Confrey, J., diSessa, A., Lehrer, R., & Schauble, L. (2003). Design experiments in educational research. *Educational Researcher, 32*(1), 9–13.

Collins, A. (1992). Towards a design science in education. In E. Scanlon & T. O'Shea (Eds.), *New directions in educational technology* (pp. 15–22). New York: Springer-Verlag.

Collins, A., Joseph, D., & Bielaczyc, K. (2004). Design research: Theoretical and methodological issues. *Journal of the Learning Sciences, 13*(1), 15–42.

DBRC (2003). Design-based research: An emerging paradigm for educational inquiry. *Educational Researcher, 32*(1), 5–8.

Dewey, J. (1938). *Logic, the theory of inquiry.* New York: H. Holt.

Gagné, R. M., Briggs, L. J., & Wager, W. W. (1992). *Principles of instructional design* (4th ed.). London: Harcourt Brace.

Gravemeijer, K. (1998). Developmental research as a research method. In J. Kilpatrick and A. Sierpinska (Eds.), *Mathematics education as a research domain: A search for identity (An ICMI Study)* (book 2, pp. 277–295). Dordrecht, Netherlands: Kluwer Academic.

Jaworski, B. (1994). *Investigating mathematics teaching: A constructivist enquiry.* London: Falmer Press.

Kelly, A. (2003). Theme issue: The role of design in educational research. *Educational Researcher, 32*(1), 3–4.

Lave, J., & Wenger, E. (1991). *Situated learning: Legitimate peripheral participation.* Cambridge: Cambridge University Press.

Schoenfeld, A. (2006). Design experiments. In P. B. Elmore, G. Camilli, & J. Green (Eds.), *Handbook of complementary methods in education research* (pp. 193–206). Washington, DC: American Educational Research Association.

Sfard, A. (1994). Two metaphors for learning mathematics: Acquisition metaphor and participation metaphor. *Educational Researcher, 27*(2), 4–13.

Skemp, R. (1971). *The psychology of learning mathematics.* Harmondsworth, UK: Penguin Books.

Swan, M. (2000). GCSE mathematics in further education: Challenging beliefs and practices. *Curriculum Journal, 11*(2), 199–233.

Swan, M. (2005). *Improving learning in mathematics: Challenges and strategies.* Sheffield: Teaching and Learning Division, Department for Education and Skills Standards Unit.

Swan, M. (2006a). *Collaborative learning in mathematics: A challenge to our beliefs and practices.* London: National Institute for Advanced and Continuing Education (NIACE) for the National Research and Development Centre for Adult Literacy and Numeracy (NRDC).

Swan, M. (2006b). Designing and using research instruments to describe the beliefs and practices of mathematics teachers. *Research in Education, 75,* 58–70.

Swan, M. (2008). A designer speaks: Designing a multiple representation learning experience in secondary algebra. *Educational Designer: Journal of the International Society for Design and Development in Education, 1*(1), article 3.

Swan, M., & Green, M. (2002). *Learning mathematics through discussion and reflection.* London: Learning and Skills Development Agency.

Swan, M., & Lacey, P. (2008). *Mathematics matters: An executive summary.* London: National Centre for Excellence in the Teaching of Mathematics.

van den Akker, J. (1999). Principles and methods of development research. In J. van den Akker, R. Branch, K. Gustafson, N. Nieveen, & T. Plomp (Eds.), *Design approaches and tools in education and training* (pp. 1–15). Dordrecht, Netherlands: Kluwer.

van den Akker, J., Graveemeijer, K., McKenney, S., & Nieveen, N. (Eds.). (2006). *Educational design research.* London: Routledge.

Can researchers 'see' creative learning and can their research help others to 'see' it?

Chapter 7

A conversation with Kathleen Gallagher

Kathleen Gallagher is a Professor, Canada Research Chair, and the Academic Director of the Centre for Urban Schooling at the University of Toronto. Dr Gallagher's book *The theatre of urban: Youth and schooling in dangerous times* (University of Toronto Press, 2007) is based on a three-year ethnographic study of four secondary schools in New York City and Toronto. Her book *Drama education in the lives of girls: Imagining possibilities* (University of Toronto Press, 2000) received the American Education Research Association's book award for a significant contribution to Curriculum Studies in 2001. Her two edited collections are *How theatre educates: Convergences and counterpoints with artists, scholars, and advocates* (University of Toronto Press, 2003) and *The methodological dilemma: Creative, critical and collaborative approaches to qualitative research* (Routledge, 2008). Dr Gallagher has published many articles on theatre, urban youth, pedagogy and gender, and travels widely, giving international addresses and workshops for practitioners. Her research continues to focus on questions of engagement and artistic practice, as well as the pedagogical and methodological possibilities of learning through the theatre.

What is your professional background?

I studied theatre, and French theatre in particular. I did my graduate degrees in education during the time I was, for ten years, working as a drama teacher in a high school. I was really interested in better understanding the practice I was engaged in and also the sociology of the context in which I worked. This was a particularly interesting place – and perhaps unusual even for Canada. It was a publicly funded single-sex school for girls. While it had all the vestiges of its private-school Catholic heritage, it was populated by mainly refugee students and those from 'working poor' families. So it was a really contradictory place that had this history that didn't correspond to its current reality, and all of the work that I'd looked at, to that point, in terms of girls' education, was set in relatively homogeneous contexts. So a lot of what people understood about how girls learn, and how girls learn in the arts, seemed to come from a context that was entirely different from the one I was working in.

So I thought about how the questions of sociology and the questions of education and theatre came together for me because I was trying to make sense of an unusual place where I thought a different kind of learning was going on. That probably set me on my ethnographic course and I would say that in my career – although I'd done some impact studies in the arts and I've done case studies and I'm doing those currently – my real evolution as a researcher has come through my ethnographic experiences.

I have spent a lot of time in other people's classrooms, paying attention to the interesting and the mundane of their work in theatre and I feel like I'm still asking questions about the intersection of the aesthetic and the social in those environments.

What is your current research about?

In my current study, which is a collaborative and multi-site ethnography situated in Toronto, in New York, in Lucknow and in Taipei, the agendas of theatre and theatre makers and the relationships between theatre teachers and their students has become enormously interesting to me. These are very different contexts, but the question of harnessing the social agenda to the theatre practices is relevant in all of these different places. And with all of the schools – although these are very diverse sites – what unites them is that they are all in so-called disadvantaged communities and so they are all places where teachers, administrators and researchers are trying to raise the bar in some way and make school more meaningful for those who are relatively disengaged by it. That's not so much the case in India, however, because in India the most disengaged students are desperate to be engaged by school: they're girls – and they are the lowest caste of girls – and so school is the opposite of what it is in North American or Western contexts: it's a refuge; it's a place for an opportunity that wouldn't otherwise be had. So we all come at the term 'disadvantage' with very different histories, understandings and experiences.

I would say that one of the tensions in drama education over many, many years has been this question of purpose, what often plays out as a tension between the aesthetic and the social. I guess most recently, in looking at my two Toronto sites, one, on the surface, would have been very much understood by most researchers and observers as being engaged in the social emancipatory goals of what is possible pedagogically, artistically and socially for kids in arts classes who are otherwise disadvantaged in school. And the other space was a sort of 'last resort' school; it's filled with young people who have not achieved academically in at least three other schools and so this is a last chance at a high school diploma. So in that school, unlike the other school we're working in, and because of the politics of the teacher, the theatre they made did not focus on their lives outside the classroom. Making drama there afforded a kind of 'escape' from their 'real' lives. Depending on where you sit politically and pedagogically with these things, you come, as a researcher, with different assessments and assumptions about those two different kinds of pedagogical spaces: one represented a real emerging curriculum where the stuff of their lives was the stuff of the classroom, and the other was explicitly about leaving the outside world 'where it belonged' and finding a refuge and a space in the classroom; to disconnect from certain aspects of identity and experience that maybe 'got in the way'.

So we watched two really different pedagogical processes: one that is probably more common, the drama room, where students draw regularly from their personal, cultural knowledges; and the other, doing a musical production and rehearsing dance numbers and singing and keeping the knife fights and other social problems that existed, *outside* the room. So you can come into that as a researcher with a whole set of ready-made analyses and a whole set of ready-made assumptions about what you're seeing. And what happened, in fact, was that there were some interesting parallels between these two seemingly different worlds. And then there were some insights from students because the youth voices in this research are absolutely central to everything that we do. And so we spend a lot of informal and formal time in discussions with the youth, and maybe I'll just add this point that when

I say 'informal time', I do mean ethnographic things like chats in hallways and side comments and informal kinds of engagements, but I also mean using art to engage. And by that, I mean using the theatre as a kind of meta-space for researchers and youth to have conversations that are different from the classic ethnographic interview. These improvised spaces that we intentionally create significantly change the terms of engagement and the forms of communication possible in a research relationship.

How do you use drama as part of your research process?

We would create extended improvisation and roles using understandings from the data we had and put these ideas back to the youth and say that we were going to work with these ideas theatrically. And what that meant was that it was no longer someone simply stating their views or opinions, but having instead to work artistically with their own and others' perspectives on ideas that seemed to be of significance based on the data that we had already gathered from working with them.

And there was no secret about this process. We would say, 'We've come across these powerful themes and a lot of you seem to speak to these kinds of issues and we want to work with these issues and see if we can extend our understanding and go further with them and nuance them in ways that a straightforward one-on-one or a focus group interview doesn't necessarily allow for.' In other words, we wanted to harness to our research process itself, the power of working with theatre.

So that's what I mean when I say that the research itself, in addition to being collaborative, which is a highly problematic term in and of itself, is also very experimental. What we are attempting to understand together is a little bit of a surprise to all of us. How do we make sense of the relationship between what we're thinking and seeing and feeling and what we have created through the distancing mechanism of the stage? How do we then draw a relationship between a 'reality' and a so-called fiction? In the field, we spend time creating with young people and then we try to account for that different way of working in our analyses.

What are the issues in researching theatre with and for kids 'at risk'?

This response may not fall in line with the well-rehearsed notion that the arts, and theatre in particular, are good for kids who are 'at risk'. I think there's lots of qualitative understanding that that is the case and I think there are some fine hypotheses about why that is the case, but it is not drama itself, it is what is *done* in drama pedagogy, the ways in which the space of drama might help them to challenge the labels of 'failing' or 'underachieving'. I think, on the surface, it creates a possibility to wear other identities and try them out and to try and treat the drama classroom as a bit of a social and academic rehearsal space.

I think pedagogical experiments of this kind are very good because school is increasingly less like an experiment, and those spaces that you can find to try things out are really important and fewer in number and should be encouraged, especially in so-called underachieving schools or disadvantaged communities.

One of the things that was prevalent across the two really diverse Toronto sites in my current project was this sense of disappointment – in ourselves, in others, in our work. Although there were successes of all kinds for individual students and pedagogical successes for teachers (and these could be as simple as 'there are still forty people in this class; I started with sixty and I usually end up with twenty', so that was a success), there was still a great sense of disappointment, a prevailing feeling of – and I took this line from one of the teachers – 'it could have been so much better'. And this became something that we really hung our analysis on because this feeling of disappointment and almost melancholia, I think, is a common experience for drama teachers, especially those working with 'at risk' young people – this sense that it always could have been better, even though there have been successes. So, we were trying to get at what it was exactly that could have been better. Could the learning have been better? Was it the performance that could have been better? What are they meaning, exactly, when they say it could have been so much better? It could have been better if they had the same twenty students consistently coming every day? This never happened. So what is it that is at the heart of that melancholia that teachers feel when they are working in the arts with students?

And the other really fascinating thing about that is that we were imagining – probably based on our own biases and assumptions – that students prefer to have their lives engaged in the curriculum and that they want to feel as though their world has some place in the privileged space of a classroom. But that wasn't always the case.

In our so-called last resort school, many of the students had addiction problems. This was an issued identified by students themselves and by their teachers. For these students, they often wanted a space in which the trials of their lives were not fodder and they wanted a space that was, in a sense, artificial, and one girl particularly said, 'I remember when I was five I used to like to dance and I haven't danced in a long time. I've struggled with addiction and I want to remember my five-year-old self and this was a class that let me do that.' So, as researchers, we have to confront our own interests and biases in terms of the arts and pedagogy, and sometimes the best you can do for some students is to create an artifice so that what you're not doing is privileging the social agenda and you're saying that this is a moment to immerse yourself in a craft. And that matters as much to some students as feeling like their worlds are not absent from the curriculum does for others.

So it was a really nice lesson for us as researchers to realize again that we cannot simply take things at face value. Sometimes, getting outside your life is as important as having your life 'included' in the work of a classroom.

Poverty is also a really big issue in our research schools. So, when I would interview kids, I would say, 'on the days that it is hard to come to school, what makes it hard?', and more often than not I got an answer like 'I don't have a bus token and the drivers don't always let me on when I ask.' So, in other words, some students were getting there by begging for a free ride on the subway or the bus and it didn't always work and that, alone, is why they weren't there. So, you know, I was confronted a lot by my own assumptions and understandings and by the simplicity of what school is or is not in their lives, and, more specifically, what role drama plays or doesn't play in their engagement in schools. Have I rambled enough?

Are there any key issues arising from the ethnographic processes you have used?

There are moments that arise in research classrooms and, just like the experience of a teacher, there are these moments that stand out for one reason or another and that require further investigation, not simply by you as a researcher but by everyone who is involved in that moment. I can share with you one such moment from one of the sites in the current study. There was a performance from an Ibsen scene study unit going on in one of the classrooms, and this was a pretty transient group of students fairly disengaged with school generally, but for some reason they hooked into this Ibsen scene study unit, and when we were watching one of the scenes, there was a young seventeen- or eighteen-year-old black boy who, in the middle of the scene, quite obviously forgot his line and there was no audience and this wasn't a high-stakes thing, but they were performing – he and his partner – and we watched a moment of silence and mounting anxiety and frustration on his face and then he turned around and he punched his fist unbelievably hard into the wall and I thought he'd broken it for sure. And the anger was extreme and there was a terrible silence in the room.

Now these kinds of things happen – and I'm not pulling this out as a particularly dramatic event because we've also pursued quite undramatic events and found amazing things. So, the teacher and the students found a way to move around this: the two students sat down and they didn't pursue their scene for the rest of that class but came back at it another day, but with very little deconstruction of what went on. That was a moment that stayed with me for months, and so I found myself watching that young man pretty closely over the rest of the semester, and we moved from winter into spring and then into summer and we were finishing with some individual interviews and I asked this particular young man if we could do an interview. We sat on the grass outside the school. He had been, to my mind, very disaffected in the classroom; he sat always on his own and he was seldom in 'the circle' with the rest of the students. He wasn't lured in very much by the teacher; she periodically would ask whether he wanted to sit with us but he would always find a way to pull himself out again. And he gazed out the window a lot.

So I wanted to ask him about what looked like, to a researcher's eye, his marginal presence in the classroom, and when I described to him what I saw and asked him to shed some light or give us some insight about what was going on, he was genuinely surprised and said, 'Do I?' And I said, 'Yes, you sit on a chair on your own away from the group almost every day that you're there.' 'I do?' 'Yes, that's what I see.' 'Oh, that's interesting. Well, I like to observe, so I'm not surprised that I'm sitting back because I like to observe.'

And then I didn't really know how to go to this one episode, which was a very vulnerable moment, and uncharacteristically so, because he wasn't a student who generally showed emotion in the classroom. So I said, 'I'm going to ask you a question now and you can tell me if you don't want to talk about this and you can tell me if this isn't something that we should be discussing, but I'm going to take a chance', and he said, 'I know where you're going.' I told him that he could stop me but I said, 'I think I want to tell you how I understood that moment; I think I want to tell you how I've been thinking about it for the last few months and you can tell me whether I'm right or wrong.' Because frankly I didn't know how to say to him, 'Tell me what was going on.' I really thought that this was going down a research avenue that is really predictable and probably unproductive, perhaps even invasive, so I said I was going to tell him what I think I saw and I started to explain and I didn't get very far into my analysis of that moment and he said, 'Wrong, wrong, wrong, totally wrong!' And I said, 'OK, well what was going on?'

And basically what he wanted me to know about that moment was that his anger was not at his own failure or his disappointment in himself, because he had clearly worked very hard at this and he wasn't a student who had given a lot up to this point. So he wasn't mad at himself for not pulling through or for failing the assignment. He was angry at himself that he'd brought someone down with him. So his anger was about this white girl he was working with who he didn't seem to know particularly well. It was OK in his mind to screw up himself, but it wasn't OK to screw someone else up, and his failure had done just that, in his mind. And that wasn't my analysis of what was going on, so we came to this really interesting kind of negotiation of what he saw and what I saw and what we thought was going on and how misinterpretation allowed for a pretty honest and candid discussion about things.

And that's what I think ethnography is: it's being in a space with a group of people who are inside it in a different way from you, although you're inside it too, and together you are bringing your understandings of the remarkable and the banal of that space into a conversation.

How does this relate to using drama as a method?

I guess, for me, using drama methodologically is really important because you get a different sort of leverage on your position as a researcher. And, in a way, the drama space puts you in a different relationship both to one another as people and to the ideas that you're investigating and communicating. So I like that we can all be, in some sense, at a remove from our roles as researchers and students in a given context, with all the baggage that that implies – the weight of our identities.

And I get some leverage when we can stand back and, in that instance, put my interpretation on the line and say, 'Speak back to my interpretation with your interpretation.' And what we're not coming out with is: he's right and I'm wrong. The responses simply tell me more about the ethnographic research relationship and the multiple stories contained in every ethnographic moment; it really adds some empirical weight to the theoretical postmodern idea of multiplicity.

It's different from the impact stuff that I have to do, where the outcomes are much clearer at the outset, and it's also different from my case-study work that seems to go down more biographical or life history lines. Using drama ethnographically makes you sensitized to the space in a different way; you have to have sensibilities open and, in this particular case, when I'm doing it with three or four graduate students and there are three or four or five of us in a room, we come away having to have very rich discussions about our different perspectives on what we were participating in and then we can check that with teachers and with students themselves. It seems a very layered activity to me and something that resonates with how I think understanding comes to be socially shaped and formed.

What are your views on the accountability of researchers?

There are two examples I would give to get at this question. One is that in my last ethnography, one of the things I explicitly did – because it happened implicitly and then I formalized it – was actually have the students interview each other and interview us as researchers. I did this because there seemed to be – at the end of three years – a lot of lingering questions about who we were; where this knowledge would go; why they'd never heard of people (researchers) before who do this kind of work. There were all kinds of interesting questions that underscored their detachment from higher education generally and from knowledge about them specifically. And so there are all kinds of methods that

I tried to introduce that would both get at different knowledge and get at knowledge differently. In other words, I want to be accountable, in the first instance, to those with whom I am collaborating. We cannot have equal power in this relationship but we can shift the balance of power to engage with each other in ways that challenge the traditional lines of research and knowledge flow.

And this year what is very fascinating is that we decided that, in one of the sites, in working with the teacher – and, obviously, as an ethnographer, to do this kind of thing you have to have a teacher who is incredibly open, and that's not [to be found at] every site – so we, with this teacher, decided that we would do a verbatim theatre unit and I have been engaged with that for the last number of weeks with workshop leaders and having them see verbatim theatre. I don't know if you know much about verbatim theatre?

Well, the verbatim theatre piece *Talking with terrorists* that really brought verbatim theatre to the fore premiered in London at the time of my last ethnography in 2002. It's taken hold as a kind of theatre genre that has interesting implications for researchers. What we decided to do was work theatrically – through verbatim theatre – with one of the themes emerging from the data: that old-fashioned notion of 'cliques' in schools, or different affiliations of groups and what constitutes an affiliation and why. So the students expressed a real interest and talked about how their school was divided and categorized in these ways. They then took this as their verbatim theatre project and have taken to the streets (or hallways of their school) to interview their peers about this subject. So while we're interviewing the students, we're also interviewing them about their experiences of inter-viewing *their* peers. So, in a sense, we're having a conversation as researchers and I'm trying to get at what their experience of researching their peers is: what the problems are with that; the ethical dilemmas; what they're learning or not learning; their frustrations with the interview process.

And they're kind of living through a lot of what we, as ethnographers, are living through. And now we're having a conversation not just about what we are all learning about this area of interest but what we're all engaged in, in terms of being knowledge makers. And that is really fascinating. What we intend to do is to work with some theatre artists – getting back to your creative partnerships – over the next year so that the students will become the directors of their research and they will pass this on to other students, who will take their words and perform what they've understood from their research process. And we, as ethnographers, in this meta-research context will be asking what it all means for research, for researcher accountability to research participants, and to the production of knowledge about and with youth.

Chapter 8

The promise of ethnography for exploring creative learning

Geoff Troman and Bob Jeffrey

Research on creative learning has normally not been the preserve of sociological researchers using ethnographic methodology and techniques. However, the 'promise' of ethnography to contribute to our understanding of what were seen to be largely cognitive phenomena has been advocated for some time. Indeed, that promise is beginning to be realized in research on creative teaching and learning.

In this chapter, we examine in what ways the promise of ethnography was used to manage research across ten cultures more usually utilized in single-site and 'lone' researcher studies. We show how we employed ethnographic approaches to develop a shared methodology and how this major focus assisted not only the research process but also the quality of the research practice. We conclude that cross-cultural research using ethnographic methodology can be carried out provided a loosely coupled approach is taken and a meta-analysis of the situated case studies is performed.

The promise of ethnography

We had striven in our previous ethnographic research in education to fulfil some of the promises of ethnography outlined by David Hargreaves (1978): its appreciative capacity to explore social action from the point of view of the actor, its designatory capacity to articulate taken-for-granted common-sense knowledge, its reflective capacity, its 'immunological' capacity to inform policy by providing knowledge and understanding of the everyday life of school, and its corrective capacity to offer a critique of macro-theories. Peter Woods (1996) has added four others: its illuminative capacity, its theoretical capacity, its policy-making capacity and its collaborative capacity.

It was an expressed intention of our European Commission-funded Creative Learning and Student's Perspectives (CLASP) project, involving ten country partners, to continue with this project. However, our problem was how to carry out research into the theme of creative learning using ethnographic methods in ten different cultures and ten different research contexts. We were sensitive to Walford's (2003) minimum requirements for ethnographic inquiry, which, in the context of education, show how policy, curriculum and pedagogy interact with teachers, learners, parents and communities. The key elements are the focus on the study of culture; the use of multiple methods and thus the construction of diverse focus of data; the direct involvement and long-term engagement; the recognition that the researcher is the main research instrument; the high status given to the accounts of participants and their understandings; the engagement in a cycle hypothesis and theory building; and the focus on a particular case rather than on any attempts to generalize (p. 4).

The problem is how to operationalize such a project, a project that emphasizes that these complex processes of data collection, analysis and writing are to be conducted individually, by the 'lone ethnographer' (Hammersley & Atkinson, 1995; Lofland, 1971; Wolcott, 1995) who is also researching as part of a team.

In previous research using ethnographic methodology, Peter Woods and Bob Jeffrey, based at the UK's Open University, had focused on a number of research projects in the area of creative teaching. The identification of creative teaching (Woods, 1995) has been the basis of a number of empirical studies that have developed the theory of creative teaching and provided many examples of its practice. In our early work on creative teaching, we were impressed by the sheer *inventiveness* of primary teachers (Woods, 1995). Their basic task was to find 'ways through' to pupil learning, and the nature of the task at times was something akin to detective work. Once that was achieved, the aim was to maximize learning. Thus, schemes of work designed to be teacher-proof, such as reading schemes, were used in creative ways, for example as subject matter for drama, advancing internalization of the reading ability. But creativity was not just important for the pupils. It was essential for teachers' own 'self-renewal' (Woods, 1995).

Creative teaching involves *ownership* of knowledge. The teacher is not simply relaying somebody else's information on to pupils, acting as a conveyer of other people's news which is then tested by instruments devised by others. The knowledge that they are concerned to produce and construct in children has been incorporated into their own life-worlds. It has become part of their own knowledge as applied to the social circumstances of their own classrooms and the social backgrounds of their students.

It follows that creative teachers have *control* of their own pedagogy. They choose what methods, and what combination of methods, to employ, and when. Creative teachers are also able to create and avail themselves of opportunities to teach creatively. They know how to exploit the 'implementation gap' between government educational policy and putting it into practice. They are also expert in taking advantage of the unexpected to promote learning.

None of this would be of any educational use unless the teaching was *relevant* to the child concerned – for the child to engage in creative learning, to make the knowledge his or her own and for it to become 'personal knowledge' (Woods, 1995, p. 116), to control learning processes, and for the learning to be innovative, to make a difference to the child. So often, 'relevance' is defined by others in terms of what *they* perceive as pupils' and society's needs.

Creative teachers are concerned with 'person-making' (Brehony, 1992), which involves the personal, social, emotional as well as the intellectual development of children: 'teaching people to be people' (Jeffrey & Woods, 2009, p. 2). It is about communicating, relating, mutual respect, working together, emotional well-being, knowing oneself and knowing others.

In earlier work, we identified a wide range of creative teaching strategies, including starting from the child; making home and school links; allowing children to revisit activities and thus develop their conceptual skills; 'teaching in the margins'; spontaneous reaction ('going with the flow'); making emotional connections; creating atmosphere and tone; stimulating the imagination; developing empathy; and devising 'critical events' – akin to the projects of the Plowden era of the 1970s (Jeffrey & Woods, 2009). These are just some of the strategies employed. They provide the flavour of everyday creative classroom teaching.

Nevertheless, international research partners have to have some common texts. They are generally located in both the substantive area of the research and the methodology they employ. However, international education is not an area of research that could be said to consist of common, tightly defined curriculums, theories of learning or a commonly shared practice. The knowledge base differs internationally, as do the various systems of organization and pedagogy, and even specific areas of research are usually open to many differing experiences and interpretations. Similarly, the validity of international common methodologies is not without its problems; for example, there are critiques of international testing (Brown, 1998), educational comparison (McLean, 1992) and the globalization of qualitative methodologies (Hammersley & Atkinson, 1995). Given that research methodologies are immanent in the research process, the CLASP project decided to develop their common text through ethnography, a methodology that has a multidisciplinary approach, one that is tentative about generalizing across different contexts and one that sees the people carrying out the research as the main research instruments.

The CLASP project

The CLASP research project was coordinated by The Open University and had ten other European partners. The research period began in March 2003 and the final report was due in October 2004. It was funded by the European Commission – Socrates Project: Action 6.1, 'General Activities of observation and analysis' – with a grant of €549,000, and the English research was also funded by the ESRC RES-000-22-0037. Ours was only one of eight projects funded that year, and each of the ten partners gained approximately €55,000. (In the event, only nine partners carried out research.)

The identification of creative teaching (Woods, 1995) has been the basis of a number of empirical studies that have developed the theory of creative teaching and provided many examples of its practice. The main features were identified as relevance, control, ownership and innovation (Woods, 1995). The emphasis on creative teaching inevitably involved some consideration of its effects, what we term 'creative learning', and the CLASP project was the first major research by us in this area.

Considering the relationship between these features, we concluded that the greater the relevance of teaching to children's lives, worlds, cultures and interests, the more likely it is that pupils will have control of their own learning processes. Relevance aids identification, motivation, excitement and enthusiasm. Control, in turn, leads to ownership of the knowledge that results. If relevance, control and ownership apply, the greater the chance of creative learning – something new is created, there is significant change or 'transformation' in the pupil: that is, innovation (Woods, Boyle, & Hubbard, 1999).

The two main theoretical frames used in our research are those of symbolic interactionism and social constructivism, although we called on other areas of theory, such as identity careers (Pollard & Filer, 1999). The linking of symbolic interactionism and social constructivism was a means whereby we could contribute towards a relevant theory of learning.

The partners, who were researching the nature of creative learning across a range of educational arenas, were situated in ten universities (Table 8.1). The aims of the project were as follows:

- to identify teachers' and students' strategies for developing creative learning in educational contexts;

- to examine the effectiveness of incorporating student perspectives into the teaching and learning process;
- to highlight the advantages to be gained for the quality of teaching and learning by examining cross-European creative pedagogic practices.

Table 8.1 Research partners and sites

Partner	Research sites
1 England – Milton Keynes	Three primary schools
2 Austria – Innsbruck	One secondary classroom and two primary classrooms in different schools
3 Belgium – Kortrijk	Uncompleted
4 Denmark – Odense	One secondary school with 450 students
5 Ireland – Dublin	Two primary schools and a special needs class
6 Poland – Łódź	All the classes at the Academy of Humanities and Economics, for students aged 18-plus
7 Portugal – Lisbon	Three classes in one secondary school
8 Spain – Cadiz	One infant school, one primary school and one secondary school
9 Sweden – Göteborg	Two secondary schools and an adult training centre
10 Scotland – Glasgow	One primary school with a specialist bilingual unit

Project strategy

Critical engagement

Our first strategy was to arrange a series of four project meetings formed of two parts. The first day focused on our methodological practice: on explicating the ethnographic method alongside some discussion of cultural interpretations of creative teaching and learning the appreciative capacity promise; a training session on a qualitative research software program, Atlas-Ti; a consultant-led meeting in ethnographic methods; and a meeting focused on the development of research findings from data coding through analysis to research findings.

The second day focused on examining and discussing partners' projects and their analysis at these meetings. Questions were asked and discussed about how far partners were applying the criteria of ethnography – articulating the taken-for-granted common-sense knowledge promise. For example, one partner was asked to provide empirical evidence for her assertions; another was asked to deepen the analysis by gaining the perspectives of all the relevant people in the research site, ethnography's appreciative capacity; another was asked to move beyond initial description and try to identify some broader characterizations; and it was suggested to another partner that the theory should arise from the data rather than be imposed upon it, applying the theoretical promise of ethnographic methodology.

The substantive research element – examination of the characteristics of creative learning and the conditions under which it thrives or is constrained – was the subject matter of partners' reports and presentations, but the development of their analysis was critiqued against the minimum requirements for ethnography. In this way, partners' 'webs of significance' were not directly or indirectly critiqued, challenged or massaged in the pursuit of a common conceptualization or theory. Each partner project retained its cultural signature but each one was refined in terms of the methodology. For example, one partner's project involved researching creative teaching and learning in a higher education college. The researchers were on the staff of the college, and at first they felt they were only accountable to the management of the college. However, after two CLASP meetings and many discussions concerning the importance of incorporating as many relevant perspectives from the site as possible, they devised a research programme that brought a class of students and their teacher into an examination of their shared practice, the collaborative capacity of ethnographic methodology. The result was a richer analysis of creative learning – ethnography's illuminative capacity – as well as a change in teacher–student pedagogic relations, evidence of the reflective promise of ethnographic methodology. This research development involved examining the culture of the classroom, using multiple methods including video and focus groups. It was possible, because of the familiarity the researchers had with the institution, that as the research instrument they could alter their approach and decide to include a wider range of perspectives from those at the research site.

A methodological framework was used creatively by the international researchers from within their own 'webs of significance'. However, this kind of loosely coupled research partnership also required some common lenses with which to carry out fieldwork.

Common fieldwork lens

Our second strategy was to establish a common fieldwork lens. Fieldwork is a work of art (Wolcott, 1995), and as with research partner relationships, the emphasis is on ensuring that the researcher has the flexibility and freedom to use his or her own imaginative tools. However, the identification of relevant research lenses through which the researcher perceives a research site is a vital element in a loosely coupled research project. The lenses we devised reflected ethnographic methodology but were directly focused on the project of creative learning: context, interaction, cognitive explorations, subjectivity and learner agency. These lenses were used to assist researchers construct the 'thick description' (Geertz, 1973) of qualitative inquiry.

The characteristics of creative teaching and learning constituted the character of creative engagement in learning. Some of the contexts that fulfilled the illuminative capacity of ethnography were as follows:

- the systems to promote creativity and creative learning, for example curriculum and pedagogic programmes, institutional timetabling and extra-curricular activities;
- the climates, cultures and environments that stimulated and developed creativity, for example classroom tones, investigative approaches and flexible learning patterns;
- the influences upon creative contexts, such as policies to prioritize learner inclusion, democratization, experiential learning and tools to assess creativity;
- the extent to which learning was made relevant to learners, for example ownership of learning and knowledge was encouraged, control was passed back to learners, and innovatory action was encouraged and valued (Jeffrey and Woods, 2009).

Our interaction lens obliged researchers to prioritize interaction between teachers and learners, between peers and between learners and other relevant adults. They were expected to record how far and in what ways teacher–learner interactions either contributed to creative learning or were the basis of it. Some of the productive interactive foci for research into creative learning included the extent to which learner voice was prioritized; the quality of open questioning, challenging and problematizing; the extent of co-participation, where knowledge, processes and problems were explored together; and the characteristics of conversational learning, the relevant learning that took place in the process of an activity and to what extent it was the driver of creative learning. This lens exemplified the 'immunological' capacity promise to inform policy by providing knowledge and understanding of the everyday life of school.

Cognitive explorations explored connection making and relationship identification; possibility thinking and possibility knowledge; playing with ideas; the discussion and evaluation of options; risk taking; the valuing of uncertainty and ambiguity; and the promotion of the construction of alternative solutions dependent on context and variables by teachers, again exemplifying illuminative capacity.

The subjectivity lens exemplified the appreciative capacity promise by focusing on feelings, emotions, the meaningfulness of creative experiences for the self and identity, and the well-being attached to social cohesion and engaging in collaborative or participative creative practices.

The agency lens examined a conception of the person as an agent of his or her own practice, someone for whom the process itself is inimical to both the experience of his or her creativity and its development, exemplifying the reflective capacity promise. As ethnographic researchers, we included data concerning:

- teachers' discussions with learners concerning their experience of learning;
- ways in which teachers include learners in the development of pedagogy and curriculum;
- teachers' and learners' evaluations of the effectiveness of learning processes and, in particular, creative experiences;
- teachers' and learners' evaluations of the effects of ideas and actions upon the individuals and groups;
- an examination of any measures, indicators and assessments of creativity used by teachers or institutions and the development of them;
- examination of the ways in which ideas are represented: visually, kinaesthetically, orally, musically, fictionally and dramatically.

These project-focused fieldwork lenses were developed through the ethnographic framework, and strengthened the 'community of practice' (Lave & Wenger, 1991) by providing a common research text.

Case-study analysis

The third strategy was to collect a series of analysed case studies, one for each research site, detailing:

- the nature of creative learning taking place within them;
- the strategies used by teachers and students to develop creative learning practices;
- how teachers responded to the use of student perspectives to improve teaching and learning;

- ways of consulting pupils about teaching and learning;
- the commencement and maintenance of student participation;
- ways of involving students as co-researchers;
- how teachers can help improve the social conditions of learning.

In the main, partners were working in-depth in their own cultures and heavily influenced by their previous experience of qualitative research. The CLASP study did not seek, at this stage, to compare differences in processes or events, as is the role of much comparative research. Rather, it sought to identify common features of a particular form of pedagogy and from these features to create something that was 'more than the sum of their parts' (Alexander, 2001, p. 511) and 'to tease out the universal . . . by the trading and migration of ideas and practices across national borders' (pp. 513–514).

We therefore established a loosely coupled relationship (Weick, 1989), because of the differing cultural 'webs of significance' (Geertz, 1973). International research in which partners from different cultures investigate a common subject is fraught with problems concerning different languages, discourses, perspectives and interpretation, policy and peda- gogic texts, research methodologies, working practices and academic criteria. Some of these differences enhance project collaboration in situations where international groups find enjoyment in doing things differently, use differences as opportunities to be more critical and find engaging with different methodologies a source of learning. However, these enhancements often develop during the process of the project and cannot be part of the original research design (Troman & Jeffrey, 2007).

We received nine partner reports and other papers from the partners, and each of these was first combed for common characteristics of both teacher strategies to develop creative learning and students' experiences of it. These features were then categorized. For example, the teacher strategies to stimulate creative learning were found to be *the establishment of real and critical events, the creative use of space, modelling creativity, encouraging par- ticipative strategies and learner inclusiveness* and *providing relevant pedagogies and discourses.* The students' common experiences of creative learning were categorised as *open adventures, intellectual analysis, engaged productivity* and *process and product reviews* (Jeffrey, 2006), all enhancing the theoretical promise of ethnography. This categorization approach we called collective synthesis (Troman & Jeffrey, 2007), for it was in effect a list of common features.

A second, and more interpretative, approach was then used to select some partner conceptualizations that appeared to have some commonality across partners' reports, embellish them and interrogate them with the data from the other partners. The project director carried out this form of analysis across the dataset, revising and reconstructing it as he searched back and forth among the reports for additional features and contradictory factors to devise categories that inclined towards a theorization of creative learning across the partners – the collaborative capacity of ethnography. For example, one of the partners wrote about creative learning being a *meaningful experience.* The reports were then trawled to find examples of this. The young participants responded to creative learning by indicating the extent to which the experience was meaningful to them, the way they felt about the learning experience and the importance it had for their self-identity and their sense of inclusion. The relevance of the experience of creative learning to their 'self' was seen in their subjective reactions – their joy of engagement and the quality of the authentic relationships they developed towards their work. Their identities – the social character they inhabit – resulted in their feeling more confident about their labour and more confident about their place in the class and school in terms of relationships and belonging through the experience of co-participation. The participants also expressed some satisfaction concerning the quality of the social relationships that developed during creative learning, although their reactions were not always positive, particularly in situations where the top-down national policies were seen as ineffective and sometimes damaging. From this trawl, we developed empirical categories of *self-affirmation*, *social identity*, *social role* and *social relations* that were significant areas of meaning for the young participants (Jeffrey, 2006).

This second analytical strategy – which we termed 'grafted synthesis' – takes one idea from the one or more of the partners, and a search was done to develop its characteristics from the reports and papers provided by the other partners. They may not have actually mentioned the meaningful nature of creative learning but their data contained some examples of its existence, and the project director developed the conceptualization from their empirical data and analysis.

The whole final report was then returned to the partners for their validation. This respondent validation process strengthened the participants in their work as they shared in the criticality of the research and tested the significance of higher-order constructs (Woods, 1996). In this case, the respondents were not those who were researched, as in some other well-known research projects (see, for example, Mac an Ghaill, 1988), but the loosely coupled research team using all the promises of ethnography in a meta context. Inaccuracies were identified, obfuscatory analysis was questioned, arguments over inclusions and interpretations took place and were resolved, and the limitations of the loosely coupled project were also discussed. The final result was an analytical research report that had been validated by the researchers of each project. On completion of this process, and when the descriptions and categories had been further interrogated, we developed a report (Jeffrey, 2005a) that had been agreed by all the partners and was published. More detailed exemplifications were published in an edited collection (Jeffrey, 2005b). Each partner's own report in the collection showed the case-study data upon which the common characteristics of creative learning were derived, acting as a corrective capacity to psychological theories of creative learning.

Conclusion

While the project realized many of the promises discussed earlier, it also fulfilled the specific promises of the application and development of ethnographic methodology in a cross-cultural project. This achieved a looser collaboration, allowing for individual development within a single object; a contingent methodology – according to context; learning from each other and collaborating in developing ethnographic methodology; and the celebration of cultural differences in research outputs.

Prioritizing the research methodology, in this case ethnography, as the common approach throughout the process of the CLASP project:

- provided opportunities for inter-national cultures to maintain ownership of new knowledge, in this case the characteristics of creative learning, and at the same time offered the possibility to draw upon these autonomous analyses to provide tentative common features;

- maintained the focus of the research on the minimum requirements for research, which are, in any case, immanent in research outcomes;
- provided a vehicle for critique and reflection of each partner's findings without appearing to construct differing culturally based interpretations.

The influence of ethnographic principles can obviously be detected in these findings, but methodological visibility can also be seen in the common framework and lenses for fieldwork that we established at the beginning of the research project. This international research was closely linked through methodology while retaining a loose coupling to maintain the autonomy of cultural webs of significance.

References

Alexander, R. (2001). Border crossings. *Comparative Education, 37*(4), 507–523.

Brehony, K. J. (1992). What's left of progressive education? In A. Rattansi and D. Reeder (Eds.), *Rethinking radical education: Essays in honour of Brian Simon*. London: Lawrence & Wishart.

Brown, M. (1998). The tyranny of the international horse race. In R. Slee, G. Weiner, & S. Tomlinson (Eds.), *School effectiveness for whom: Challenges to the school effectiveness and school improvement movements* (pp. 33–48). London: Falmer Press.

Geertz, C. (1973). *The interpretation of cultures: Selected essays by Clifford Geertz*. New York: Basic Books.

Hammersley, M., & Atkinson, P. (1995). *Ethnography: Principles in practice*. London: Routledge.

Hargreaves, D. H. (1978). Whatever happened to symbolic interactionism? In L. Barton & R. Meighan (Eds.), *Sociological interpretations of schooling and classrooms: A reappraisal*. Driffield, UK: Nafferton Books.

Jeffrey, B. (2005a). *Creative learning and student perspectives: European report*. Report for The Open University (Milton Keynes, UK).

Jeffrey, B. (Ed.). (2005b). *Creative learning practices: European experiences*. London: Tufnell Press.

Jeffrey, B. (2006). Creative teaching and learning: Towards a common discourse and practice. *Cambridge Journal of Education, 36*(3), 399–414.

Jeffrey, B., & Woods, P. (2009). *Creative learning in the primary school*. London: Routledge.

Lave, J., & Wenger, E. (1991). *Situated learning: Legitimate peripheral participation*. New York: Cambridge University Press.

Lofland, J. (1971). *Analysing social settings*. Belmont, CA: Wadsworth.

Mac an Ghaill, M. (1988). *Young, gifted and black: Student–teacher relations in the schooling of black youth*. Milton Keynes, UK: Open University Press.

McLean, M. (1992). *The promise and perils of educational comparison*. London: Institute of Education, University of London.

Pollard, A., & Filer, A. (1999). *The social world of pupil career*. London: Cassell.

Troman, G., & Jeffrey, B. (2007). Qualitative data analysis in cross-cultural projects. *Comparative Education, 43*(4), 511–525.

Walford, G. (Ed.). (2003). *Investigating educational policy through ethnography*. Vol. 8, *Studies in educational ethnography*. Oxford: Elsevier Science.

Weick, K. E. (1989). Education systems as loosely coupled systems. In T. Bush (Ed.), *Managing education: Theory and practice* (pp. 118–130). Milton Keynes, UK: Open University Press.

Wolcott, H. F. (1995). *The art of fieldwork*. London: Sage.

Woods, P. (1995). *Creative teachers in primary schools*. Buckingham, UK: Open University Press.

Woods, P. (1996). *Researching the art of teaching: Ethnography for educational use.* London: Routledge.

Woods, P., Boyle, M., & Hubbard, N. (1999). *Multicultural children in the early years: Creative teaching, meaningful learning.* Clevedon, UK: Multilingual Matters.

Chapter 9

'Now it's up to us to interpret it'

Youth voice and visual methods in creative learning and research

Sara Bragg

Introduction

This chapter explores visual methods – using, generating and disseminating images and artefacts as drawings, collages, diagrams, maps, still photographs, video, installations – within research, within creative learning and within 'youth voice' or participatory practices. New digital and web technologies mean, of course, that most of these visual methods are increasingly available, accessible and affordable. However, their increasing popularity is not determined by technology alone: it marks broader material, conceptual and social-political shifts that have directed attention to the visual, multiplied the contexts in which it is used, and brought about changes in what and how research questions are asked, in who creates visual material and how it is interpreted.

Many resources on visual research and methods already exist, and this chapter points readers to some of them (such as Banks, 2001, 2008; Denzin & Lincoln, 2005, 2008; Hamilton, 2006; Emmison & Smith, 2000; Knowles & Sweetman, 2004; Pink, 2007; Prosser, 1998; Prosser & Loxley, 2008; Rose, 2006; Visual Learning Lab, 2007). While there is nothing new about social scientists generating visual data for and by themselves within a research process, there are some distinctive demands and assumptions being made about visual methods now, particularly in relation to young people, and it is on these that this chapter focuses (see also Thomson, 2008).

The visual in contemporary culture

It is something of a truism to say that Western culture has become increasingly dominated by the visual: the proliferation of television, cinema, photography, computer games, the role of advertising images in urban consumer landscapes, and the widespread use of CCTV are just some examples that substantiate this claim. However, there is considerable dissent concerning its extent, its significance, its nature and its definition. Edited collections and introductions to the academic field of 'visual culture' represent it quite differently and thereby reveal diverse understandings of creativity and cultural practice. Some, for instance, focus primarily on the photographic or cinematic image (Evans & Hall, 2001), some embrace other technologies such as medical or scientific imaging (Sturken & Cartwright, 2001), and others expand the field of 'the visual' to include architecture, environment, clothing and body adornment (Emmison & Smith, 2001). Sometimes the term is applied to distinctively aesthetic practices, such as sculpture, craft, fashion, design, fine art, video and performance art (Rampley, 2005; Barnard, 2001), or to explore the newer forms of graphic novels and computer games; at other times, it is the ordinary, everyday, or domestic uses and contexts of images that are held to supply their significance (Frosh, 2003; Murray, 2008; Rose, 2006). Mirzoeff (1999, 2002) aligns visual culture – 'the tendency to represent things visually that are not themselves visual' – with the postmodern and its crises of representation and authority; an interdisciplinary, tactical understanding that may more readily accommodate recent emphasis on material or spatial cultures and on 'sensory' methodologies that extend beyond the visual (Pink, 2006).

However, as Hill (2008) points out, in the humanities and social sciences the visual attains the status of academic knowledge within the university principally through written form. He outlines four approaches to writing the visual, each of which addresses and thereby constructs a different kind of reader or student. The humanist or art-historical approach, dominant until the mid-twentieth century, focuses on individual artistic talent traced through compositional elements, simultaneously affirming the 'cultivated individual' able to appreciate them. From the 1960s emerged the overtly political 'critical-theoretical', which exposed visual (including popular) culture's ideological role in perpetuating inequalities and injustice, through both its content and its spectatorship practices, and in so doing assumed a 'politicized' student subject. More recently, a third approach deals explicitly with methodological issues, reflecting both the 'cultural turn' in the social sciences, and the high value placed on methodology by an increasingly dominant audit culture, thereby developing the 'skilled' student-worker required by the knowledge economy. Finally, in the 'postmodern', studies of reception, audiences and fandom explore the meanings and enjoyment visual culture provides, addressing the student as pleasure-seeking 'consumer' in both leisure and education.

These approaches continue to coexist, rather than superseding one another, and Hill's categorization may help contextualize some of the themes, concerns and silences of different kinds of academic work with, or of, the visual. They may also be relevant at school level, to the various rationales for 'creative' practices and media/film/art curricula that have been offered over the years.

Outside academia, we should note the contradictoriness of attitudes to the visual. One dominant trend in popular discourse deplores it, invariably depicting child or youth audiences in particular as 'bombarded', 'saturated' and 'assaulted' by (commercial) images. By contrast, another welcomes it as more accessible than the printed or spoken word, and thus as being able to 'give voice' to marginalized, socially excluded and powerless groups, including people with disabilities, children and young people. Yet another celebrates young people's 'natural' affinity for and innate skills in negotiating visual cultures, which are claimed to outstrip those of older generations. Both the latter suggest, although not for the same reasons, that youth 'voice' can be 'heard' more 'directly' through images, and thus that visual methods give a more privileged 'inside' perspective than others, allowing young people to 'speak for themselves' – as if images are transparent in a way that words are not. Such emphasis on 'voice' to enable participation, when contextualized within the rights- and consumer-based discourses of contemporary neoliberal societies, helps account for the use of visual methods to generate data for strategic use in policy formulation and public service provision, by local authorities, government and voluntary-sector bodies, advocacy groups, charities, and so on, and within commercial marketing practices as well as academic research.

Visual methods in research, learning and participatory processes

This section explores how and why visual material might figure in research, learning and participatory processes, discussing these together to indicate their points of connection despite their apparently different objectives and contexts. The overview here is selective: it generally focuses on examples that relate to or involve young people and reflect some common preoccupations with how young people are positioned and addressed, rather than all possible methods. We begin with one 'visual method' – the scrapbook – that is briefly outlined below and then referred to repeatedly in the following discussion to illustrate how it might meet diverse aims.

A visual method for different contexts?

'Scrapbooks' appear, in different forms, in a range of research, learning and other contexts, as well as having a long history as a domestic craft. The term is used here to identify an approach that gathers together material generated privately (such as photographs) or existing texts and objects (such as magazine and newspaper articles, leaflets, tickets, greetings cards), usually accompanied by personal writing, drawing or other commentary.

'Memory books' evolved as a biographical research method, alongside interviews, in a longitudinal, qualitative study of young people's transitions to adulthood (referred to henceforth as YTA). Participants were given a notebook and some stickers with suggested headings, a disposable camera and a folder in which to put paraphernalia. They were asked to bring it to their second interview, nine to twelve months after the first (Thomson & Holland, 2005).

Research into children's views on 'love, sex and relationships' in the media (referred to here as LSR) asked participants to keep a diary or 'scrapbook' over one or two weeks. They were provided with a blank notebook in which they were asked to provide some information about themselves and their family and then to record their encounters with the themes of 'love, sex and relationships' in the media, including examples of newspaper or magazine articles, advertisements and other material (Bragg & Buckingham, 2004, 2008).

This scrapbook approach was subsequently adopted for teaching purposes in a unit of work called 'Media relate: Teaching resources about the media, sex and relationships', designed for use in schools with 12- to 14-year-olds (Bragg, 2006). Students were asked to carry out research at home investigating and recording media portrayals of love, sex and relationships as a starting point for more extended work and discussion in class.

What might visual methods aim to achieve? There are many possible answers, beginning with the following.

To answer a question

Rose (2006) argues that visual research methods involve images 'as a way of answering a research question', and that they should be consistent with the theoretical framework for the research. While one might argue that methods actively *produce* understandings and research objects, nonetheless the principle that visual methods should be motivated by a research or learning focus, rather than randomly adopted, is sound. In relation to the projects above, the YTA memory books were clearly a form appropriate to biographical investigation, while the LSR media scrapbooks aimed to be to some extent 'private' and personal in a way that mirrored social understandings of sex and relationships. To give further examples, a research perspective on sexuality as embodied and performed was reflected methodologically by asking participants to make video diaries, which demonstrated how identities were narrativized and variable (Holliday, 2004). Allen (2009) argues that visual methods facilitated research into the sexual cultures of schools, an issue that would have been hard to address by more conventional means. Conversely, when 'youth voice' about issues such as service provision is represented by a short video of a handful of presentable young talking heads (examples of which can be seen on YouTube), one might wonder whether different methods would have produced deeper understanding and wider engagement.

As will be apparent, visual methods are rarely used alone, but form part of a mixed methods approach – alongside other qualitative methods such as narrative, semi- or unstructured individual or group interviews or participant observation, or mixing interpretative and participatory approaches (Hemming, 2008), or with quantitative methods such as surveys. Their purpose is to generate different data from different perspectives, rather than more of the same. Many qualitative researchers have adopted the concept of 'crystallization' (Richardson, 2005) rather than the positivist one of 'triangulation' of data; while the latter seems to suggest that a 'truth' can eventually be reached through different methods, the former admits that the knowledges and insights generated by different approaches may not cohere smoothly while still enriching the outcome of the research. As we discuss later, however, one might ask whether this metaphor glosses over the real difficulties of using and interpreting visual data.

Beyond this overarching rationale, visual methods may have multiple overlapping purposes, including the following.

To generate talk: the visual as 'elicitation tool'

Visual material, in the form of 'found', or already, existing images, or those created specifically for the purpose, can be used as a stimulus that not only provides a way into talking about particular topics but can also generate different kinds of talk and conversation (Harper, 2002). As well as talking about individual images, participants might undertake exercises such as ranking sets of images according to particular criteria, engaging in dialogue with each other and/or the interviewer as they do so – practices that are similar to 'creative' (but familiar) classroom strategies to promote discussion. While there are longer traditions of, for instance, using children's drawings as a diagnostic tool in psychotherapy, what distinguishes the approaches here is the interest in seeking participants' own perspectives and interpretations of the material.

In the YTA research, memory books completed by the research participants were used as a basis for discussion and served as a reminder of events or issues that might have been omitted from more conventional narrative interviews. In LSR, scrapbooks were collected and read in advance of the first interview, so researchers could prepare a general set of questions about the process of making them, and some specific follow-up questions about interesting or unclear elements in individual cases.

In other work, family photographs or images of the self have been used in sociological and geographical studies of emotions (see Harper, 2002; Rose, 2004), oral history and biographical work (Spence & Holland, 1991) and within education (Cohen, 1990). Coates (2004) discusses children's drawings, and Bagnoli (2009) discusses the use of drawing and graphic approaches (e.g. timelines) in biographical interviews. Media researchers and educators screen television extracts to provoke group discussion and interpretation (e.g. Buckingham, 1993), or use young people's existing representations of self on social networking sites such as Bebo (Willett, 2009). In educational contexts, Scratz and Steiner-Loffler (1998) discuss children taking photos in school self-evaluation, and Mitchell and Weber (1998) use school photographs both to elicit narratives from teachers and to reflect on professional practices; see also Prosser (2007) and a number of school-based examples in Thomson (2008). However, the case study at the end of the chapter indicates some important limitations to this approach in some contexts, which might include research into creative learning; it cannot be assumed that those who produce images will automatically be able to articulate or even recognize the insights and understandings implicit in them.

To document or provide evidence

Anthropologists and ethnographers have made visual images of the communities they study ever since the technology became available. These constitute an archive that has been critically reinterpreted in the light of changing perspectives and theories, showing not least how such images actively produce the realities and power relations they claim simply to reflect. Assembling visual materials and records, then, is not an 'innocent' process, and I indicate some of its dilemmas below (including the impact of degree of 'finish' required and the intended audience). However, it can prove powerful and useful in a number of ways: as a narrative of a process (of creative learning or of joint action, and so on); as memories of the self or of others; as a guide around one's world, for another; as a portfolio of achievements; in social action projects; as evidence of problems requiring solutions; and so on. Thus, the memorabilia collected in the biographical YTA project illuminated young people's daily routines, modes of communication (valentine cards, emails, notes exchanged in lessons, etc.) and aided recall of less obviously significant social activities. In the LSR research, examples of media material helped the researchers to grasp young people's actual cultural experiences and, where the same material reappeared in different scrapbooks, the diversity of their responses to it.

To make room for tacit knowledge (and creativity)

Media audience research has long acknowledged the inadequacy of asking participants to express their understanding of visual forms only in words, and has tried to develop more appropriate approaches. For example, MacGregor and Morrison (1995) asked participants to edit news material, to demonstrate their comprehension and judgements about current affairs programming. For similar reasons, most forms of media education employ practical production work (where students work within the conventions of a specified genre to produce short texts such as advertisements, trailers or introductory sequences) in order to mobilize the implicit knowledge young people have accumulated from familiarity with media forms. These may well demonstrate creativity, which gives them particular relevance here, although this is not the main objective in media education, and nor is assessment based on the romantic notion of 'originality' beloved by creativity discourses, which all too often proves to be a codeword for avant-garde, alternative or 'approved' forms. Instead, intelligibility and appropriateness provide evidence of understanding; and the overall purpose is to help students learn *from* the experience of creating media, about concepts such as representation (Buckingham, Grahame, & Sefton-Green, 1995). In addition, by allowing informal learning to be expressed other than through conventional essays, they might contribute not only to students' motivation and confidence, but also to their success at school (especially where such work forms part of assessment) – much as expressive arts have often been advocated as alternatives to existing formal curricula that alienate too many young people from learning. Debates about what constitutes a 'creative curriculum' explore how it might connect with and draw vitality from students' out-of-school interests; reckoning with the forms of visual culture that are now likely to figure prominently there suggests the importance of visual methods for accessing and understanding the learning they provide.

These arguments informed the development of the LSR scrapbooks, where young people's creativity in compiling their collages and their ability to parody or make use of media conventions, such as the layout, tone and language of teenage magazines, demonstrated their comprehension and interpretative skills more effectively than if they had been required to write about them.

To explore identities and the non-rational

Talk-based methods, in classrooms or research, are often held to be insufficient for dealing with emotional, private dimensions of subjectivity and experience, with issues that are hard to articulate fully or that participants lack the vocabulary to discuss. Visual methods are argued to do this more effectively, by facilitating symbolic, non-verbal communication of meanings or drawing on now well-established 'private' visual genres, such as the video diary. They have developed, therefore, in part because of the greater interest in subjective experience and processes of identity construction that has marked recent theory and practice in the social sciences (for an educational-related example, see Allan, 2005). In this respect, their processes may approach those of art therapy, where creating visual images or narratives aims to help patients work through traumatic experiences; but while the comparison may also help account for the satisfactions (and sometimes distress) generated even by 'pedagogic' versions of creative expression, it also points to the potential dangers of inviting personal explorations without the capacity to handle the emotions these can evoke.

The YTA memory books were modelled in part on the 'memory boxes' developed in child therapy to help children cope with major life events such as bereavement or adoption. Scrapbooks, too, have been used in therapeutic contexts for 'narrating' life stories; in LSR, they often conveyed emotional meanings through the way images were juxtaposed, or how colour and letter size was used. However, there is clearly a need for sensitivity in how these elements are addressed with participants and in how they are interpreted.

To explore the non-verbal: context, space, style and bodies

Interdisciplinary work examining environment, place and embodiment has turned to visual images to capture these material aspects of the world. Thomson and Holland (2005) reflect on how the photographs in their young participants' memory books foregrounded the physical changes of growing up, which would have passed virtually unnoticed within verbal data alone. Flewitt's audio-visual recordings of pre-schoolers show how visual data can draw attention to body language and gesture, focus and direction of gaze, and relations between learners, and thus counter the bias towards spoken and written language within education – revealing, for instance, that a child considered to lack verbal skills was in fact able to communicate with ease non-verbally (Flewitt, 2006).

Many studies have taken a participative approach, inviting children and young people to photograph, draw or create maps and to comment on these in relation to (for instance) play spaces (Burke, 2008), health (Hemming, 2008), bullying and safety, territoriality and social exclusion (Kintrea, Bannister, Pickering, Suzuki, & Reid, 2008), routes, travel, learning, ideal schools and more (see Prosser, 2007). Their power lies in highlighting the very different experience young people may have of their surroundings; even an apparently shared space such as a school building contains many areas into which adults rarely venture (such as student toilets), or that students put to unsuspected uses. This interest in space is increasingly significant in relation to creative learning, especially where school buildings or playgrounds are being redesigned, which offers genuine opportunities for realizing ideas developed with students (see, for instance, the accounts in Deveson, 2008).

To be inclusive

As we have already noted, visual methods are frequently presented as more inclusive, allowing the expression of views and perspectives by groups and individuals who are often excluded from research, consultation or learning, such as the very young (Clark & Moss, 2001). Another interpretation of inclusivity stresses the importance of diversity in terms not only of the range of participants but also of the kinds of 'voices' and 'selves' that can be expressed by those involved. Some formal, word-based consultations with young people, for instance, may require responses phrased in 'correct' language and a presentation of self as a serious, responsible citizen. By contrast, both the YTA and the LSR research stress how the relative openness of the scrapbooks allowed young people to present themselves quite differently there as compared to in the interviews, and to play with the divergent 'voices' that emerge from different creative and writing genres. In LSR, for instance, participants could express and display the pleasures they gained from the media, which was sometimes more difficult in the school contexts of interviews; relying on only one method would have restricted understanding of their media cultures and of their identities.

Visual methods also lend themselves to collaborative approaches, both in the sense of participants working together to create materials (such as videos), and in the sense of working with others (researchers, teachers, youth workers, facilitators, and so on) in making decisions about the images they create, what happens to them, and in discussing and analysing them, constructing shared interpretations. This has led to some large claims about the inherent participatory possibilities of visual approaches, their potential for minimizing power hierarchies, promoting involvement in decision making and empowering those using them, which I address in sceptical vein in what follows.

To promote reflection: a 'tool for thinking with'

Those engaged in using visual methods frequently comment on how the practices involved (such as creating, viewing, editing, selecting, assembling, exhibiting and arranging) and the company and interest of others help to generate new perspectives, connections and thought processes. Consider this creative learning project with secondary school students in an area targeted for urban regeneration:

> [The students] did a whole promenade performance from the school through the subway, which they made into [a] time tunnel . . . they had re-imagined what their shopping arcade and community would look like in 10 years time. They had got an empty shop front that they had taken over [to show] how they would like it to look . . . the local people from the council, some parents, the teachers from school that were not involved in the project, other students – a range of people [came to it]. It was very visible so you had people walking past, who were just at the shops, saying oh what's going on . . . and they had to go and speak to the market traders, now normally the market traders hate the young people because they are a pain in the neck to them and so they had to have a different kind of conversation which was interesting.
>
> (Creative Partnerships Regional Director, 2008; quoted in
> Bragg, Manchester, & Faulkner, 2009)

This creative project illustrates how 'visual methods' might constitute valuable resources for reflection and thinking, both for those producing them and those viewing and working with them. Asking students to visualize urban regeneration in a hands-on, creative, collaborative way, using and adapting objects and familiar surroundings, may have brought the debate alive and engaged a wider range of young people than more formal, verbal methods would have done. In addition, both the process and the product involved visibility, a tangible presence in public space for young people and their ideas, making them available for others to analyse and reflect upon.

Central to this argument is not only that visual methods are a 'tool for thinking with' but also that the thinking they stimulate is different from that stimulated by other tools such as language (compare Knowles & Cole, 2008). One educational dilemma, however, is their role in learning. Visual and other creative production in media education, as already noted, allows tacit knowledge to be expressed; but students are also asked to write about the process, a 'translation' aiming to make that knowledge available for reflection and self-understanding, and to aid conceptual learning. This raises again the question of how visual material is used and interpreted, which I address below.

To disseminate

Chaplin asked, in 1994, whether the use of visual methods within a research process should find a counterpart in a creative presentation of findings, attending to visual impact even if only in such minor areas as choice of typeface. Since then, the development of hyper-media has overcome many of the previous cost-based restrictions on publishing visual materials, although it has generated new ethical questions touched on below. Pink, Kürti, and Afonso's 2004 collection on visual ethnography is itself accompanied by a website where still and moving images can be viewed, and discusses a range of dissemination modes such as project websites, online journals, interactive discussion forums, and so on. However, it is worth recalling Hill's argument about the role of the written in validated university knowledge referred to at the start of this chapter.

The relation of text to image raises interesting issues: one might ask how far visual materials carry an argument, as opposed merely to illustrating it, for example (see Hurdley, 2007). Conversely, in participatory, social action and educational contexts the fairly common practice of making (for instance) a video for public exhibition without encouraging interpretation and discussion might indicate an instrumental or rhetorical deployment of the image whose function requires interrogation.

Issues, risks and limitations in the use of visual methods

This section points to some of the dilemmas raised by visual methods, although it does not do so exhaustively. In particular, technical matters related to the 'how' of visual methods are not addressed, since these quickly become redundant as new technologies or software provide solutions and create different affordances.

Ethics, power and participation

Gaining genuine and informed consent has been a recurrent concern in working with children and young people (e.g. David, Edwards, & Allred, 2001), which visual methods may intensify. Children's and/or parental consent is now more frequently required for taking images involving children, even by other children, and there are increasingly tight controls on publication of images, or reluctance to publish at all. Anonymity is harder to maintain in relation to visual images and correspondingly raises questions of safety, the right to privacy, how far the audience for images can be predicted now and in the future, and the appropriateness of online publication rather than more limited forms (on CD or DVD, for example). The International Visual Sociology Association has recently produced its own code of research ethics (Papademas & International Visual Sociology Association, 2009); and see also TeacherNet, 'Schools: Use of photographs and video for publicity' (www.teachernet.gov.uk/wholeschool/familyandcommunity/childprotection/usefulinfor mation/photosandvideos). A useful discussion about ethics can be found in Prosser and Loxley (2008).

These concerns about the visual can create paradoxical situations – for instance, where newspapers can take and publish images of schoolchildren, and indeed children can do so online, but researchers cannot – or a stand-off between ethical principles, where one (protection of minors) conflicts with another (involving and enabling a wider range of participants). Indeed, research may now be generating its own distinctive aesthetic of childhood: if familiar Western representations of happy, energetic children construct childhood as 'innocence', the 'ethical' solution of anonymizing children through pixellation produces an uncanny effect, of ghostly figures without faces, which perhaps above all communicates a notion of childhood as always and everywhere 'at risk'.

The informed consent, anonymity and confidentiality of individual research participants are not the only relevant issues here, however: broader ethical concerns are also at stake in debating the truth claims of visual images, their embedded values, the kinds of gaze they invite or resist. Another ethical dimension concerns the effects of visual methods on those who create them. They are repeatedly described as 'empowering', which is an overused and under-analysed term, as Buckingham (2009) argues. It may be that the process of making images places the producers in more powerful roles, in which they can see themselves as creators or directors, develop new (technical, interpersonal, creative) skills or draw on hitherto untapped and unrecognized skills in new ways and contexts. Or it may be that the public communication enabled by images, or the settings in which images are used and displayed, can provide a route by which to enter debates with policy and decision makers. Questions about how far this constitutes (or is experienced as) empowerment, how often any of this happens in practice and how long this empowerment lasts often remain unanswered, however. Such claims may even obstruct critical reflexivity about the larger contexts and power relations at play in 'participatory' practices and the compulsorily therapeutic. In the example below, a photography project had worked with 'underachieving' girls in a generally high-achieving secondary school, culminating in an exhibition of their work. However, only one teacher turned up to view it. The speaker, who had supported the project as regional director of Creative Partnerships (the English body promoting creative teaching and learning in schools), interpreted this as the school's institutionalized reluctance to address the girls' negative experiences, and as a result he reflects critically on the ethics of self-expression. While his argument could apply to other methods as well, it could be that the public display of images here made the failure of others to engage with their meaning all the more visible and painful:

> Part of the reason these children were seen as underachievers was that nobody seemed to take any interest in them, and they've been shown a lot of interest now, and they've been nurtured and supported. Now what happens when we go? Is it worse that we've done this, or worse that we've not? . . . You raise these issues and actually it means they [the school] have got to do something about it, they're just not prepared to go there. . . . So sometimes you think, what's our responsibility in supporting young people to have a voice, and to say something about themselves, but at the same time the environment which they will go back into, isn't interested?
>
> (Interview, 2008; quoted in Bragg *et al.*, 2009)

Dilemmas of product and process in visual methods

Discussing the way some commentators on new technology celebrate children as 'digital natives', Facer (2008) remarks that their competencies derive not from their youth per se but from 'their participation in a complex set of networks and their access to diverse material and cultural resources' (such as access at home to computers, broadband, diverse software packages . . .). To ignore – and fail to counteract – these very real factors, she argues, could actively disadvantage young people who lack such facilities in their lives, and further entrench other young people's existing privileges. In relation to visual methods, there is a similar danger of assuming that young people are all already skilled and willing 'creators' of visual culture, whether with pen or with pixels.

However, questions that seem merely technical – how much support should participants receive in generating visual materials? – quickly become more conceptual ones. Rejecting the argument that technologies such as cameras are instinctively understood by anyone also involves denying that photographs represent a purer and more authentic 'voice'. But at what point does 'scaffolding' to aid effective visual communication shade into an elaborate ventriloquy of conventional or dominant perspectives and meanings? Does a refusal to impart skills actively undermine participants, leaving them frustrated at their inability to realize their ambitions and preventing them from reaching audiences?

These questions may be particularly acute when visual methods are used in activist contexts, such as arguing for change in policy or practice. Are visual methods here a means or an end? Is it the quality and coherence of the product that counts, or its content (the issues it tries to address), or the collaborative process of making it? If an end product is crucial and likely to be exhibited publicly, it may be more closely scrutinized, and more effort put in to ensure that it meets a certain visual standard – sometimes at the expense of critically analysing the arguments it presents. Creative professionals in supporting roles may be constrained by how far their own reputations or future commissions are seen to rely on the 'quality' of outcomes. The intended audience may shape the process from the outset, as when schools, for instance, select their star students for high-profile youth voice projects, hoping they will present the best public face possible, or when institutions are concerned about potential dissemination of negative images. Such practices and anxieties are underexplored, although they are understandable in contexts of school and other public-service marketization and performativity, where one of the most common uses of images is therefore for (good) publicity.

Working with visual data: analysis and interpretation

The final dilemma to be addressed here is the most important yet often the most neglected, and it can be simply expressed: our capacity to generate visual data far outstrips our capacity to analyse them.

Flewitt (2006) offers some useful insights into the demands of audio-visual data in research, including the time and cost involved in transcribing, the information conveyed and omitted by different transcription notations, and the theoretical foundations and skills needed to work productively with them. Recording hours of data on DVD is all too easy; but the distinct possibility that the material will never be viewed again should caution against investing time and effort – one's own or, worse, others' – in creating such data without clear purposes and boundaries. Software packages have been developed specifically for handling such data in research contexts, but, as Coffey, Holbrook, and Atkinson (1996) comment insightfully, there is a marked contrast between the problematizing and diversifying of data generating and representing, and the orthodoxies emerging in computer-aided analysis informed by the suppositions and procedures of 'grounded theory' on which such software often draws.

Interpreting the outcomes of visual methods can prove problematic even where they have an immediate purpose and a receptive audience. At a 2007 youth voice conference in the English Midlands, for example, students worked with creative practitioners to discuss questions put to the conference by the local authority, based on its draft Schools Improvement Plan. They expressed their responses by drawing on large Perspex panels, which were then assembled in a striking display. Surveying the results, one of the conference organizers remarked, 'what's noticeable is that words are missing . . . now it's up to us to interpret it' (cited in Bragg *et al.*, 2009). It was by no means clear how the local authority might use the drawings within such a formal process as development planning; nor would it have been easy to analyse them in creativity research.

Nonetheless, Piper and Frankham (2007) identify a tendency for researchers to treat participant-generated visual images as unproblematic, failing to analyse them at all, or producing interpretations that support their own preconceptions and pre-scripted narratives while simultaneously gushing over the 'raw power' of such 'visual voice'. There is a vast discrepancy between this treatment of the visual and the sophisticated, multifaceted approaches within visual culture studies to which I referred at the start of this chapter. This may be because qualitative researchers lack an intellectual grounding in these areas, although in some cases not allowing time for analysis, dialogue and interrogation suggests a decorative rather than a substantive interest in 'youth voice'.

The issue of interpretation is particularly important to researching creative learning in schools. People come to image making with different levels of skill and of familiarity with visual forms and conventions. The cultural repertoires and textual styles available to them will refract and mediate what is 'said' or communicated, and what positions or identities they make available. Meanwhile, schools have a specific relationship to cultural values and judgements, arguably informed by bourgeois moral and aesthetic standards, which may obstruct appreciation of creative learning from contemporary forms of spectacular and 'disreputable' visual culture. Questions of cultural competence, cultural capital and taste are all invoked in working with images: my final example, below, aims to indicate some of the complexities here and to encourage reflexive, critical attention to analysing the visual.

'A wrestling move': learning to see learning

My doctoral research focused on classroom teaching about the horror genre in post-compulsory education, in order to explore the sometimes uncomfortable encounter between contemporary popular youth culture and the discourses and practices of media education. As discussed above, the latter include media production, and here students were asked to produce a video cover and a storyboard for the opening sequence of a horror film of their own devising. They used a digital camera to create a series of still images, which were edited on to video with a musical soundtrack. These, together with a written commentary analysing the sequence in relation to genre conventions and media concepts, were part of their formal assessment.

One 17-year-old, Richard, produced a video sequence depicting a 'psycho killer' abducting a young man and (in two final ketchup-laden shots) slitting his throat. It was preceded by a written scenario and hand-drawn storyboard that relished similarly spectacular violence. The first draft of his accompanying commentary revealed an extreme lack of confidence with analytical academic writing; instead, he recounted wittily – but in assessment terms, irrelevantly and too colloquially – how circumstance had conspired to prevent him achieving quite the death scene he had wished for.

When I showed the video to other teachers, they were often negative; while they pointed to the killer's lack of motivation to justify their low opinion, they seemed primarily worried about its violence – moralistic concerns of the sort often voiced in debates about popular culture but which carry particular import in the pastoral 'habitus' of the school. In conjunction with the inadequate written explanation, it looked unlikely that the piece would be marked highly. However, the story was communicated clearly, the images well framed and shot; I enjoyed its exuberance, and noted the hilarity and esteem with which it was received by his peers. It seemed to me that Richard was exactly the kind of non-traditional student whose abilities and visual literacy 'creative' approaches aim to accredit. The dilemma was that for his creative achievement to be recognized, Richard himself had to account for it; yet he lacked the words to do so (so much for elicitation), and since we were not sure of the film's exact genre, neither

I nor his teacher could help him (my inept references to 'Grand Guignol' left him mystified).

A solution came through another long-advocated media pedagogy, of feedback from other audiences. In a slightly elaborated version, I showed the students' work in another school; rather than evaluative judgements of quality, I asked for descriptions of the storyline, who the film was for, and so on. In Richard's case, the student group immediately identified the soundtrack as taken from a Tarantino film (which I had not), which cued them into the kinds of genre (and person) behind it – and also helped me see the value of interpretation by those who share cultural reference points. And while they understood and enjoyed it, they also commented insightfully on some contradictory elements, such as the childishness of the woolly gloves donned by the killer, which put the overt violence of the storyline (and indeed of its creator) into perspective.

I shared these responses before the final evaluations were written; 'reflecting back' in this way aimed to open up a space where students could view their images through the eyes of others and thereby grasp meanings they had generated unconsciously. Space permits just one illustration here (Figure 9.1). Richard's first draft described the villain 'putting a Million-Dollar Dream' on the victim, an expression that I and his teacher ignored since it was meaningless to us. In the second draft, however, he added to it the comment 'a wrestling move'.

Figure 9.1 'A wrestling move' still from 'Psychokiller' film made by Richard.

This explanation, at last taking into account an audience that could not be assumed to share his implicit understandings was, for me, revelatory. It allowed me to understand the particular image to which it refers, to re-view what could have seemed a dangerously uncontrolled violent gesture as instead choreographed, skilled and staged. Even more importantly, it guided me in how to appreciate the film as a whole, to learn how both its aesthetics and its random psychopath are typical of wrestling; which furthermore, as Roland Barthes argued in 1957, is a 'spectacle of excess' but not a 'sadistic spectacle: it is only an intelligible spectacle' (Barthes, 1972). My argument here is not to outlaw other interpretations – although evaluating images according to irrelevant aesthetic values does risk unfairly penalizing students. It is to point to the opaqueness of the visual, to the difficulty of creating conditions that enable conversations about meanings, as well as to their rewards. Creative learning is always, and at least, two-way.

Conclusion

This chapter has aimed to challenge the notion that visual methods provide unmediated access to an 'authentic' creative response, or indeed any kind of singular 'voice'; even their role as 'self-expression' is questionable. In assessing both the learning and the creativity involved in visual image making and research, it is important to be aware of factors such as the context of productions, the 'genre' of the artefact (whether explicitly acknowledged or not), the producers' sense of their audience, and the biases and perspectives of those interpreting the material. Nonetheless, visual methods have rich potential and there are many sound reasons for using them in exploring less easily verbalized aspects of experience, creativity, informal knowledge and learning.

References

Allan, A. (2005). Using photographic diaries to research the gender and academic identities of young girls. In G. Troman, B. Jeffrey, & G. Walford (Eds.), *Studies in educational ethnography*. Vol. 11, *Methodological issues and practices in ethnography* (pp. 19–36). Oxford: Elsevier.

Allen, L. (2009). 'Snapped': Researching the sexual cultures of schools using visual methods. *International Journal of Qualitative Studies in Education*, 22(5), 549–561.

Bagnoli, A. (2009). Beyond the standard interview: The use of graphic elicitation and arts-based methods. *Qualitative Research*, 9(5), 547–570.

Banks, M. (2001). *Visual methods in social research*. London: Sage.

Banks, M. (2008). *Using visual data in qualitative research*. London: Sage.

Barnard, M. (2001). *Approaches to understanding visual culture*. Basingstoke, UK: Palgrave.

Barthes, R. ([1957] 1972). *Mythologies*. Translated by A. Lavers. St Albans, UK: Granada.

Bragg, S. (2006). 'Having a real debate': Using media as a resource in sex education. *Sex Education*, 6(4): 317–331.

Bragg, S., & Buckingham, D. (2004). *Young people, sex and the media: The facts of life?* London: Palgrave Macmillan.

Bragg, S., & Buckingham, D. (2008). 'Scrapbooks' as a resource in media research with young people. In P. Thomson (Ed.), *Doing visual research with children and young people* (pp. 114–131). London: Routledge.

Bragg, S., Manchester, H., & Faulkner, D. (2009). *Youth voice in the work of Creative Partnerships*. London: Creativity, Culture and Education.

Buckingham, D. (1993). *Children talking television: The making of television literacy*. London: Falmer Press.

Buckingham, D. (2009). 'Creative' visual methods in media research: Possibilities, problems and proposals. *Media, Culture & Society*, 31, 633–652.

Buckingham, D., Grahame, J., & Sefton-Green, J. (1995). *Making media: Learning from media production*. London: English & Media Centre.

Burke, C. (2008). Play in focus: Children's visual voice in participative research. In P. Thomson (Ed.), *Doing visual research with children and young people* (pp. 23–36). London: Routledge.

Chaplin, E. (1994). *Sociology and visual representation*. London: Routledge.

Clark, A., & Moss, P. (2001). *Listening to young children: The mosaic approach*. London: National Children's Bureau.

Coates, E. (2004). 'I forgot the sky!' Children's stories contained within their drawings. In V. Lewis, M. Kellett, C. Robinson, S. Fraser, & S. Ding (Eds.), *The reality of research with children and young people* (pp. 5–21). London: Open University/Sage.

Coffey, A., Holbrook, B., & Atkinson, P. (1996). Qualitative data analysis: Technologies and representations. *Sociological Research Online*, *1*(1). Online, available at: www.socresonline.org.uk/1/1/4.html.

Cohen, P. (1990). *Really useful knowledge: Photography and cultural studies in prevocational education*. Stoke-on-Trent, UK: Trentham Books.

David, M., Edwards, R., & Alldred, P. (2001). 'Children and school-based research: 'Informed consent' or 'educated consent'? *British Educational Research Journal*, *27*(3), 347–365.

Denzin, N. K., & Lincoln, Y. S. (2005). *The Sage handbook of qualitative research* (3rd ed.). Thousand Oaks, CA: Sage.

Denzin, N. K., & Lincoln, Y. S. (2008). *Collecting and interpreting qualitative materials* (3rd ed.). London: Sage.

Deveson, T. (2008). *Engaging students in school design and rebuild projects: CP London East and South case studies*. London: Creative Partnerships. Online, available at: www.creative-partnerships.com/area-delivery-organisations/anewdirection/research/engaging-students-in-school-design-and-rebuild-projects-102.pdf (accessed 7 August 2009).

Emmison, M., & Smith, P. (2000). *Researching the visual: Images, objects, contexts and interactions in social and cultural inquiry*. London: Sage.

Evans, J., & Hall, S. (Eds.). (2001). *Visual culture: The reader*. Thousand Oaks, CA: Sage.

Facer, K. (2008). What does it mean to be an 'adult' in an era of children's rights and learner voice? Draft Working Paper. Warwick: presented as Closing Keynote at the 'Why Learner Voice?' Conference, Warwick University, 23 October 2008.

Flewitt, R. (2006). Using video to investigate preschool classroom interaction: Education research assumptions and methodological practices. *Visual Communication*, *5*(1), 25–50.

Frosh, P. (2003). *The image factory: Consumer culture, photography and the visual content industry*. Oxford: Berg.

Hamilton, P. (2006). *Visual research methods*. London: Sage.

Harper, D. (2002). Talking about pictures: A case for photo elicitation. *Visual Studies*, *17*(1), 13–26.

Hemming, P. J. (2008). Mixing qualitative research methods in children's geographies. *Area*, *40*(2), 152–162.

Hill, A. (2008). Writing the visual. CRESC Working Paper 51. Centre for Research on Socio-Cultural Change (CRESC), The Open University, UK. Online, available at: www.cresc.ac.uk/publications/documents/wp51.pdf.

Holliday, R. (2004). Filming the closet: The role of video diaries in researching sexualities. *American Behavioral Scientist*, *47*(12), 1597–1616.

Hurdley, R. (2007). Focal points: framing material culture and visual data. *Qualitative Research*, *7*(3), 355–374.

Kintrea, K., Bannister, J., Pickering, J., Suzuki, N., & Reid, M. (2008). *Young people and territoriality in British cities*. York: Joseph Rowntree Foundation. Online, available at: www.jrf.org.uk/bookshop/eBooks/2278-young-people-territoriality.pdf.

Knowles, C., & Sweetman, P. (2004). *Picturing the social landscape: Visual methods and the sociological imagination*. London: Routledge.

Knowles, J. G., & Cole, A. L. (Eds.). (2008). *Handbook of the arts in qualitative research: Perspectives, methodologies, examples and issues*. London: Sage.

MacGregor, B., & Morrison, D. E. (1995). From focus groups to editing groups: A new method of reception analysis. *Media, Culture and Society*, *17*, 141–150.

Mirzoeff, N. (1999). *An introduction to visual culture*. London: Routledge.

Mirzoeff, N. (2002). *The visual culture reader* (2nd ed.). London: Routledge.

Mitchell, C., & Weber, S. (1998). Picture this! Class line-ups, vernacular portraits and lasting impressions of school. In J. Prosser (Ed.), *Image-based research: A sourcebook for qualitative researchers* (pp. 197–213). London: Falmer Press.

Murray, S. (2008). Digital images, photo-sharing, and our shifting notions of everyday aesthetics. *Journal of Visual Culture, 7*(2), 147–163.

Papademas, D., & International Visual Sociology Association (2009) IVSA Code of Research Ethics and Guidelines. *Visual Studies, 24*(3), 250–257.

Pink, S. (2006). *The future of visual anthropology: Engaging the senses.* London: Routledge.

Pink, S. (2007). *Doing visual ethnography: Images, media and representation in research* (2nd ed.). London: Sage.

Pink, S., Kürti, L., & Afonso, A. I. (2004). *Working images: Visual research and representation in ethnography.* London: Routledge.

Piper, H., & Frankham, J. (2007). Seeing voices and hearing pictures: Image as discourse and the framing of image-based research. *Discourse: Studies in the Cultural Politics of Education, 28*(3), 373–387.

Prosser, J. (1998). *Image-based research: A sourcebook for qualitative researchers.* London: Falmer Press.

Prosser, J. (2007). Visual methods and the visual culture of schools. *Visual Studies, 22*(1), 13–30.

Prosser, J., & Loxley, A. (2008). Introducing visual methods. Review Paper NCRM 010. ESRC National Centre for Research Methods. Online, available at: http://eprints.ncrm.ac.uk/420 (accessed 31 January 2010).

Rampley, M. (2005). *Exploring visual culture: Definitions, concepts, contexts.* Edinburgh: Edinburgh University Press.

Richardson, L. (2005). Writing: A method of inquiry. In N. K. Denzin & Y. S. Lincoln (Eds.), *The Sage handbook of qualitative research* (pp. 398–421). Thousand Oaks, CA: Sage.

Rose, G. (2004). 'Everyone's cuddled up and it just looks really nice': The emotional geography of some mums and their family photos. *Social & Cultural Geography, 5*, 549–564.

Rose, G. (2006). *Visual methodologies: An introduction to the interpretation of visual materials* (2nd ed.). London: Sage.

Spence, J., & Holland, P. (Eds.). (1991). *Family snaps: The meaning of domestic photography.* London: Virago.

Scratz, M., & Steiner-Loffler, U. (1998). Pupils using photographs in school self-evaluation. In J. Prosser (Ed.), *Image-based research: A sourcebook for qualitative researchers* (pp. 235–251). London: Falmer Press.

Sturken, M., & Cartwright, L. (2001). *Practices of looking: An introduction to visual culture.* Oxford: Oxford University Press.

Thomson, P. (Ed.). (2008) *Doing visual research with children and young people.* London: Routledge.

Thomson, R., & Holland, J. (2005). 'Thanks for the memory': Memory books as a methodological resource in biographical research. *Qualitative Research, 5*(2), 201–219.

Visual Learning Lab (2007). Visual research methods in education. Nottingham: University of Nottingham Visual Learning Lab. Online, available at: www.visuallearninglab.ac.uk/publications.php (accessed 31 January 2010).

Willett, R. (2009). 'As soon as you get on Bebo you just go mad': Young consumers and the discursive construction of teenagers online. *Young Consumers, 10*(4), 283–296.

Chapter 10

When only the visual will do

Pat Thomson

Visual and auditory senses dominate schools. Children are expected to look at the board, their books and the teacher. They are watched to see that they do not get into any mischief. Children must listen carefully to instructions in lessons and speak only when it is appropriate, and in acceptable ways. (Dinner and toilets smell, but this is to be ignored.)

Movement is highly regulated. Children must line up for class, stand when visitors or the headteacher enters the room, move around only with approval, play games according to set rules. There are places in school where children cannot go and places they do not want to go.

Children must not touch, fiddle, push, poke or stroke out of turn or out of place. Only in the yard at appointed times, and in designated lessons and places, can they run around, dance, creep, jump, yell out.

Creative learning breaks out of these visual and auditory barriers.

Creative learning opens up the sensory and sensual environment of the school.

Suddenly, there are dark, secret and hidden places to explore and to inhabit. There are dens, tents and tree-houses.

There are props for make-believe games. There are things to pick up and move around, to experiment with. How do they work?

There is dirt to dig and plants to carefully place, to smell, to feel. Some are smooth and some are rough and some are prickly and some stink and some sting.

There is a room where there are wings and shells that are real and they are mixed up with wings and shells made from cardboard, paper and tape which can be put on and you can crawl around and feel how it must be to live as a snail.

There are lights and sounds that respond to touch and to loud and soft and high and low voices and movements big and little.

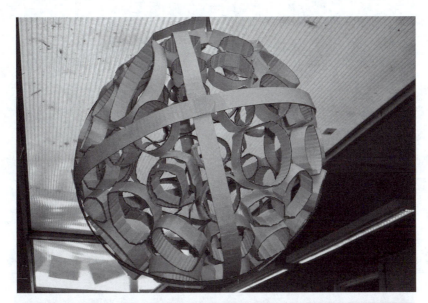

There is equipment that helps you to make animations from sticky dough and paper plates. You can make a musical soundtrack by banging tin cans together and no one says STOP THAT NOISE!!

There is room to run and space to jump, cartwheel, tumble, stretch and pirouette.

Creative learning gives permission and encouragement for the curious and the shy to investigate, to take risks, to have wonderful ideas. Creative learning opens up the marvellous in the everyday.

Images appear to capture these experiences. Images invite the viewer to imagine – to engage in *play without action*, as Vygotsky had it – as the children in the school might. And as they do.

Chapter 11

Less elusive, more explicit

The challenge of 'seeing' creativity in action

*Erica McWilliam, Shane Dawson
and Jennifer Pei-Ling Tan*

Introduction

Creativity has always had an association with the social sciences *in spirit*; however, we are now well into a decade in which creativity is being understood as a powerful *body* of ideas for driving economic and social change. Recent research (see Kaufman & Sternberg, 2007; McWilliam, 2008) has unhooked creativity from artistry, revealing it as economically valuable, team based, observable and *learnable*. As the ability to 'move an idea from one state to another' (Jackson, 2006a: 8), creativity is argued by David Perkins (1981) and others to be evident in skills such as pattern recognition, creation of analogies and mental models, the ability to cross domains, exploration of alternatives, and problem solving. It has displaced routine 'industrial' thinking and doing as the most relevant workplace capacity in an increasingly complex, challenge-ridden and rapidly changing economic and social order. In Mihaly Csikszentmihalyi's (2006) terms, creativity is 'no longer a luxury for the few, but a necessity for all' (p. xviii).

For the widespread dissemination of this 'second generation' thinking about creativity we can thank post-millennial economic and social analysts such as John Howkins, Charles Leadbeater, Stuart Cunningham, Mihaly Csikszentmihalyi, Teresa Amabile, John Hartley and Richard Florida. They have built in double-quick time a set of understandings of creativity that have moved it on from the romantic province of arts-based idiosyncratic genius into the cut and thrust of innovative entrepreneurship. Most prominent among them has been Richard Florida, whose *Rise of the creative class* (2002) generated much intellectual ferment around the nexus between creativity and productivity at the turn of this century. While debates continue, as they should, around the extent to which Florida's claims are overblown in relation to the factors influencing the rise of a 'creative class', nevertheless his insistence on creativity's centrality to productivity – '[p]laces that succeed in attracting and retaining creative class people prosper; those that fail don't'[1] – is a message that has resonated worldwide. It has seen policy makers at all levels rushing to discover what new combinations of skills count as 'creative' and how more precisely they can turn into real economic advantage in the form of new business opportunities and regional growth.

The growing trend to value creative and relational capacities over narrow instrumental skills is reflected globally, with employers seeking 'multi-competent graduates' (Yorke, 2006, p. 2) who have 'high-level expertise . . . emphasising discovery and . . . exploiting the discoveries of others through market-related intelligence and the application of personal skills' (p. 5). Underneath these trends is a more fundamental recognition that productivity in the twenty-first century requires 'a deep vein of creativity that is constantly renewing itself' (NCEE, 2007, p. 10). This sort of creativity is not limited to the creative industries but includes all those employed in a wide variety of professional work, including computing, engineering, architecture, science, education, arts and multimedia.

The burgeoning interest in creative capacity building in and through formal education is an outcome of this new 'creative' imperative in professional work, but it is also a response to evidence about the new ways that young people learn (Hartman, Moskal, & Dzuiban, 2005; Seely Brown, 2006). A report issued by the European University Association (2007) directs the sector to consider 'creativity' as central to their research and their teaching:

> The complex questions of the future will not be solved 'by the book', but by creative, forward-looking individuals and groups who are not afraid to question established ideas and are able to cope with the insecurity and uncertainty that this entails.
>
> (p. 6)

The problem that now bedevils educators is not that creativity needs to be 'sold' as an educational outcome. Indeed, as Norman Jackson (2006a) sees it, creativity in education is omnipresent but is not taken seriously in designing systematic approaches to teaching and learning. In other words, while glossy brochures for attracting enrolments from the brightest and best trumpet creativity as a valued graduate attribute, teaching-for-creativity is 'rarely an explicit objective of the learning and assessment process' (p. 4). This is a problem that is born, in part, out of the lack of imagination that underpins what it is that we see as worthy of assessment, and, thus, the means by which we go about the business of designing instruments for assessment and evaluation of educational outcomes. Put bluntly, creativity is, in educational terms, the emperor's new clothes: admired but never actually seen.

Creativity research as 'unscientific'

While we do not intend to expand here on the historical development of theories about what makes for 'effective' educational assessment, it is important to acknowledge the power of the scientific tradition of validation through measuring test results. This tradition ties any and every evidentiary claim to laws that allow generalizable explanation or prediction. The core business of this tradition has been to offer principles, practices and types of evidence through which credibility is established using numbers and their interpretation. As a method for validating evidentiary claims, quantitative inquiry questions all approaches that researchers might adopt that fall outside this logic. Numerical scores allow quantitative researchers to make comparisons between like others, and this makes them valuable to educational leaders and policy makers who want to know how individuals and groups compare when ranked in terms of a particular skill – for example, literacy or numeracy. The rankings that can be produced provide a rationale for funding certain projects and refusing or cutting funding to others. In other words, a high ranking on desirable skills is *the* 'valid' measure of quality educational outcomes.

The hegemony of measurement in and for scientific validation has weakened any credibility that 'alternative' approaches might have by marginalizing them as 'cases where the common interpretation and validity inquiry do not hold' (Moss, Girard, & Haniford, 2006, p. 112). Indeed, as Rob Cowdroy and Erik de Graff (2005) understand it, the dominance of measurement as the means of validation has obliterated any chance of 'seeing' creativity altogether:

> Pressures for conformity with conventions of assessment in other fields of education, and reinforced by global quality assurance demands for objectivity, uniform standards and transparency, reinforce focus of assessment on the demonstrable execution and the tangible product and preclude assessment of *creative ability.*
>
> (p. 511)

It has only been in relatively recent times that some wiggle room has been opening up in relation to 'seeing' creativity in action. There has been a breakthrough of sorts from the widely held view that creativity is too vaporous and multidimensional to be amenable to empirical scrutiny. This came with the insistence of both Teresa Amabile (1996) and Mihaly Czikszentmihalyi (1999) that creativity is better understood as a process that occurs *outside* an individual rather than being the mysterious product of an unknowable inner world. With creativity exteriorized theoretically, it has become possible for independent observers to agree that what they are observing either is or is not creative. This has paved the way for developing criteria through which we can formalize systematic observations into an evidence base through which the processes of building creative capacity can be 'seen' to be operating. This means that, while simplistic quantification measures will continue to be unhelpful in any systematic inquiry into creativity in action in education, we can and should be taking cautious 'scientific' steps towards 'seeing' creative capacity building in action.

'Creatives', according to Richard Florida (2002), spend little time on routine problem solving using conventional knowledge. Instead, they focus on interactivity, navigation capacity, forging relationships, tackling novel challenges and synthesizing 'big picture' scenarios for the purposes of adding a competitive commercial edge to an organization or business. Moreover, they are more likely than other workers to be located in digitally enhanced environments (including 'home' or 'garage' environments). With few transportable templates for project design, they *unlearn* 'solutions' to higher-order problems as quickly as they learn them (see McWilliam, 2005), so they can quickly jettison ideas and formulae that do not 'add value'.

All this demands mental agility but it also demands a capacity to move, either literally or virtually, to where the action is, and away from where the action was. In what follows, we report on two studies that address each of these capacities – an agile learning disposition and an advanced capacity for social networking – in turn, showing how such capacities may become more visible without doing violence to the complex social processes through which creativity may be fostered.

'Seeing' creative learning dispositions

The capacity for engaging in creative thinking and doing – serious intellectual play that throws concepts into the air – is what Jennifer Pei-Ling Tan (2008) has termed cognitive playfulness. Her study of cognitively playful individuals shows them to have a predisposition to curiosity, inventiveness and the desire to play with novel ideas and innovations, all of which can result in increased levels of personal innovativeness and individual learning. In her inquiry into students' learning dispositions (Tan, 2008; Tan & McWilliam, 2008, 2009), she posits cognitive playfulness as having two dimensions: intellectual curiosity (or level of inquisitiveness) and intellectual creativity (or level of imagination and spontaneity). Both dimensions emerged in her study as highly significant in explaining the extent to which students are predisposed to take up 'creative' learning opportunities in their formal schooling.

Tan's mixed-methods study design incorporated a quantitative self-report student questionnaire administered to a senior school student population of approximately 600 students. The questionnaire was implemented in mid-2007, by which time a new student-led digital learning innovation, known as the Student Media Centre (SMC), had been in operation for approximately one year. The SMC was endorsed by school leadership and designed and implemented by a group of student leaders to provide their fellow students with opportunities to create and to learn, in ways that go beyond what was afforded by the dominant model of transmission-based, exam-oriented classroom learning and teaching activities at the school.[2] The numeric data from the questionnaire pertinent to this chapter included socio-psychological scales that measured students' learning dispositions and their usage behaviours related to the new SMC. Simply put, Tan wanted to know what learning dispositions underlay students' varying levels of engagement with the SMC learning innovation as part of their schooling practice.

A classification and regression tree (CART) technique of analysis[3] (Briemann, Friedman, Olshen, & Stone, 1984) was used to inquire into the statistical relationships between students' learning dispositions (predictor variables) and their levels of usage of the SMC (target variable). The learning dispositions measured include *cognitive playfulness* and two other dispositional constructs: *personal innovativeness* and *achievement goal orientations*. *Personal innovativeness* is defined as 'one's willingness to change, an openness to new experiences and the propensity to go out of one's way to experience different and novel stimuli particularly of the meaningful sort' (Leavitt & Walton, 1975; Rogers, 1995). *Achievement goal orientations* is defined in terms of two sub-dimensions, *learning goals* and *performance goals*, following social psychologist Carol Dweck's (2000) work on self-theories. Dweck's inquiry into the paradoxical nature of educational outcomes gave rise to her distinction between an individual's *performance goals* (focused on 'winning positive judgments of your competence and avoiding negative ones') and *learning goals* (characterized by a desire to develop 'new skills, master new tasks or understand new things'; pp. 16–19). Dweck expressed concern that when young people prioritize their performance goals in ways that negatively impact on their learning goals, it can lead to the sort of fixed mindset that seeks to avoid the challenge of learning through experimentation and play.

Measurement scales for the variables of interest described above, which consisted of both self-developed items and items adapted from previously validated studies, reported strong reliability and validity for test results.[4] Figure 11.1 provides a visual representation of the statistical results that demonstrate the extent to which learning dispositions influenced the students' usage of the media centre to further their learning opportunities and extend their learning experiences in school into more 'creative' learning options.

The results reported in Figure 11.1 can be interpreted as follows. First, all the individual-level variables (i.e. *learning goals*, *performance goals*, *cognitive playfulness* and *personal innovativeness*) emerged as significant predictors that together explained 44 per cent of the variance in the target variable SMC usage. Second, the predictor variable that emerged as the first child node, positioned at the top of the tree (Cognitive Playfulness: Curiosity), is referred to as the primary or best splitter variable for this optimal solution, and is, therefore, the strongest predictor of SMC usage. The CP: Curiosity cut-off score of 27.5 partitioned

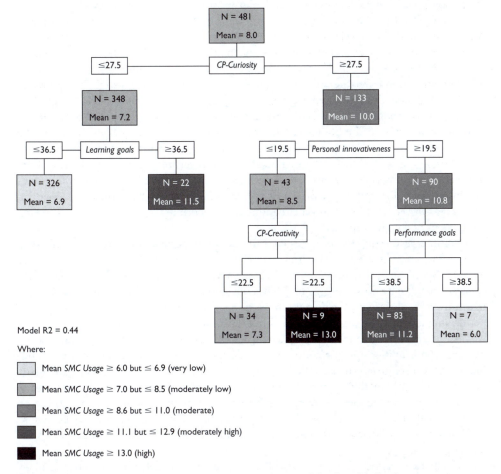

Figure 11.1 Optimal decision tree: learning dispositions and Student Media Centre usage.

the student respondents into two groups: 'low cognitive curiosity' ("27.5) and 'high cognitive curiosity' (≥27.5). The 'low cognitive curiosity' group consisted of 348 students and yielded a predicted mean SMC usage value of 7.2 (moderately low; SD = 5.1). The 'high cognitive curiosity' group consisted of 133 students and yielded a predicted mean SMC usage value of 10.0 (moderate; SD = 6.5).

The 'low cognitive curiosity' group was split further into two groups according to their learning goals orientation: 'low learning goals' ("36.5) and 'high learning goals' (≥36.5). The 'low learning goals' group consisted of 326 students and yielded a predicted mean SMC usage value of 6.9 (very low; SD = 4.8). The 'high learning goals' group consisted of 22 students and yielded a predicted mean SMC usage value of 11.5 (moderately high; SD = 6.6). *Learning goals* therefore emerged as a variable that had mediating effects on the relationship between cognitive curiosity and SMC usage. If a student was low in *cognitive curiosity* but high in *learning goals*, then they would still engage with the SMC to a comparatively high degree. On the other hand, students who reported very low levels of SMC usage ranked low on both *cognitive curiosity* and *learning goals*.

In sum, these results suggest that, first and most importantly, *cognitive playfulness* in terms of intellectual curiosity is the best predictor of SMC usage. In other words, students who exhibited higher levels of intellectual inquisitiveness – a learning disposition that mobilizes them to explore and play with a problem until it is solved (see Dunn, 2004; Glynn & Webster, 1993) – were most likely to engage with the creative affordances of the digital learning innovation to a larger extent when compared with the general student population. Second, students who exhibited higher levels of cognitive playfulness relative to their peers, in terms of both intellectual curiosity and intellectual creativity, emerged as the learner category that reported the highest usage of the SMC (mean = 13.0, SD = 5.8). On the other hand, students who reported low levels of engagement with the SMC (mean = 6.0, 6.9, 7.3; SD = 6.1, 4.8, 5.1) exhibited relatively low levels of cognitive playfulness (both intellectual curiosity and creativity) and learning goals orientation. This finding underscores the importance of cognitive playfulness as a learning disposition that motivates individuals to engage with and embrace novel situations and inventions, a disposition that is a vital component of creative capacity.

Two other interesting trends emerged from the results shown in Figure 11.1, which call attention to the value of being healthily learning oriented rather than merely performance focused. Specifically, the profile of the lowest SMC user-group (mean = 6.0, SD = 6.1) suggests that despite possessing an above-average level of cognitive playfulness and personal innovativeness, an individual who tends towards being highly performance driven may value performing in ways that overwhelm the former learning dispositions, and this in turn may well be a barrier to the individual's capacity to experiment with new ideas, innovations and learning opportunities. On the contrary, as indicated by the profile results of the second-highest SMC user group (mean = 11.5, SD = 6.6), individuals who may not be particularly dexterous or agile in the cognitive domain but exhibit robust levels of learning goals orientation may nonetheless be open to experiencing new ways of living and learning by engaging with innovative technologies available to them. Once again, they may be able to self-fashion in ways that incorporate both academic achievement and new strategies for learning.

Overall, Tan's results show that individuals who are intrinsically motivated to learn new things and acquire new skills are likely to appreciate the opportunities presented by innovations such as online and/or digital tools to extend their range of abilities and competencies. By contrast, individuals who are primarily focused on 'getting the right answer' and winning positive judgements of their competence while avoiding 'looking dumb' are likely to resist experimenting with new learning technologies that challenge the comfort zones of traditional pedagogical practices. This resistance or unwillingness to take on new ways of learning and engaging may militate against the sort of robust learning disposition needed for twenty-first-century digital-age life-worlds characterized by forces of rapid change, shifting and multiple identities, and exponential technological advancements and growth.

'Seeing' agile networking

As much as Tan's study begins to put meat on the bones of empirically assessing creativity at an individual level, there still remains the problem of developing methodologies for evaluating and identifying creativity within the collective. To assist us in the task of identifying creativity, there is an emerging consensus within the research literature that the skills and attributes associated with creativity relate to originality, imagination, communication, seeing connections, problem solving and team and individual leadership (Tierney, Farmer, & Graen, 1999; Robinson, 2000; McWilliam, 2008; Burt, 2004; Jackson, 2006b). Interestingly, most of these skills and attributes are focused on the importance of teamwork and developing opportunities for interactivity. Simply put, creativity as a process is enhanced through sustained interactions within a collective of active, agile and enterprising networkers.

Recent research in social networks has much to offer in terms of identifying the key individuals, attributes and relationships that are commonly associated with the process of creativity (Tepper, 2006). For instance, sociologist Ronald Burt (2004) has demonstrated that individuals located in key positions within an organizational network (see Figure 11.2) have greater and earlier access to information and resources than their less strategically connected peers. In Ronald Burt's terms, individuals located within these key brokering positions have opportunity 'to see early' and 'see more broadly' the information and resources accessible throughout the whole network. Thus, individuals occupying these brokering positions have access to 'a vision of options' that are 'otherwise unseen' (Burt, 2004, p. 354).

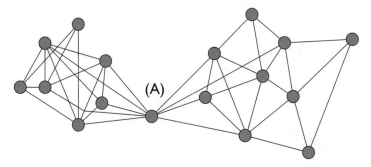

Figure 11.2 Example social network – illustrating an individual (A) occupying a key brokering position with the network.

The actors occupying these network positions are essential for building creative capital within the organization. This manifests through their ability both to control knowledge dissemination in more value-adding ways and to form new 'boundary spanning relationships' (Geletkanycz & Hambrick, 1997, p. 654) within and external to the existing organization. It is for this reason that the identification and monitoring of social networks and the actors who bridge network gaps (i.e. brokering roles) are central to our understanding of creative capacity.

In empirically demonstrating the relationship between creativity and social networks, Burt's work has provided a foundation for developing the necessary tools for visualizing and evaluating creativity in process. The identification of the network at large and the individuals occupying certain roles and positions provides a valuable quantifiable set of indicators for determining creativity in action. In the education context, creativity may be evidenced in the positions students hold in their various peer networks and the artefacts that evolve from learning and teaching practices that promote student-to-student interactivity. The application of social network analysis within the field of education can start to develop more quantitative – and therefore explicit – evidence of creativity, while also providing opportunity for evaluating the learning and teaching activities that are designed to foster creative capacity more generally.

Harvesting student interactions

Although social network analysis provides a sound methodology for evaluating creativity, the identification and subsequent capturing of the network relationships are complex and time-consuming. This is further complicated as the network size grows and when relationships are established beyond the organizational environment (Brooks, Hansen, McCalla, & Greer, 2007). Thus, it represents a complex challenge for educators attempting to evaluate the impact of any learning and teaching activity designed to promote creativity through the development of student networking agility. However, a solution to this impasse may be found in the increasing adoption of information and communication technologies (ICT) across the education sector.

At a global level, universities have been increasingly adopting various ICTs to supplement or entirely replace prior traditional models of teaching delivery. For example, learning management systems (LMS) such as BlackBoard, Moodle and Sakai are increasingly a core component of the student learning experience. These systems have been largely adopted for the provision of more flexible opportunities to access content delivery and engage and interact with peers regardless of time or place. While there are a high number and diversity of tools available within any given LMS, Macfadyen and Dawson (2010) demonstrate that the discussion forum is the primary resource by which educators aim to develop more online socially engaging learning activities. Consequently, any study relating to student social networks, or online learning communities, will commonly include discussion forum archives as an essential data source.

The common reliance on discussion forum data is in part due to the readily attainable archived discussion via the recorded LMS logs. A key feature of all LMS is their capacity to track and record student interactions. Thus, the captured logs associated with a specific teaching unit can be harvested in order to provide a representation of the student social network that has developed through the peer–peer discussion forum interactions. Dawson (2006a, 2006b, 2007) has previously discussed the pedagogical benefits that can be leveraged from the analysis of student LMS activity logs. For example, he demonstrates how student discussion forum activity can be used to reconstruct visualizations of the social network. His study identified a relationship between student sense of community and an individual's learning network position. The constant interrogation of the evolving LMS data can be readily used to inform educators of the levels of student interaction and engagement, and provide proactive and timely lead indicators of individual student skills and attributes in action.

In building on this prior research, Dawson has been involved in further developmental work[5] to design the necessary tools and resources for teachers to reconstruct the extracted LMS log data into more readily interpretable formats for reflection and action (see Figure 11.3). The visual generation of the student social networks, or sociograms, provides for rapid identification of students who are central to the network, peripheral and disengaged, or linking previously disparate clusters into a networked community (see Figure 11.3). These linking students are critical for uniting these prior fragmented clusters of small-world networks into a broader, more substantial community. This provides greater opportunity to

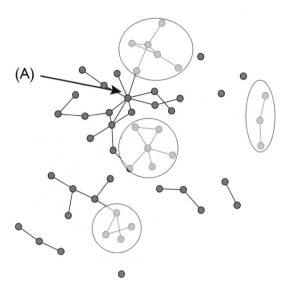

Figure 11.3 An example student social network constructed from student discussion forum interactions. Clusters of small-team student networks and a student (A) occupying a linking position are illustrated.

draw upon the resources, information and strengths of the entire collective. In elaborating upon the types of pedagogical models that enhance creativity, McWilliam and Dawson (2008) have described these pivotal individuals as 'border-crossers'. They note that border-crossers commonly display the enterprise and agility skills necessary for bridging network gaps (or, as Ronald Burt has termed them, structural holes) in order to fertilize the broader network with new ideas, knowledge and processes. Through these visualizations, educators can start to identify the key networked individuals and the changing dynamics of the network in order to distinguish indicators of creative capacity that are developing within the student cohort. Importantly, this process of extraction and visualization of student behaviour provides an instrument for evaluating the impact of implemented learning and teaching activities. Educators can observe network behaviour and then design future learning interventions informed by the actual student behaviour and the developing network properties.

Evaluating creative practice

Above, we have argued that the process of creativity is enhanced through sustained and diverse interactions. Given this, the visualization of the student social network, derived from online activities, not only provides an insight into the skills and attributes of the individuals situated within the network, but also acts as an evaluative tool that can assess the impact of any implemented learning activity congruent with creativity-enabling practice. The contrast between Figures 11.4 and 11.5 well illustrates this premise. Figure 11.4 highlights the lack of student engagement and diversity established through the social discussion forum activities. In this instance, the instructor (A) has largely established a one-way communication flow: instructor to student. Thus, the implemented learning activities have contributed little in developing the sorts of engaged interactions that lead to the development of creative capacity. By contrast, Figure 11.5 represents the sorts of diverse engaged interactions that we would argue are lead indicators of well-designed creativity-enabling practice.

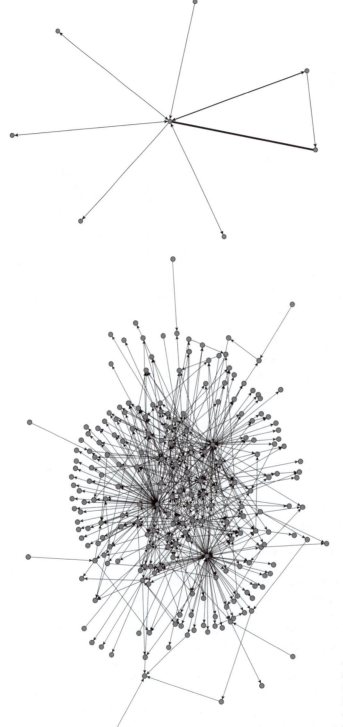

Figure 11.4 Sociogram of student discussion forum interactions, highlighting the minimal level of student interaction and the dominant role of the instructor (A). Thicker lines represent a greater number of communication exchanges.

Figure 11.5 Sociogram of student discussion forum interactions. The diagram highlights the diverse and engaged interactions among the student cohort.

Through this process, educators have an early and timely opportunity to implement learning interventions to promote diversity of student interactions and thereby reduce possible incidences of homophily. As noted above, while diverse and engaged networks are critical for developing creative capacity, there is a propensity for individuals within an organizational network to form connections based on similar attributes or characteristics (McPherson, Smith-Lovin, & Cook, 2001). The promotion of similarities such as occupations, demographics, etc. within an establishing group does provide for rapid relationship development and initial early growth of the network. However, if left unchecked, these ongoing interactions with similar individuals can also lead to what the business community has frequently described as *group-think*. In these instances of strong homophily, creativity is essentially strangled out of the network. By monitoring the evolution of the student online networks, educators can initiate the necessary learning interventions in order to combat group-think – promote diversity and cultivate a community that comprises agile and enterprising networkers. It is through these sorts of proactive practices that education can begin to meet the challenges associated with developing graduates imbued with the sorts of skills and capacities necessary for the conceptual age.

Conclusion

The two studies summarized above are illustrative of a second generation of inquiry into creativity as a set of dispositions and processes that are learnable and possibly even teachable. They demonstrate how we can begin to 'see' with more confidence the capacity young people have to engage in value adding through creative co-production. This capacity is likely to be optimally displayed in groups and cohorts of students co-creating, co-editing and co-evaluating in conjunction with each other and with their teachers and mentors, rather than in giving the correct answers to one-shot examination questions. It can also be seen through the application of tools that can distinguish a learning disposition from one focused more squarely on performance.

When taken together, studies such as those documented above can allow better judgements to be made about whether a prospective employee will measure up in terms of all the desirable skills and attributes of a 'creative' worker. Creativity for employability is not simply a matter of accumulating undergraduate degrees in business and information technology and/or a degree in the creative industries or the creative arts. With all that we now know about creative capacity as a complex set of dispositions, high-level aptitudes and unique lifestyle preferences, we can and should be looking to a second generation of tools for making creative worker potential visible and calculable. This chapter opens up just two of many new ways for doing so.

Notes

1 Retrieved on 12 February 2008 from www.washingtonmonthly.com/features/2001/0205.florida.html.
2 A comprehensive description of the digital learning innovation's technological and pedagogical design is provided in Tan (2008) and Tan and McWilliam (2008, 2009), and can be made available on request.
3 CART modelling was first developed more than twenty years ago as a statistical method of analysing relationships among variables and has since been used widely in fields that engage primarily with complex and non-linear data sets, such as finance and banking, social welfare policy and

epidemiology. In brief, CART predictive modelling aims to examine each predictor variable through a process of binary recursive partitioning of data to obtain the most accurate prediction of the dependent variable that has the lowest error cost and highest explanatory power. This process is considered binary because each split of a group of participants or cases (parent node) results in two groups (child nodes). The predicted value at each node is the mean of the target variable for all cases included in that node. A comprehensive discussion of CART can be found in the definitive text on this statistical technique (Briemann, Friedman, Olshen, & Stone, 1984).

4   Scale validation procedures and results are beyond the scope of this chapter but can be made available to interested readers on request.

5   Bakharia, A., & Dawson, S. (2009). Social Networks Adapting Pedagogical Practice (SNAPP) (Version 1.2). Brisbane, Australia. For more information, see http://research.uow.edu.au/learning networks/.

References

Amabile, T. (1996). *Creativity in context.* Boulder, CO: Westview Press.

Briemann, L., Friedman, J., Olshen, R., & Stone, C. (1984). *Classification and regression trees.* Belmont, CA: Wadsworth.

Brooks, C., Liu, W., Hansen, C., McCalla, G., & Greer, J. (2007) Making sense of complex learner data. In Workshop of Assessment of Group and Individual Learning through Intelligent Visualization (AGILEeViz). Thirteenth International Conference on Artificial Intelligence in Education (AIED 2007). Marina del Rey, Los Angeles.

Burt, R. (2004). Structural holes and good ideas. *American Journal of Sociology, 110,* 349–399.

Cowdroy, R., & de Graff, E. (2005). Assessing highly-creative ability. *Assessment and Evaluation in Higher Education, 30,* 507–518.

Csikszentmihalyi, M. (1999). Implications of a systems perspective for the study of creativity. In R. Sternberg (Ed.), *Handbook of creativity* (pp. 313–335). Cambridge: Cambridge University Press.

Csikszentmihalyi, M. (2006). Foreword: Developing creativity. In N. Jackson, M. Oliver, M. Shaw, & J. Wisdom (Eds.). *Developing creativity in higher education: An imaginative curriculum* (pp. xviii–xx). London: Routledge.

Dawson, S. (2006a). Online forum discussion interactions as an indicator of student community. *Australasian Journal of Educational Technology, 22,* 495–510.

Dawson, S. (2006b) Relationship between student communication interaction and sense of community in higher education. *The Internet and Higher Education, 9,* 153–162.

Dawson, S. (2007) Juxtaposing community with learning: The relationship between learner contributions and sense of community in online environments. Thesis, Queensland University of Technology, Brisbane.

Dunn, L. L. S. (2004) Cognitive playfulness, innovativeness, and belief of essentialness: Characteristics of educators who have the ability to make enduring changes in the integration of technology into the classroom environment. PhD dissertation, University of North Texas, Denton.

Dweck, C. (2000). *Self-theories: Their role in motivation, personality and development.* Ann Arbor, MI: Psychology Press.

European University Association (2007). *Creativity in higher education: Report on the EUA Creativity project 2006–2007.* Brussels: European University Association.

Florida, R. (2002). *The rise of the creative class.* New York: Basic Books.

Geletkanycz, M. A., & Hambrick, D. C. (1997). The external ties of top executives: Implications for strategic choice and performance. *Administrative Science Quarterly, 42,* 654–681.

Glynn, M. A., & Webster, J. (1993). Refining the nomological net of the Adult Playfulness Scale: Personality, motivational and attitudinal correlates for highly intelligent adults. *Psychological Reports, 72,* 1023–1026.

Hartman, J., Moskal, P., & Dzuiban, C. (2005). Preparing the academy of today for the learner of tomorrow. In D. G. Oblinger & J. L. Oblinger (Eds.), *Educating the net generation: An Educause e-book* (Chapter 6). Retrieved from www.educause.edu/educatingthenetgen (accessed 8 July 2007).

Jackson, N. (2006a). Imagining a different world. In N. Jackson, M. Oliver, M. Shaw, & J. Wisdom (Eds.), *Developing creativity in higher education: An imaginative curriculum* (pp. 1–9). London: Routledge.

Jackson, N. (2006b). Creativity in higher education: Creating tipping points for cultural change. *SCEPTrE Scholarly Paper*, 3, 1–26.

Kaufman, J. C., & Sternberg, R. J. (2007). Resource review: Creativity. *Change*, 39(4), 55–58.

Leavitt, C., & Walton, J. (1975). Development of a scale for innovativeness. In M. J. Schlinger (Ed.), *Advances in consumer research* (pp. 545–554). Provo, UT: Association for Consumer Research.

MacFadyen, L., & Dawson, S. (2010). Mining LMS data to develop an 'early warning system' for educators: A proof of concept. *Computers & Education*, 54(2), 588–599.

McPherson, M., Smith-Lovin, L., & Cook, J. M. (2001). Birds of a feather: Homophily in social networks. *Annual Review of Sociology*, 27, 415–444.

McWilliam, E. (2005). Unlearning pedagogy. *International Journal of Learning Design*, 1(1), 1–11.

McWilliam, E. (2008). *The creative workforce: How to launch young people into high-flying futures.* Sydney: UNSW Press.

McWilliam, E., & Dawson, S. (2008) Teaching for creativity: Towards sustainable and replicable pedagogical practice. *Higher Education*, 56, 633–643.

Moss, P., Girard, B., & Haniford, L. (2006). Validity in educational assessment. *Review of Research in Education*, 30, 109–162.

NCEE (2007) *Tough choices or tough times: The report of the New Commission on the Skills of the American Workforce.* Washington, DC: National Center on Education and the Economy. www.skillscommission.org

Perkins, D. (1981). *The mind's best work.* Cambridge, MA: Harvard University Press.

Robinson, K. (2000). *Out of our minds: Learning to be creative.* Oxford: Capstone.

Rogers, E. M. (1995). *Diffusion of innovations* (4th ed.). New York: The Free Press.

Seely Brown, J. (2006). New learning environments for the 21st century: Exploring the edge. *Change*, 38(5), 18–25.

Tan, J. P.-L. (2008). *Contestations and complementarities: An investigation of the adoption and diffusion of a student-led online learning initiative within a mainstream schooling context.* Brisbane: Queensland University of Technology.

Tan, J. P.-L., & McWilliam, E. (2008). Cognitive playfulness, creative capacity and generation 'C' learners. Paper presented at the ARC Centre of Excellence for Creative Industries and Innovation: Creating Value between Commerce and Commons Conference, Brisbane, Queensland, 25–27 June.

Tan, J. P.-L. and McWilliam, E. (2009) From literacy to multiliteracies: Diverse learners and pedagogical practice. *Pedagogies: An International Journal*, 4(3), 213–215.

Tepper, S. (2006) Taking the measure of the creative campus. *Peer Review*, 8, 4–7.

Tierney, P., Farmer, S. M., & Graen, G. B. (1999) An examination of leadership and employee creativity: The relevance of traits and relationships. *Personnel Psychology*, 52, 591–620.

Yorke, M. (2006) Employability in higher education: What it is – what it is not. In M. Yorke (Ed.), *Learning and employability series one.* York: The Higher Education Academy. Retrieved from www.heacademy.ac.uk/assets/York/documents/ourwork/tla/employability/id116_employ ability_in_higher_education_336.pdf

Chapter 12

Snapshots and portraits

The re-presentation of case-study research findings about creative learning and change

Christine Hall, Ken Jones and Pat Thomson

This chapter is about the later stages of research projects: it focuses on the impact of different decisions about modes of analysis, and, particularly, about how the various findings from social scientific inquiries are represented and shared. We try to combine two kinds of account. The first concerns the process of writing a report of the research (including the choices and trade-offs that are involved); the second a series of 'takes' on the work of a single school, one of the many that we studied, that aims to show the multiple ways in which we sought to represent the 'subjects' of our research, and that also – we hope – illustrates the distinctiveness of what our project tried to achieve. To put it in theatrical terms, we aim to offer an insight into the mechanics of research 'staging' and to show something of the achieved work, the 'play' itself.

Our interest in these issues arises from a mixture of principled positions and practical concerns. Our principled position is that we believe that researchers should take responsibility for disseminating and communicating what they have found. In the social sciences, this means making sure that findings are shared with relevant 'stakeholders', including participants in the research, professionals in the field, agencies and policy makers, as well as a wider public. We also think that ongoing dialogue about the nature of the evidence as it emerges is likely to sharpen the analysis, raise new lines of investigation and deepen understandings.

We recognize that in the everyday realities of conducting research, there are sometimes difficulties in putting principles into practice. In our experience, the practical difficulties are likely to relate either to time factors, or to the nature of the data, or to access to stakeholders who are prepared to engage meaningfully with the research process and its emerging outcomes. Often, the various difficulties will combine: the size and/or sensitivity of data sets will create problems and it will prove difficult to identify exactly how or when to engage stakeholders. The final stages of research projects are often highly pressured and sometimes truncated by the need to meet deadlines for reporting or submitting the completed work. The pressures of time restrictions, a natural desire to bring a complex project to a conclusion and, often, the demands of new work that needs attention can, paradoxically, lead to situations where researchers have less time to analyse and disseminate what has been found than they gave to justifying the importance of the research questions and devising the means of answering them in the first place, when they wrote the original bids for funding and worked out the research design.

These issues – about communicating and discussing research findings, about managing data, time and relationships with participants and stakeholders – are the concerns of this chapter. We illustrate and discuss these concerns in an account of a project that set out to research the relationship between creative learning and school change. Working through this illustration allows us, we hope, to draw out some of the complexities of marrying principles and practice. We begin by offering an overview of the research project.

The Creative School Change project

The aim of the research project, which was funded by the Arts Council, was to investigate institutional change in schools that had become involved in creative learning initiatives. The focus was on schools that had taken up the resources offered to them at that time by the English initiative Creative Partnerships (see Chapter 17). We were interested in the kinds of school change that were occurring (e.g. to school cultures or structures, to teaching and learning practices), who was involved and the level at which any changes occurred (e.g. the classroom, the whole school). Since the Creative Partnerships (CP) programme was designed to encourage partnerships between the educational and the cultural sectors, we wanted to know about the models of partnership schools were using and the impact of these partnerships on capacity building within the school.

The research was fundamentally about school change, but what it means to say that a school has changed is not easy to define. In some basic respects, schools are constantly changing, as students and staff join or move on from the institution. In other respects, the basics of a school – the buildings, the organization of the curriculum, the way of doing things – often seem to stay the same over many years. Different members of a school community will have different views on whether or not a school has changed, depending in part on the particular aspect of change being discussed, the person's experience of the school and who is asking the question. It was clear from the start of the project that we would be trying to understand these complex issues in widely varying sites and conditions, and that each of the schools involved with Creative Partnerships would have its own history and reasons for engaging in the programme. We also knew that we had a three-year period, from the autumn of 2006 to the summer of 2009, to conduct the research.

So, there were very real questions of representation, communication and time management to address from the start of the Creative School Change project.

Establishing the research

The research was organized into two main phases. The initial phase involved a large sample of forty schools from across England; the second phase focused in greater depth on twelve of the schools. We were clear from the outset that the sample was not intended to be representative; we were seeking to study schools where school change had occurred, in order to find out more about what had happened and why. Our aim was to look at interesting cases to see what might be learned from them – what Connell (1995, p. 90) calls 'strategic sampling' with a potentially 'high theoretical yield'. The selection of the sample of schools for the first phase immediately confronted us with the need to address fundamental issues about the definition of school change: how would we know whether change had occurred in a school? Whose opinions on this would count? How would we know whether the changes were related to involvement in the Creative Partnerships programme?

We resolved these questions, in part, by leaving definitions open and involving a subset of knowledgeable individuals – in this case, the regional directors of the Creative Partnerships programme – in helping us construct the sample. For its own organizational purposes, Creative Partnerships had divided England into thirty-six regions, each of which had a regional director. We asked each director to nominate a priority list of three schools from his or her region which could be considered good examples of school change supported by involvement in the Creative Partnerships programme. The regional directors responded well to this request for nominations; they had their own views about school change and did not ask for clarification. The research team then selected the sample from the regional directors' lists to include schools of different types, including pupil referral units and special schools, and to ensure a balance of primary, secondary, rural and urban, and a diversity of language and cultural heritage in the school populations. We then worked our way through the nominated schools on the list, inviting them to participate in the research and substituting equivalent schools if for some reason one school was unable to accept, until forty schools had agreed. Like the regional directors, the school leaders whom we approached to gain consent for the research felt no need to seek further explanation of the nature of the changes we were investigating; they responded readily to the suggestion that their school had changed and that the Creative Partnerships programme had something to do with that change.

Each of the forty schools in this first phase of the data collection participated in a research encounter that occurred over two consecutive days. The first school visits were conducted by pairs of team members, in various combinations, to ensure reliability in the data collection procedures, but the bulk of the visits were carried out by single researchers. We called this the 'snapshot' phase.

Taking snapshots

In the early stages of the work, the issue was not so much about having substantive findings or theoretical interpretations to feed back to funders; it was more about building the individual profiles of schools and assuring the accuracy of the data. We amassed a lot of data on each of the forty schools, including Creative Partnerships material, newsletters, reports to governors, annual reports, documentary evidence on websites and news clippings. We conducted individual interviews with the head or a relevant member of the senior management team and, where possible, with other individual teachers, a key school governor and the creative agent or practitioner. We held focus-group discussions with teachers and with students of mixed ages. These interviews were taped and transcribed. We took photographs of the entrance areas, playgrounds and relevant displays. We had informal conversations in the staff room, play areas and offices, observed lessons and extra-curricular activities and kept extensive field notes as records of the visits.

We were grateful to the staff who had allowed us access to their schools and we found much to admire in the schools we visited. We wanted to encourage the sharing of ideas. We were also interested in respondent validation of the data we were working with. This led us to the idea of creating 'snapshots'. We conceived of the snapshots as a series of anonymized synopses, no more than 1,000 words long, written to a five-part template that began with some details about school context, identified the origins of the school's involvement with Creative Partnerships, outlined the creative learning projects, discussed the impact of these projects and finished with something about future plans. We illustrated the snapshot with one or two photographs from our data set and made an 'album' of the snapshots on the web so they could be browsed or downloaded. The box that follows offers an example of one of the forty snapshots, that of Rowan Tree School.

We chose to call these synoptic accounts 'snapshots' to emphasize the fact that we were presenting an image of the school 'taken' fairly rapidly from a particular perspective at one moment in the school's history. We presented these likenesses back to the schools to see whether they recognized them, and encouraged the schools to use them if they wanted to. The process of reducing and summarizing the data imposed a discipline on the research team which, on the whole, we relished as we worked on the fuller cross-case analysis. We were pleased, too, with the website, which allowed us to offer schools as much or as little engagement with the project findings as they chose. However, the need for brevity and individualized representations of each of the schools limited the scope for analysis, and the invitation to schools to browse the snapshots encouraged us to adopt a standpoint that tended to affirm, rather than critique, the schools' work. However, reading across the snapshots created a picture of the kinds of work that were generally going on in schools under the rubric of 'creativity'.

Example of a snapshot: Rowan Tree School

The school

Rowan Tree Nursery and Infant School is located within a large local authority housing estate on the outskirts of a city in the English Midlands. The area is within a former mining community. Many families are still feeling the effects of the decline of industry in the area over the past three decades and in many cases are finding it difficult to make ends meet.

The headteacher has been in post for eighteen years, and there is high staff retention. There are a large number of teaching assistants as well as a group of arts practitioners on staff. One of the school's creative practitioners is on the board of governors.

Creative Partnerships' involvement

Origins

The school has recognized creative approaches to teaching and learning as a necessary part of its commitment to providing significant and individualized learning experiences for its students.

The school became involved with Creative Partnerships at the pilot stage and was active in the establishment of partnerships with other schools in its locality.

Projects

Creative Partnerships has funded a number of projects in this school. These include the work of a dancer, a musician and a sculptor. The sculptor has worked collaboratively with children in the nursery on such projects as the sculpture of animals and cardboard furniture; the current focus is on a bamboo structure in the outside space of the nursery. The dancer has been involved in the development of the skills of the youngest children to an advanced level. Each class within the school has an artist working with it once a week for half a term, reinforcing the continuity of experience which is at the heart of the school's approach to teaching and learning.

Impact

Creative Partnerships has had a positive impact on school development. Within the school, the arts are seen as a vehicle for experiential learning. Although certain practices have been part of school life for some time, such as a whole day each week devoted to individual learning, Creative Partnerships' involvement has encouraged further modelling of teaching and learning around creative practices. It has opened possibilities for the school to work with a group of artists who have proven to be a great asset and have remained working with the school on a series of projects, to the point where they are now funded by the school itself.

Careful and regular planning takes place between teachers and creative practitioners in order to incorporate creative approaches across the curriculum and to maximize their impact on the students' learning experiences. Examples of the artists' involvement across the curriculum include the teaching of maths and science through the measuring of sculptures and the examination of the properties of the materials used to create the sculptures. The artists' involvement is also seen as part of the teachers' and teaching assistants' professional development.

It is reported that the students' work with the artists has also had a clear impact on their ability to deal more appropriately with personal problems and difficulties. This is partly attributed to an increase in both opportunity and capacity for self-expression. Parents have responded positively to the experience received by their children, attending performances based on project work:

> We are getting an awful lot of our curriculum but in a different way and in a more hands-on way, and the language that they will use, as a result of that, is fantastic. To have a 6-year-old use the word 'translucent' in the correct context is impressive.
>
> (Teacher)

> When you look at the sculpture and the progress that the children have made, [it] is more than we could have expected.
>
> (Headteacher)

The students are actively engaged in their sessions with artists and acknowledge the way in which the artists bring different experiences to their school day:

> It wouldn't be so much fun. We wouldn't do the singing.
> > (Year 1 student, reflecting on what school would be like without the artists)

> I wish I was never poorly because I like school.
>
> (Year 1 student)

All students are enabled to engage meaningfully in the activities. Artists have built effective relationships with their groups. This is partly due to the consistency in the school's approach to employing the artists to work regularly with all groups.

The future

The school has ambitious plans to continue to base its curriculum around creative teaching and learning. In view of the precarious future of Creative Partnerships' funding, the school has drawn from alternative budgets, such as that for behaviour support, or Gifted and Talented funds, in order to maintain the consistency of involvement at its current rate. The main challenges to this approach at the school may lie in the response of the local authority and of Ofsted (the Office for Standards in Education), although it is hoped by the staff that the school's improving academic standards will demonstrate the effectiveness of the creative approach.

It can be see from this snapshot of Rowan Tree that as a representational genre it is largely descriptive and is light on critique, but gives a sense of the activities being undertaken and the reasons why they are being undertaken. Importantly, it places the activities in their local context.

Our other publication was an Interim Report (available on www.artsandcreativity research.org.uk) that offered a cross-case analysis of the data from the first phase of the project. This presented our analysis of all of the documentary and photographic data we had gathered, the interviews and the field notes. Our analytic approach to the interviews combined discourse analysis with thematized coding (Silverman, 1993). We were interested in what interviewees took as creativity and as whole-school change, what examples they produced and how they represented the changes that they attributed to Creative Partnerships. We used a schedule to analyse field notes where we recorded information such as the structures supporting Creative Partnerships in the school; the relationship between Creative Partnerships and broader professional development; any changes in student grouping, timetabling, budget or staffing; and the types of evaluation practices carried out. We were particularly concerned to see what steps the school had taken towards making changes sustainable in the longer term when funding for the programme finished.

In this cross-case analysis, we were looking for what Bassey (1999) calls 'fuzzy generalizations' about the kind of school change that was supported by Creative Partnerships. The report was based largely on self-reporting at the school level, since researcher verification was limited by time and design factors. The size of the research team meant that there was little opportunity in the first phase of the project for all of the researchers to work together; it was therefore likely that there would be variations in the data produced simply through differences in approach to school investigation. We did our best to minimize these variations by conducting two separate analyses of the snapshot corpus, but the initial researcher effect could not be ignored. Despite these caveats, certain themes emerged from the analysis, and numbers of schools appeared to have 'things in common'. The focus of the Interim Report was on the identification and discussion of these commonalities.

Illustrating the cross-case analysis

The Interim Report was conventionally organized into an introduction, which set out the remit and methods of the research, followed by five sections entitled 'What counts as school change?', 'Who is involved in school change?', 'Building the capacity for change', 'Thinking about change' and, as a conclusion, 'Making a difference?'. Clearly, at this point it was necessary to offer our own understandings and assumptions about 'school change' and to clarify how the definitions we had adopted affected the report we were presenting.

Because the readership of the Interim Report was, in the first instance, the project funders, the focus was on dealing directly with the initial research questions about the nature of change in schools engaged in the Creative Partnerships programme. This was in contrast to the presentation of the snapshot data, which left the reader to browse the accounts and make connections and comparisons. Whereas the snapshots presented individual, named (but anonymized) schools, the Interim Report presented synthesized findings in which the schools were referred to by phase rather than picked out separately. Once the data had been thematized, they were then mined to find salient examples of the issue or idea. In this sense, the quotations from the interview transcripts or field notes were used to *illustrate* the analysis; that is, to offer an example or demonstration that helps to clarify or explain the point.

We have chosen two examples from the report where data from Rowan Tree, the infant school presented in the snapshot above, were used to illustrate particular parts of the analysis. These examples are intended to demonstrate how information from the same data set was re-presented for a different audience and to suit a different mode of analysis and genre of writing.

The first example comes from a discussion about funding in the section of the report titled 'What counts as school change?'. All of the schools in the sample were worried about the fact that the extra funding provided by Creative Partnerships might dry up. They wanted to sustain the work they had started, so the budget holders in the schools were committed to deploying resources in ways that embedded the changes they were making. Some of the schools thought that this was best done by adopting an apprenticeship model of professional development, in which teachers learned from the artists and then adopted the new practices they had learned. Other schools took a different view. Anonymized quotations from the data are used here to illustrate the different school positions; in this case, Rowan Tree offers a clear example of the contrary view.

Use of data to illustrate different views of teacher professional development in the Interim Report

They [the schools] shared the widely voiced view that one-off projects did not, on the whole, provide good value for money. But rejecting the one-off project led to different views of how best to use the budgets, depending on how the school viewed the work and role of the creative practitioner/artist. Some schools took the view that teachers' professional development was the best financial investment. They saw the artists as having skills and dispositions that could be passed on to the teaching and support staff and focused on pedagogic processes:

> A lot of what we do tends to be much more about process than about any finished product and I think that is possibly quite different to other schools . . . if you looked at how we spent our budget, it's very different to how other schools have spent theirs. Other schools will come up with project-based work where there is a lot of

money spent on artists coming in and doing a project and there is a finished product, but our budget has been spent on lots of CPD [continuing professional development] for teachers and for us to have time out either to do joint planning together or to talk together to come up with ideas. A lot more thinking time and getting people to come in to talk to us about working in different ways.

(Creative Partnerships coordinator, primary school)

Less common, but stemming from the same desire to sustain the impact of CP, was the attempt to find ways of funding the continued involvement of artists in the day-to-day work of the school. One headteacher was forthright in rejecting the apprenticeship model proposed by the regional CP, which she saw as promoting the idea that teachers could develop 'all singing, all dancing' practice from the artists and pass it on to the children:

It is very disrespectful to any of our artists to imagine that we could ever do what they do. I mean [the dancer] is very tall, very lithe and he's not yet 30, and black as well. And, yes, I might be able to absorb everything he does but, by gum, I'd look a fool trying to do what he does! I wouldn't have the same impact or passion. It's the passion that is coming through the artists as well as their absolute knowledge of their own subject.

(HT, infants school)

This analysis, which saw the skill sets of artists and teachers as distinct and drew heavily on the artists as alternative adult (largely male) role models in the feminized early years school environment, underpinned the headteacher's decision to abandon the compensatory support programmes offered to schools in economically deprived areas (e.g. SEAL [social and emotional aspects of learning] resources, extra support for gifted and talented pupils). Making a judgement about overall value, she chose instead to divert the funds into employing the artists:

The school now employs its own artists using funding from different pots such as, gifted and talented, behaviour management and school development.

(Field note, infants school)

Despite the fact that this decision had been viewed favourably in the school's inspection, it created tensions with the local authority representatives, who took the view that the school's statistical profile indicated the need for the officially endorsed compensatory programmes. Local authority influence over financial management, in small schools particularly, tended to be used in favour of the belt and braces approach – behaviour management programmes and arts projects – rather than to support more radical changes to established patterns of spending.

The second example comes from a discussion in the report about the limitations of what could be claimed from the evidence that had been gathered. Here the Rowan Tree illustration is offered alongside similar comments from teachers in two other schools to illustrate how loose connections were being drawn between student attainment and Creative Partnerships' involvement. Again, the point was to highlight the status of the evidence for the claim rather than to associate the view with a particular school, so the school pseudonyms were not included.

Use of data to offer multiple illustrations of teachers' theories in the Interim Report

Few schools claimed a causal link between the implementation of CP-related changes and the results that the children achieved in statutory tests, but still some were prepared to make tentative connections between the two:

> We'd gone into a whole year of sculpture and at the end of that year . . . our SAT results had gone up and the second year they'd gone up again, particularly around the boys, and we thought, 'This isn't a fluke.' So, the following year sculpture wasn't done and there was a dip in their maths again. Back came the sculpture and up it went again. So that, in a way, was sort of proving that this was happening, and this is what we put in our document because sometimes somebody will read these.
>
> (Teacher, infant school)

> Going back a few years, you would have only a handful of students doing A level but last year we had seventeen and next year there will be well over twenty who want to do A level maths, and in this sort of school that is really unusual.
>
> (Headteacher, secondary school)

> [We had an] unexpected higher achievement in SATs and attributed that to the fact that children had experiences to write about.
>
> (Teacher, primary school)

After working for approximately one year on the Creative School Change project, then, we had produced an album of school snapshots and an Interim Report that offered indicative findings illustrated by data from the forty schools we had visited in the first phase of the research. The aim of the next phase of the work was to achieve deeper understanding of the relationship between school change and creative learning through a concentration on just twelve of the schools from the original sample. These were the 'case-study' schools, each of which was visited by two researchers for a further twelve days spread over two school years (one calendar year). We set out to get to know these sites very well and track their development over time as they implemented and debated – and sometimes experienced unforeseen – changes.

Presenting the case studies

The research project was funded until the summer of 2009, so our Final Report was due at that point. It had been clear from the outset that the research was about creative learning and school change, and that it did not in any sense involve evaluating the Creative Partnerships programme. Nevertheless, we felt we were faced with a challenge in representing the findings as effectively as possible.

We made two decisions about how to represent our findings. The first decision related to the Final Report. We wanted to support both the development of policy making in the area of creative learning and the continuing professional development of the staff who were leading initiatives in schools and in the wider community. This led us to develop a series of heuristics and tables as part of the Final Report in an attempt to condense complex data into usable forms to aid thinking about how to promote creative learning effectively at the national and local levels and also at the level of individual schools. But this same desire to promote creative learning also prompted our second decision, which was to produce narrative accounts – in some senses the opposite of heuristics and tables – which were also intended to help in developing better understanding of the issues and of the process of change itself.

We understood school change as neither linear, nor smooth, nor evenly spread across institutions; instead, we saw it as proceeding jerkily and with difficulty, taking wrong turns, needing refreshing and happening often in 'pockets of innovation'. Our theory of 'vernacular change' – that is, change which is responsive to and made possible by local contexts needs and resources – led us to try to capture both the commonalities and some of the distinctiveness of the sites we studied. We continued to look for ways to represent the vernacular. This became, in our view, more an assertion than a representation in the cross-case work, and we looked back to the snapshots with some regret that the particularity they showed, and that we now knew much more about, we could not evidence.

In the introduction to the report, we confronted the changes to Creative Partnerships and set out our aim of building on the Interim Report to produce a useful resource:

> We are mindful of the problems associated in reporting on events that are now part of a previous incarnation of the Creative Partnerships programme. There is certainly a point in assembling evidence that assesses what the first phase of Creative Partnerships accomplished. However, our goal in this report has not only been to report our findings, but also to attempt to develop heuristics which may be useful as Creative Partnerships continues in its new form. Our intention is to develop a vocabulary and categories of activities which might be mobilised in professional development and diagnostic support of schools engaged in the next phase of the programme.
>
> (*Creative School Change Research Project Final Report*, p. 5)

Two examples are offered to clarify how these intentions were realized in the main body of the report itself. Heuristics are interpretative categories that arise from immersion in experience, and from reflection upon it. At least so far as we used them, they were intended to initiate conversations rather than assert conclusions. We tried to describe and analyse what was happening in the schools in ways that were strongly conceptualized (and informed by the research of others) but also attentive to context. We hoped that we would thus provide resources for reflection by teachers on their own practice.

In seeking to condense complex information to make it more available for exploration and interpretation, we set ourselves the discipline of building summary tables that allowed the different features and characteristics of the case-study schools to be set alongside one another. This had two main benefits. First, it brought together the analysis of each of the different elements of the final report as they related to the individual schools. This allowed us to look again at our interpretation of the way the school had taken up and developed creative learning. In a sense, it produced a better-informed, sharper, shorter version of the earlier school snapshots: it emphasized the features of the individual school and tried to bring elements of the history and context of the school into play with the actions of key individuals and the take-up of particular ideas and projects. Unlike the snapshots, though, the summary tables cannot be easily understood without reference back to the more substantive discussion in the relevant sections of the full report.

We present, by way of an example, the summary table for Rowan Tree School as Table 12.1 (p. 136). It will be clear that, for instance, the summary description of the 'change modality' as 'devolved' will require the reader to return to the discussion of these labels in the report (see www.creativitycultureeducation.org/data/files/creative-school-change-final-report-nov-2009-184.pdf).

The second benefit gained from condensing the data into table form was that it allowed comparisons to be drawn between the characteristics and approaches of different schools. This helped us build theories about clusters of characteristics and actions that influenced change; it also allowed us to present the data in a form that is open to readers to interrogate further. Even in this reduced form, the tables are unwieldy, but Table 12.2 (p. 137), an extract from one such comparative table, indicates some of the ways in which Rowan Tree might be compared with other schools in the sample.

These kinds of comparisons go beyond simply mapping what happens in schools, as was the case with our interim snapshots. Here we focused on heuristic categories that we hoped would be useful to others who wanted to understand the processes of school change. We imagined that another researcher or a consultant could go into a school and ask questions about 'beginning points', for example, or 'affiliation'. This representation of change, then, was intended to guide others in synthesizing information and diagnosing school 'stage of change'.

The Final Report, like the Interim Report, was conventionally presented; it focused on the case-study phase of the work since we had already reported the first-phase findings; it built on the themes of the earlier work, explicated a fuller theory of change, set the work in regional, national and international contexts, discussed school leadership and classroom-level approaches to teaching, learning and assessment, and made recommendations about policy and practice. Nevertheless, as we have suggested already, we felt that these forms of reporting did not entirely do justice to our experience of being in the schools, where we had witnessed some powerful and intriguing changes, which we thought were best represented as narratives.

This led us to the work of Sara Lawrence-Lightfoot on portraiture in the social sciences.

Narrative portraits

Lawrence-Lightfoot broke new ground with her 1983 study *The good high school*, in which she drew portraits of six American schools, concluding the book with a 'group portrait', a meditation on what constitutes 'goodness' in schools. Lawrence-Lightfoot sees portraiture as 'a genre whose methods are shaped by empirical and aesthetic dimensions, whose descriptions are often penetrating and personal, whose goals include generous and tough scrutiny' (1983, p. 369). She proposed portraiture as a new and creative approach to qualitative inquiry, a dialogue between art and science, 'a methodology that hopes to bridge aesthetics and empiricism and appeal to intellect and emotion, and that seeks to inform and inspire and join the endeavors of documentation, interpretation and intervention' (Lawrence-Lightfoot, 2005, p. 7). Her portraits are based on systematic social scientific inquiry and require deep engagement with the school or subject, but they are not, she argues, the same as rich descriptions produced by ethnographers since they operate in a limited time-frame. They must always therefore be impressionistic and be about capturing

Table 12.1 Example of school summary table from Final Report

ROWAN NURSERY AND INFANTS	Small school in high-poverty suburban estate.
Context	Experienced head, stable staff, clear philosophy of teaching and learning, strong relationships with local community. Possibility of amalgamation with nearby junior school. Ofsted 'good' school.
Priorities for change	Extend early childhood pedagogies. Develop arts curriculum.
CREATIVE PARTNERSHIPS	Substantive affiliation.
Starting points for Creative Partnerships-related change	Changing the way pupils learn, changing what counts as learning, changing who teaches.
Creative approach	Employing artists to work alongside teachers for sustained periods.
Creative Partnerships engagement	Aimed to increase number of adults working in pedagogical roles with children to include artists and thus broaden learning and experiences. Rejected teacher apprenticeship CPD model of working with artists.
Creative agent	Community member type, focused on evaluation.
Regional focus	Tactical orientation: school-focused and arts-based improvement in teaching and quality of learning.
PEDAGOGICAL APPROACH	Exploratory, negotiated and creative approaches.
Student voice	Self expression/identity building. Therapeutic engagement in arts. Academic: collaborative evaluation through discussion and negotiated curriculum.
View of community	As assets rich.
LEADERSHIP AND MANAGEMENT	Strong bonds between more experienced staff, including head, and strong commitment to bringing newer staff into school community.
Change modality	Devolved.
Staff participation in decision making	Emphasis on whole-staff involvement (including artists).
TEACHER LEARNING	Emphasis on learning together within and about the school community. Opportunities for systematic analysis and reflection built into school schedule. Strong culture of professional inquiry and developed beyond traditional CPD offering, e.g. attendance at Appleby Horse Fair to better understand traveller families' issues.
Reorientation	Detailed analysis of artefacts and pedagogies across whole staff including support staff. Full complementarity between teachers and artists.

Table 12.2 Extract from cross-school summary table from Final Report

School	Beginning points	Creative approaches	Affiliation	Pedagogical approach
Oak Tree Primary: large multicultural primary.	Changing school organization	Focus on teachers' understanding of creativity	Substantive	Creative approaches primarily to learning environments and extra-curricular activity
Plumtree College: Secondary comprehensive serving deprived estate plus older, more established middle-class community. Poor building stock.	Changing school culture, changing the way pupils learn	Big collaborative productions	Affiliative but opted out	Creative approaches in extra-curricular activities and gifted and talented enhancement
Rowan Tree Nursery: small nursery and infant school in high-poverty suburban estate.	Changing the way pupils learn; changing what counts as learning	Employing artists to work alongside teachers for sustained periods	Substantive	Exploratory, negotiated and creative approaches
Silver Birch Secondary: Catholic secondary school (non-grammar) in area with selective secondary system. Specialist arts college.	Changing school culture	Through big collaborative productions	Symbolic	Creative approaches predominantly, but not exclusively, in extra-curricular activities
Sycamore Secondary: medium-sized specialist business and enterprise college. Located in middle-class area but serving nearby estate. Comprehensive in grammar school system.	Changing the way learning is organized; changing what counts as learning	Linking creativity, enterprise and entrepreneurialism	Affiliative	Creative skills, creative approaches in extra-curricular and vocational specialism

a likeness or – more controversially – an 'essence' (English, 2000, p. 21; Lawrence-Lightfoot & Davis, 1997, p. 4; Lawrence-Lightfoot, 2005, p. 6). They aim to be holistic and combine the outsider's distance with the insider's immediacy. The quest is for the big themes, key events and important people, as well as the texture of everyday life. The style draws on literary tropes as well as social scientific language: 'The personal dimension of the portraits and their literary, aesthetic qualities create symbols and images that people can connect with, offer figures with whom readers can identify, and ground complex ideas in the everyday realities of organizational life' (Lawrence-Lightfoot, 1983, p. 378).

Central to Lawrence-Lightfoot's interpretative method is a focus on paradox (2005, p. 9). This focus made good sense to us as researchers who had witnessed schools trying to reconcile what sometimes seemed like opposing government agendas that encouraged them to promote creativity and independence of thought in systems where they were being judged overwhelmingly by test and examination results. Lawrence-Lightfoot also sees a paradox in the linking of 'private intimate storytelling which is at the center of portraiture, with the public discourse that it hopes to affect' (p. 11), and this chimed strongly with our own intentions. Lawrence-Lightfoot set out to write vivid descriptions that provided material 'to work with', in ways that scholarly abstractions and lengthy reports often do not. We had experienced this tension early in our own project and had resolved it by producing both the snapshots and the Interim Report. We would, we hoped, be able to offer our portraits back to the schools we had studied, while also using them to communicate with a wider set of stakeholders. If 'heuristics' enabled a condensed conceptualization of particular practices, then the more extensive space of the portrait offered room for reflection on context, experience and the complex 'sprawl' of institutional life.

Like the snapshots, the notion of a portrait foregrounds the fact that the representation is one 'take' on reality; inherent in the form of representation is the idea that different interpretations would also be valid. While this is, of course, true of representations in the social sciences generally, and huge efforts are made, for example, to ensure that sources and methods can be scrutinized, a story has a different kind of impact because it works with the particular, allows in more of the affective dimensions of engagement and suggests different kinds of interpretation and response. Lawrence-Lightfoot herself set out 'to find the goodness and talk about the successes' of schools and to 'honor' them (1983, pp. 10, 22; 1986, p. 13). While the portrait methodology does not necessarily need to be employed in this positive way, we had the privilege of witnessing thought-provoking and sometimes inspiring work in different schools, and disseminating these experiences was part of the responsibility we felt we had taken on with the research project. We considered it important to schools and teachers that researchers tell stories of health as well as of pathology, and so Lawrence-Lightfoot's approach supported our own.

We end, then, with a short extract from the portrait of Rowan Tree School, the school that has been represented in different forms and genres throughout this chapter. The portrait was constructed entirely from the field notes, interviews and photographic and documentary evidence gathered at a school over our two and a half years of engagement with it.

Portraiture of Rowan Tree Nursery and Infants School

Making a difference

Ringo, the sculptor, has long sideburns, is slight, sockless and dressed in an Irish surfing T-shirt. His manner is intense; he leans forward to listen to the children, speaks mildly and is very positive. He hated school himself; he was always being accused of things he hadn't done. He has no formal training as an artist; he worked first as a helper in a community arts project, then found himself leading the sessions. When CP came along, his work was extended to schools. He says of CP, 'You couldn't ask for better professional development.' He sees sculpture as lending itself particularly to maths and science work. He wants the children to have the experience of working with the different materials and techniques. He sees himself as adding to their repertoire of skills.

The children are sitting on the carpet and Ringo is talking to them about a new project. They are going to make a structure from bamboo garden canes in a palm-tree shape and plant ivy inside it.

Ringo says, 'It's going to live outside, and instead of decorating it, we're going to let nature decorate it.'

Audible gasp of pleasure from the children.

Ringo produces the plant he has brought along. 'It's not just any old plant. It changes colour.'

Louder gasp from the children. They spend a minute or two suggesting what colours it might change to and, when someone hits upon red, the 'oooh!' is even louder, and several children agree that it's 'like magic'.

In the nursery, the reward the children particularly prize is a seat during story-time on the cardboard sofa they made with Ringo.

All the teachers have a favourite anecdote about a dramatic piece of learning that they've witnessed in one of Ringo's sessions, from a little boy with Down's syndrome who made his first triangle, to a 6-year-old who talked about translucence. Kaye, the head, says:

> When you look at the sculpture, the progress that the children have made is more than we could have expected. . . . We'd gone into a whole year of sculpture and at the end of that year we thought it was a fluke because our SATs results had gone up. And the second year they'd gone up again, particularly around the boys. And we thought: this isn't a fluke. So, the following year sculpture wasn't done and there was a dip in their maths again. Back came the sculpture, and up it went again.

The artists work with the children for extended periods of time. Lee, the dancer, said:

> I'd been doing a lot of early years work always on the premise that we had to work twenty minutes with this age group because of attention spans. . . . I thought that was kind of piffle myself. . . . What we do now is I work for a full morning.. . . . We feel it and see how it goes.

The artists' sessions are pacy and physically engaging: Lee dances with a huge elastic band that encircles the class; Pete, the musician, works on developing 'a much more embodied sense of rhythm'; Steve uses Meyerhold's 'biomechanics' approach to actor training to help the children use their bodies to tell stories. Kaye mentioned that the staff are much fitter since the artists joined the school.

All the teachers agreed that their teaching had changed, 'because we are having to follow up these very creative lessons' and because of the standard of the artists' work. 'Take the dance. [Lee] is working with the kids now at GCSE level so all the staff, including the TAs [teaching assistants], are working at an advanced level.' The artists drew frequently on theory from within their particular arts disciplines; they were interested in form and excellence and process, rather than more diffuse notions of creativity, or self-expression through performance. Lee insisted that 'the idea of creativity isn't actually creativity, it's actually arts-based learning'. And Steve said:

> I have felt in some schools that you really compromise the art form and what the art form can bring. And the art form is kind of chipped away to fit into an education format. I personally have fought against that, because what I think the children here pick up on is, one, my enthusiasm for the art form but also the fact that the art form, in itself, is exciting. And it's that excitement which is the spark to anything that follows. Once you dampen down or shave your art form to fit the need, then that's when the work becomes a little bit generic for me. I find that really frustrating because it loses its edge: it becomes a dull blade.

The artists' commitment to their work influenced the teachers. Jill felt more confident about learning through drama: 'I'm spending a three-hour session doing drama with [Steve] and that's fine because I can tell people exactly what those children have got out of those three hours.' Linda echoed this feeling of independence:

> You're not always thinking I must get something into a book, to back it up. You know that people will see our children working and they're using the skills. It's not a case of filling in a worksheet or doing something like that, just to be seen to do something. That's fine if there's only one piece of writing out of a fortnight's work to do with something. It doesn't matter that there's no hard copy at the end of it.
>
> Whereas before, we were all very conscious, you know, looking in a maths book and realizing you've not got anything written in for the week. 'We must do some on Friday.' But now, we know that these children are using those skills practically, all the time, and that's far more important.

As Lee settled in to his new role as chair of Rowan Tree's governing body, Kaye (the head) summed up the school's commitment to their particular form of teacher–artist partnership:

> We believe in this, and my great thing now is to ensure that it doesn't stop here. I absolutely believe that this is the right thing for our school and our kids. It's becoming clear we are going to need artists forever.

Conclusion

In this chapter, we have focused on the question of representation. Using examples from a long-term case study-based research project into creative school change we demonstrated the use of:

- snapshots: short descriptive writing that gives a flavour of the context, the activities and their rationale;
- discursive discussion, which uses data from one site to illuminate a cross-case theme obtained from reading systematically across the data set; we call these illustrations;
- cross-case tables, which provide analytic heuristics for further work, as well as summaries that provide evidence for conclusions to be drawn; and
- portraits, which use data from one case to develop rich and appreciative narratives of activities.

We have argued that there are multiple ways for research findings to be represented and that choices about representation are tied to intended readerships and their interests. We suggest that the conventional notions of 'communication' or 'dissemination' of findings could be usefully exchanged for the concept of representation, which focuses attention on textual choices and the processes of meaning making that they make possible.

References

Bassey, M. (1999). *Case study research in educational settings*. Maidenhead, UK: Open University Press.

Connell, R. W. (1995). *Masculinities*. Cambridge: Polity Press.

English, F. W. (2000). A critical appraisal of Sara Lawrence-Lightfoot's *Portraiture* as a method of educational research. *Educational Researcher, 29*(7), 21–26.

Lawrence-Lightfoot, S. (1983). *The good high school: Portraits of character and culture*. New York: Basic Books.

Lawrence-Lightfoot, S. (1986). On goodness in schools: Themes of empowerment. *Peabody Journal of Education, 63*(3), 9–28.

Lawrence-Lightfoot, S. (2005). Reflections on portraiture: A dialogue between art and science. *Qualitative Inquiry*, 11(3), 3–15.

Lawrence-Lightfoot, S. and Davis, J. H. (1997). *The art and science of portraiture*. San Francisco: Jossey-Bass.

Silverman, D. (1993). *Interpreting qualitative data: Methods for analysing talk, text and interaction*. London: Sage.

Part 3

Can creative learning be measured and evaluated?

Chapter 13

An interview with John Harland

John Harland, an experienced English arts researcher, was interviewed by Julian Sefton-Green in July 2009; he was asked to describe and explain the range and impact of his work, especially at policy level. The interview has been edited to give a sense of an arts-research career and what it means to spend a working life in this field.

John has been a full-time educational researcher for nearly thirty years, mainly with the National Foundation for Educational Research (NFER), where he was head of the Northern Office in York. This interview describes the work of many of his publications in more detail.

After a study of a theatre-in-education residency in a special school (Harland, 1990), arts education became a major focus for John's work. He is now a freelance researcher with LC Research Associates. His recently completed projects include research into moving image projects with the British Film Institute and the NFER (Lord *et al.*, 2007), an evaluation of the BBC's news report in schools project (Bazalgette, Harland, & James, 2008) and an audit of practice within the national initiative, Creative Partnerships (CP) (Pringle & Harland, 2008). He is currently leading an evaluation of CP's Enquiry Schools Programme and a study of the Human Scale Schools initiative.

Becoming a professional researcher for the NFER

I was a former teacher and I used to teach drama, and so I guess that role is quite germane to how I developed an interest in arts research. I trained in the '60s – late '60s – and I did my initial teacher training at Bretton Hall, which had a very strong arts background, but I was doing English at the time and not drama. But it was steeped in the arts and I had artists all around me, and I loved that sort of community of artists. Then I went off to teach drama for four years in a large comprehensive. Then I did a short spell in a special school but carried on teaching drama in a youth club, and then I got into higher education because I'd already done my university degree to complement my teacher training certificate. And then I went off to do a doctorate at the University of York in the sociology of education. I guess that led me into research in a stronger professional way. In fact, after doing my MA and doctorate I never went back into teaching, at least not within schools.

By the time that I did my doctorate, it was about 1980, and my first full-time research job was in the college of education sector, which later became the college of higher education sector, and for four years I was studying the diversification of colleges at the College of St John in York. And after that I joined NFER as a senior research officer. I think I went in there with a kind of ambition to help build up the qualitative side of it and to change some people's perception of NFER as being largely a number-crunching research organization.

NFER's claim was that it was the largest independent educational research organization in the UK. It had a reputation for being heavily policy orientated, almost devoid of theoretical development, and so it was a kind of empiricist paradise, in a way. That was how it was largely seen: as empirical, policy related. . . . Central government couldn't reach out or influence NFER and there was a very good, legal distance from government at a national level which allowed its researchers to examine policies and initiatives from an independent perspective.

My initial work was on an interesting project, which was evaluating the very first initiative that the Department for Education – or the DES, as it was known then – ran itself directly. It was called 'The Lower Attaining Pupils Programme' and was initiated by Sir Keith Joseph. I was on a large team of about seven or eight researchers evaluating that for four years. It wasn't the easiest of research experiences: it was on a large team and I didn't feel that my training or background in research got adequate expression within that. I had to be a team player . . . I couldn't write very well and my reporting was not good, and although I had a few things published, I wasn't pleased with them because we had to go through an editorial process which had a very strong team management structure.

At the end of that project, I got an opportunity through an academic at the University of York, where I was based, who had received an invitation to bid for the evaluation of an arts project at a special school and he couldn't do it, but he asked if I wanted to submit a proposal for it. So I took the opportunity, and it was funded by Yorkshire Arts, and a new colleague called Dick Downing was sponsoring it. . . . I called it an arts 'experiment' and I should never have done that, but it was an evaluation and report of a theatre group called Whitehouse & Fleming who were working in this special school on a residency for a term; the Royal Opera House was also involved.

And I did it solo; I did it totally by myself. I think it was only about sixteen days' work and I kept it entirely to myself and I loved it, and some colleagues have said that the paper that it led to was the best thing I've ever written. It was my first piece of work in the arts and it was a very significant step. It was published in a journal of special education . . . but it was ultimately about an arts group having a residency in a school, and from that flowed a whole load of work, and through it I felt that I was able to go back to using the ethnographic technique that I wanted to use.

Researching the arts

I had not come from a background steeped in a study of the literature on arts research. But this experience did create in me a desire to want to do some larger-scale work in the arts.

I felt that, within NFER and nationally, research into arts education was something of a Cinderella area. I felt there were opportunities here for bringing the arts into research as they needed more empirical data and more theorizing behind them. And I put together a proposal because I got interested in the whole data – or the lack of data – on how many young people participate in the arts and what sort of arts they do and what's the difference between young people's home and street art and what they do at school, and the relationship between the two. I sent the proposal round various sponsors and eventually a group got together to fund it, and that became the publication *Arts in their view* [Harland, Kinder, & Hartley, 1995]. And one sponsor I've done a lot of work with since, the Gulbenkian Foundation . . . had already been doing work with Ken Robinson and Paul Willis, and I was added to the stable in a way, which was great.

There was a continuation in terms of the methodology from my 'arts experiment'. It was not just my excitement about the arts which was encouraged by involvement in the special school study, but it was the technique. Although I wanted to ask questions about young people's involvement on a larger scale, I still wanted to hang on to a qualitative element, and that's where a lot of people felt I was mad for pushing that, because if you had a normal methodological solution to what I wanted to do, it would be to have a survey of young people. But I felt that a survey would be biased towards certain constituencies within the population of young people. We're talking about young people from the ages of, I think, 14 to 24, and I felt that if there was a written survey, that would alienate several elements, and a lot of young people wouldn't bother with that and it would only scratch the surface. So I was adamant that I wanted to do one-to-one interviews, and so I think it was one of the largest interviewing one-to-one qualitative pieces of work of anything I've ever undertaken. To actually go out there and have interviews – and some of these interviews were about an hour and a half each . . . all transcribed . . . and sponsors paid for that. I convinced them to do it in that way and to not go down the survey route.

As well as seeking to hold on to a qualitative interview experience, I was trying to solve those sorts of pressures for representativeness, and we looked carefully at the sampling techniques, and it was quota sampling where we had so many male/female; so many from different socio-economic groups; so many ethnic minorities – and we actually weighted the ethnic minorities. But it was all done statistically so you had that statistical credibility to it but, at the same time, the interface with the young people was very much a kind of interactive one; a human one.

The reality was that sponsors were more likely to be influenced by quantitative numbers rather than just the one case study. In their minds, that is only one case and it is kind of anecdotal, and therefore you had to find ways of putting numbers on it, which gave it much more credence, and that was another reason why I was keen to find ways of producing studies in the arts that had some big numbers to them but had the qualitative element that I was trying to hang on to because I firmly believe that, particularly in areas like the arts, you're talking about very complex human stories and reactions and you have to find ways of actually getting down to individuals and the reasons behind their actions.

I had a desire to bring more studies to the arts, and in the '90s I convened a symposium at one of the universities, where I invited other arts researchers to come together. So, I was always interested in actually raising the profile of arts education and research, but I think that my other drive was to try to show that it could be research that had credibility on a quantitative front as well as working in the more ethnographic work.

'Arts in Their View'

In the 'Arts in Their View' project, we were talking to young people up to the age of 24 – well beyond the school context – and these were young people that we contacted out in their communities or workplaces or leisure places, and so on. So it was not a school perspective and it came up with findings – and I guess they've become commonplace now – but we were saying that wasn't it interesting that music was the most prevalent art form among young people in that age range along with media activity and film and so on, and yet it's one of the least liked in schools and one of the least studied in schools. We were trying also to show points of participation in terms of making and critically viewing the arts – we had difficulty finding the right words for that, and I think we talked about 'participating in' and 'consuming' the arts. But that was part of the problem, and we struggled with the language to discuss it. But the report gave impetus to the whole issue about young people's participation in the arts.

The other thing the study tried to do was to pick out a few stories of people's careers in the arts and try to illuminate the ways that the arts had influenced young people's lives, either in young people being turned off the arts – and we found out that school was one of the leading factors that turned people off. We called that the arts biographies or careers, and that had an influence in saying, OK, you can look at the big numbers if you want and look at the percentages that have participated in visual arts or in music making, but by actually going out to the young people, we were able to get into the sort of musical genres they were interested in and were participating in such as mixing and so on, and dubbing and all that. But, at the same time, when you look at the individuals there's a lot to learn about what are enormously positive experiences for some young people engaged with the arts.

We just captured young people before they left school and right up to the age of 24, and the study painted a trajectory of a typical involvement in the arts which tended to fall off in the 20 to 24 age range. You could see that there was more involvement, I believe, around earlier than 17, and it would often drop off at 17 to 20. Also, the study broke the assumed myth about the high involvement of ethnic minorities in the arts and they were, in fact, under-represented in the arts, as were males.

The study did influence not so much the Department of Education and Science, as it was then, but the Department for Culture, Media and Sport, as it has become. They took it on and it started to work through into a number of policy documents that informed young people's participation in the arts and in sports. Shortly after this – about a year later – there was a report that they published on youth participation in culture and so on, and I think my study informed a lot of that and raised the profile. We were interested in the kind of art houses and the kind of provision for young people outside of formal education, but I do think that it influenced some politicians towards thinking that this is a problem and we need to generate more involvement in the arts.

Our sponsors came with their own particular politics as well, and there was that sort of confluence of interests and motives at the end. They weren't just coming to us impartially; they too had an interest, I think, in pursuing and pushing and making a case for the arts. . . . If there is anything particularly different about the studies researching the arts, it's that there has been, over the last thirty or so years . . . the need to make the case for the arts. That is not the case for other areas of the curriculum, and that's what we were running into, and the pressure then started to grow in 'Arts in Their View'. I was happy to go along with that to some extent, but it wasn't how we set up doing this.

'Arts Education in Secondary Schools: Effects and Effectiveness'

The 'Arts Education in Secondary Schools: Effects and Effectiveness' project developed in response to a growing sense of the instrumental value of arts learning (which was largely American driven), where they were making a very strong case for the arts through the new interest in the neurological work in how the brain works and responds to the arts such as music and particularly Mozart. . . . I'm thinking of Frances Rauscher, for example [Rauscher et al., 1997], who did the work where they found that listening to Mozart had a positive benefit. And then there were Martin Gardiner and Alan Fox [Gardiner, Fox,

Knowles, and Jeffrey, 1996], who produced a piece in the journal *Nature* which claimed to show that children who were able to play the keyboards did better in maths in Reception at school than other children, and they drew links and parallels between music and maths skills. This research was also beginning to have an effect here, and the whole debate about the arts was focused on: can we establish some extraneous transfer effects from the arts to other areas of cognitive growth in the curriculum? Can arts performance boost academic performance?

The Royal Society for the Arts [RSA; www.thersa.org] came to us and said they wanted to do some research which looked at the notion that students who do music at GCSE perform better at maths and other curriculum areas. They were assuming some kind of causal relation. That's what they came for us for . . . they wanted us to do . . . a statistical quantitative study to just try and test that particular thesis. We were interested because it had the scope to make a major contribution, although we were sceptical, so we persuaded them that the problem of funding a piece of work that was tied to such a narrow focus would be limited and we persuaded them to actually initiate a study that looked at all effects and not just that particular one.

. . . I was trying to broaden it out, not just from a methodological point of view but also from a political point of view because I was worried that if we did this study and it proved negative or we had problems with that correlation, then that's a real downer for the arts. And the RSA totally accepted that and, in fact, were quick to see it and to make the same point, and recognized that we needed a study where if we couldn't find evidence of the Mozart effect or something similar, there were other stories and other evidence which actually made the case for the arts on other grounds. Politically, however, 'Effects and Effectiveness' [Harland *et al.*, 2000] was really fashioned in the context of the burgeoning interest in finding ulterior instrumental benefits of the arts and justifying it within the curriculum.

There were three methodologies in this project: there was the number-crunching one which looked at the data going back for a number of years of GCSE data for most children in England. So the statistical work was massive and they [the NFER statisticians] had a very, very large database to try and look at those correlations between those taking the arts subjects and their performance in other subjects and so on. The second methodology was a survey, which was a written questionnaire to schools, and, again, that would have something like twenty-two schools. But the main qualitative work was based in five schools that were thought to have a good representation in the arts across the board. So it was biased towards good arts schools, and again the justification was that this was largely about exploring if this was the best case for the arts, then let's go to the best schools to make that case or to see if it can be justified. And then we did three years of data collection in this, and we tracked through two cohorts of young people: one group from 11 for three years to the end of what we know as Key Stage 3 and one from 14 to the end of compulsory schooling. So there were those two groups and we interviewed pupils once a year to document their experiences of the arts and the way they reacted to them and their performance within that.

We ended up with a typology which was very influential. A lot of other researchers started to use it and a lot of other people making the case for the arts use it. So people were using it as a source to justify the arts in the curriculum, as well as other researchers in the arts picking up on that sort of schema or framework for understanding the effects of the arts.

We came out very strongly at the end of the project and said that we could find very little evidence of arts involvement having a positive statistical effect on performance in other areas. In fact, we thought there was a kind of reverse association and that actually the kids that did music were largely middle-class kids . . . over in the States, Louise Hetland and Ellen Winner were doing their meta-analysis at the time and we sent them copies of our interim report, and I think we fed into their work. We gave a paper on it in the States and we weren't very popular for saying that, but we were quite clear that we felt there were real problems in trying to make that argument and, therefore, we were saying, 'Look at the qualitative evidence and you'll see an enormous range of other types of effects that the arts can have on young people, in schools where they are given proper status and good coverage.' I think the other thing was that in the five schools that we studied, although they had a very strong background in the arts, there were also problems and there were gaps in the provision. The provision of the arts is very partial and not a lot of kids really get a good deal, across-the-board arts educational experience. But where you do, it can have a fantastic effect on their maturation and growth in areas like self-esteem, the development of identity, teamwork skills, and so on. So it was those areas where we felt there was a stronger justification for the arts.

I gave about forty or fifty talks or seminars based on this report. I probably had a bigger influence through the talks that I gave or that other people gave with me than through any writing, and one of the messages from this report was the very problematic state and quality of music education in our schools. Music comes out very badly in terms of its effect; it was probably the art form that was having the least range of effects across the curriculum, and I gave lots of talks to music organizations and educators trying to explain that problem.

I think our messages about the poor state of the arts and music had an influence. For instance, on the day the report was published, a large sum of money was put by the government into music education because they had read it, or Ofsted had read it, and realized it had some dreadful things to say about music, and so, politically, they came out and put more money into music in schools.

'The Arts–Education Interface' (AEI)

'Effects and Effectiveness' looked at the provision of arts education in mainstream schools. I'd done other work for the Arts Council, and my initial piece of work that looked at the special school was about artists going into schools. Hence, the work covered the two big kind of sub-strands within arts education – namely, you're either studying mainstream arts education in the school or you're studying artists in schools (of which I think there has probably been an awful lot more, proportionately, than research into the actual provision by teachers in schools). It's very interesting how there are those two strands and, in a way, you can see 'AEI' as picking up the other strand of artists working in schools . . . using a similar type of methodology and framework to that used in 'Effects and Effectiveness'; it gave us the chance to ask the question, what sort of effects on students could be seen from artists going into schools?

The study was in two local areas. The other story behind 'AEI' is that the Arts Council was aware that Creative Partnerships was going to happen and that 'AEI' was seen as a preparatory ground for these arts agents, who would work in two areas of England – Bristol and Corby – because the Arts Council would be directly employing arts coordinators and, as I understood it, they wanted a context in which they could try out and develop their own sort of experience so that the Arts Council would have some direct involvement in organizing work in schools.

The subtitle of the book [Harland *et al.*, 2005] is *A mutual learning triangle* (coined by Kay Kinder, one of the co-authors of the report). I guess what we were trying to examine in this study was what were the artist-in-school projects that worked, and through the research we were able to study different models of interventions, some which were short one-offs, others were longer projects over two years or so. So it was an opportunity to look at a variety of models of artists engaging both with pupils and teachers in schools. We found a number of problems and reasons for projects failing. One, I guess, was the lack of engagement by the teachers with the artists and the learning they offered. Where artists went into schools and worked purely with students and saw no kind of professional development aspects with teachers, there was likely to be far less lasting input than where the school and the teachers were drawn into the project and encouraged to participate as partners. We said that if you're looking for a model of how those sorts of projects work, it's where the students and the teachers from the school see themselves as having a learning agenda in and around that project.

Reflections on the research process

I do like going with the evidence. It's just that you make these kind of surprising discoveries and you work them up and you express them, and then people say, 'Oh, we knew that anyway', but it wasn't always like that when you were looking at the data. They might have known it but I didn't know it, or it hadn't struck me so forcefully. To give an example from 'Arts in Their View', there was the sheer variation amongst young people . . . you need to speak to an awful lot of young people to capture trends because there is an enormous variation in what human beings think about things and we are in great danger when we generalize in surveys that we think we've captured it. So that was one surprise: the sheer extent to which young people can differ. But I think one finding that came up very strongly that was a surprise was the polarization of children that identified with sport and sporting activities and those who identified with the arts, and that goes back to the two cultures idea. I just didn't realize that it was so prevalent amongst young people, and we wanted to ask, 'What do schools do to perpetuate that?' Some young people talk about the problems of having a toe in one and a foot in the other and how it can cause problems for them. The stories that they [related] told of the pressures that they came up against of not being totally identified with one camp, and that was a major surprise that we still haven't thought through enough. We still haven't done enough to actually deconstruct the strong boundaries between sport and the arts.

I think with research design I'm always keen to leave the door open to unintended consequences and unintended findings, and I think that is where research is at its best sometimes. 'Effects and Effectiveness' had, I guess, surprises in and around music and its problems. I didn't realize the severity of the poor quality of music education. For me, I would love to see the whole research agenda shift from the legacy of that research, which was about trying to make a case for the arts, to one which is about trying to understand the difference between the good and bad quality of arts education that we've already got. Because of the political pressures to look for evidence to make the case for it, bad provision or simply the lack of provision hasn't been fully exposed and many children who should be getting, across the board, a great experience of the arts are not.

The debate needs to move on beyond making the case for it to look at what is actually happening in schools and begin to research and put some evidence on why it works in some cases but not others.

Bibliography

Bazalgette, C., Harland, J., and James, C. (2008). *Lifeblood of democracy? Learning about broadcast news*. London: Ofcom.

Downing, D., and Watson, R. (2004). *School art: What's in it? Exploring visual arts in secondary schools*. Slough, UK: NFER.

Gardiner, M. F., Fox, A., Knowles, F., and Jeffrey, D. (1996). Learning improved by arts training. *Nature, 381* (23 May), 284.

Harland, J. (1990). An evaluation of a performing arts experiment in a special school. *Educational Research, 32*(2), 118–129.

Harland, J. (2008). Voorstellen voor een evenwichtiger kunsteducatiemodel. In J. Harland and L. Hetland (Eds.), Gewenste en bereikte leereffecten van kunsteducatie. Special issue of *Cultuur + Educatie, 23.*

Harland, J., Ashworth, M., Bower, R., Hogarth, S., Montgomery, A., and Moor, H. (1999). *Real curriculum: At the start of Key Stage 3*. Slough, UK: NFER.

Harland, J., and Kinder, K. (1997). Teachers' continuing professional development: Framing a model of outcomes. *British Journal of In-service Education, 23*(1), 71–84.

Harland, J., and Kinder, K. (Eds.). (1999). *Crossing the line: Extending the access of young people to cultural venues*. London: Calouste Gulbenkian Foundation.

Harland, J., Kinder, K., and Hartley, K. (1995). *Arts in their view: A study of youth participation in the arts*. Slough, UK: NFER.

Harland, J., Kinder, K., Lord, P., Stott, A., Schagen, I., Haynes, J., Cusworth, L., White, R., and Paola, R. (2000). *Arts education in secondary schools: Effects and effectiveness*. Slough: NFER.

Harland, J., Lord, P., Stott, A., Kinder, K., Lamont, E., and Ashworth, M. (2005). *The arts–education interface: A mutual learning triangle?* Slough, UK: NFER.

Lord, P. and Harland, J. (2000). *Pupils' experiences and perspectives of the National Curriculum: Research review*. London: QCA.

Lord, P., Jones, M., Harland, J., Bazalgette, C., Reid, M., Potter, J., and Kinder, K. (2007). *Special effects: The distinctiveness of learning outcomes in relation to moving image education projects. Final Report*. Slough, UK: NFER.

National Advisory Committee on Creative and Cultural Education (NACCCE). (1999). *All our futures: Creativity, culture and education*. London: DfEE Publications.

Pringle, E., and Harland, J. (2008). *Creative Partnerships: An audit of practice*. London: Creative Partnerships.

Rauscher, F. H., Shaw, G. L., Levine, L. J., Wright, E. L., Dennis, W. R. and Newcomb, R. L. (1997). Music training causes long-term enhancement of preschool children's spatial-temporal reasoning. *Neurological Research, 19*, 2–8.

Robinson, K. (1982). *The arts in schools: Principles, practice and provision*. London: Calouste Gulbenkian Foundation.

Tambling, P. and Harland, J. (1998). *Orchestral education programmes: Intents and purposes*. London: Arts Council of England.

Willis, P. E. (1990). *Common culture: Symbolic work at play in the everyday cultures of the young*. Milton Keynes, UK: Open University Press.

Chapter 14

Quantitative research on creativity

Mark A. Runco, Nur Çayırdağ and Selçuk Acar

The growth in creative studies over the past twenty-five years may be most obvious in the social and behavioural sciences. Indeed, the number of empirical studies on creativity has doubled several times over in this period (Feist & Runco, 1993). The vast majority of the studies on creativity in the social and behavioural sciences have been empirical. This chapter focuses on studies of creativity that have used quantitative methods and data. It does not, then, discuss qualitative research.

This chapter was prepared for individuals who are interested in creativity but whose expertise is not in testing or measurement. Although there is some jargon, each term is defined and illustrations are provided. The coverage was dictated by several related questions: Why is the quantitative approach suitable for studies of creativity? Which of the various quantitative methods are the most useful for creative studies, and which facets of creativity can be meaningfully studied with these methods? What issues are related to the quantitative approach to the study of creativity? Finally, what are the limitations of the various quantitative methods when studying creativity?

The structure of this chapter follows Gay and Airasian's (2003) descriptive, correlational, causal-comparative and experimental research categories. One section of this chapter is devoted to each of these. The historiometric method is not included in the earlier categorization but is reviewed here since it constitutes an important part of creative studies (Simonton, 1990, 1995; Runco, Kaufman, Halladay, & Cole, in press). We also devote one section to research that is best categorized as psychometric since it relies on paper-and-pencil tests. Meta-analysis and longitudinal studies were subsumed under descriptive (survey) research by Gay and Anastasia but here are treated as distinct categories, the intent again being to do justice to the research specifically in creative studies. There is overlap among the categories used here, as well as exceptions. Longitudinal designs are, for instance, often correlational, and sometimes descriptive. Such overlap and any possible complementarity among approaches is noted in what follows. Descriptive research is a good place to start because most quantitative research begins with descriptive data.

Descriptive research on creativity

Descriptive research is extremely common in the social and behavioural sciences. Descriptive research usually details the characteristics of a variable within a certain sample (Gay & Airasian, 2003). It can also be used to compare groups, such as males and females. Self-report questionnaires are often employed, but data can be collected via telephone, surveys or interviews. Descriptive research allows the researchers to summarize the basic characteristics of a sample, categorize the information and provide information about similarities and differences (Creswell, 2005).

Educational research is often descriptive. Fryer and Collings (1991), for example, used the descriptive method to explore teachers' views on creativity. Their sample consisted of 1,028 teachers whose responses to the question 'What does creativity involve?' were rank-ordered. The top five rankings of teachers were imagination, original ideas, self-expression, discovery and seeing connections. According to the teachers, creativity can be developed but is rare, only relevant in some subjects, limitless, and is defined by each individual. These views suggest what expectations teachers may have for their students. The notion that creativity is only relevant to certain subjects, for example, implies that creativity varies from domain to domain (e.g. art versus mathematics), which is consistent with quite a bit of data, but there is the questionable implication that creativity may not be relevant to certain subjects. If an educator holds that view, he or she may not look for or encourage creativity in a domain where it is thought to be unimportant. Any descriptive research relying on reports such as these is limited. The teachers, or anyone completing measures such as those used by Fryer and Collins (1991), may have a view based on certain experiences, his or her memory of those experiences, and perhaps even socially desirable (but not sincere) ideas. Socially desirable responding is a common problem when self-report measures are used.

Mohan (1973) reported a similar descriptive study as part of a needs assessment for a course on creativity for pre-service and in-service teachers. A needs assessment questionnaire was administered to 180 graduate and senior students in teacher education and 70 experienced teachers in schools. Results showed that 169 out of 180 (94 per cent) of the students felt there was a need for such a course and 64 of 70 teachers reported that there was a need for such a course. Again these results must be interpreted in the light of possible socially desirable responding. Additionally, if the intent of the research was transparent, there is another concern. In this case, the potential problem is that responses could be slanted towards any expectations that were apparent in the questionnaires or administration of them. Reliable research should avoid transparent objectives and ensure that participants are blind to research hypotheses.

Aljughaiman and Mowrer-Reynolds (2005) worked with thirty-six elementary school teachers in a college town in northern Idaho. This sample constituted 75 per cent of all elementary school teachers in the district. This implies that the sample was representative of the entire population, which in turn bodes well for generalizations from the findings. Aljughaiman and Mower-Reynolds asked the teachers about their definition of creativity and found that 88 per cent of them chose original ideas, 35 per cent chose aesthetic product, 35 per cent chose intelligence, 29 per cent chose linguistic product and 26 per cent chose imagination. Fifty-two per cent of the teachers 'strongly agreed' and 28 per cent 'agreed' with the idea that creativity can be developed in the classroom. Forty-four per cent strongly agreed that creativity is essential for enhancing student academic learning in schools, and 42 per cent strongly agreed and 33 per cent agreed that they themselves employed many methods in the classroom to foster creativity.

Firestien and Lunken (1993) assessed the long-term effects of the Master of Science degree in creative studies. Of the fifty-three alumni, 42 per cent were employed in education, 16 per cent in business and 11 per cent in government; 13 per cent of them completed their doctorate degree; 39 per cent had published an article, 34 per cent wrote a book, 57 per cent created original educational materials and 66 per cent organized a new course for a professional organization or group. Forty-four per cent of them also reported that 75–100 per cent of their job involved specific work in creativity, and 24 per cent of them reported that 50–75 per cent of their job involved work in creativity.

Descriptive research often compares groups. West (1993), for instance, compared the work practices and creativity of advertising agencies in the US, Canada and the UK, and Fernald and Solomon (1987) compared male and female entrepreneurs in Florida. According to West (1993), the work patterns and activities for creative teams were very similar in the US, Canada and the UK. Put briefly, the effect of working in different agencies and countries on creativity was seen a positive thing for all countries (93 per cent for all three countries). Also, working on creative problems in the morning was rated higher than working on them in the afternoon or evening. Most of the participants (61 per cent) felt that professional awards were positive influences on their creative work, which is intriguing given the oft-cited *overjustification effect* (whereby rewards can distract from creativity).

Correlational research on creativity

As the name 'correlational' implies, this kind of research focuses on relationships. Such research is extremely useful because it can ensure that predictions of creative performances are as accurate as possible. If a test score is highly correlated with some index of actual creative performance, for example, it can be employed as a predictor or indicator of future performances. Correlational research is also useful when examining what is unique about creativity and creative persons. As we will see below, creativity is not strongly correlated with general intelligence, and educators can take that correlation to indicate that they should look for creative talents even in students who are not at the top of the class or whose academic performances are less than superior. Correlational research can also be used when relationships are of interest, such as those between parents' interests or family background and the development of creative talents.

The correlation coefficient is especially useful because it indicates the degree to which two variables or sets of variables co-vary. The direction of relationship is suggested by the sign of the coefficient. A positive correlation thus indicates that two things co-vary; when one is at a high level, the other is also at a high level. Negative relationships are inverse; one trait is at a high level only when the other trait under study is at a low level. Only certain kinds of data (i.e. those on a continuous scale) can be analysed with correlational techniques. Continuous data (e.g. ratio or interval scales) can be correlated; nominal scale data (mere categories, such as ethnicity) cannot. Very importantly, a statistically significant correlation does not say anything about cause and effect. Correlation is only one of several preconditions for causality (Gay & Airasian, 2003).

Still, research of this sort is very useful and enormously popular. This is especially true given the fact that different correlation coefficients can be used with different kinds of data. A *product moment correlation* can be computed for research with two variables (often a predictor and criterion, but alternatively an independent and dependent variable), *multiple regression* with several predictors of one criterion, or *canonical correlations* when there are several predictors and several criteria. There are even non-parametric methods that can be used if the statistical assumptions are not met by the data in question. Examples of each of these are easy to find and have clear messages about the nature of creativity.

A large number of correlational studies have examined the relationship between general intelligence and creativity. One view is that the correlation between creativity and intelligence is negligible. Another view is that there is a positive correlation between the two. If data support the first of these views, educators could expect to see students who are intelligent but not necessarily creative, and students who are creative but not necessarily academically advanced. A number of correlational studies have reported that the relationship between creativity and traditional intelligence tests is indeed insignificant or weakly positive (e.g. Helson, 1971; Hocevar, 1980).

An alternative is that there is a low but functional relationship between creativity and general intelligence. If this is the case, the question becomes, how much general intelligence is necessary for creative thinking? Torrance (1962) referred to *threshold theory*, with creativity highly correlated with IQ below 120, but weakly or not correlated with IQ above 120. Barron (1969) did not find a relationship between high IQ and creativity but found a correlation between average IQ and creativity. Guilford and Christensen (1973) also supported these results with data from school-age children. Runco and Albert (1986) did not find a significant relationship between IQ and various indices of divergent thinking in all IQ levels except the 131–145 IQ group. Preckel, Holling, and Wiese (2006) found a relationship between IQ and creativity; however, the correlations did not differ significantly in groups above and below 120 IQ. Note that multivariate correlational methods can be used to determine whether a relationship in one segment of a sample is different from that of a different segment of the sample. Such curvilinearity is found with quadratic variables computed specifically for a multiple regression.

One interesting extension of this work takes context (e.g. test administration) and setting (e.g. classroom) into account. Boersma and O'Bryan (1968), for example, investigated the relationship between creativity and intelligence under different testing conditions. Half of the student examinees received the Torrance Tests of Creative Thinking (TTCT) as if they were typical academic tests. The other students received the TTCT under a relaxed environment (e.g. sans evaluations, grades and time limits). There were no significant differences in intelligence between groups but the group that received the TTCT in the relaxed setting had significantly higher scores on creativity tests. When the correlation coefficients were examined, the relationship between creativity and intelligence was reduced in the relaxed environment. The message is clear: creative talents may not manifest themselves in settings where other, more traditional skills are emphasized.

Correlational research is often used to study the relationship of creative potential with characteristics and personality traits. MacKinnon (1965), for instance, reported a positive relationship between autonomy and creativity (also see Runco & Albert, 1985). Later, Griffin and McDermott (1998) revealed the relationship between creativity and rebelliousness and openness to experience. In addition, openness to fantasy and openness to aesthetic experience correlated with creative activity. Williams (2004) also found a positive correlation between creativity and openness to experience among non-academic employees of a large university. Openness to experience was positively correlated with divergent thinking, and with supervisors' and co-workers' ratings of creativity. Sheldon (1995) found creativity to be correlated with both autonomy and the personality trait labelled *self-determination*. Prabhu, Sutton, and Sauser (2008) reported that creativity was significantly and positively correlated with *intrinsic motivation* and significantly but negatively correlated with *extrinsic motivation*. Creativity was also significantly correlated with *openness to experience* and *self-efficacy*. The correlation between creativity and *perseverance* was not significant.

Joy (2008) studied sixty-eight undergraduate students to examine the relationship between personality and creativity in art and writing. When students' lyric poems were evaluated, number of words in the poem was significantly and positively correlated with *maladjustment* and number of words used only once was significantly and positively correlated with *need to be different, subjective distress* and *maladjustment. Need to be different* correlated significantly with *originality of imagery and style.* Originality of the drawings was significantly correlated with *need to be different, psychoticism* and *maladjustment.* Experts' judgements of drawings for creativity also significantly correlated with *need to be different, maladjustment* and *subjective distress.* Generalizations to other samples are limited, given the reliance on undergraduates, but then again other research confirms that originality sometimes has a cost. Since originality implies that the person is in some way unusual, it is not hard to see why there may be asocial correlates. After all, the original person is not conventional and may even be non-conforming or a contrarian.

Chavez-Eakle, Lara, and Cruz-Fuentes (2006) studied creativity and personality among thirty highly creative people, thirty staff and graduate students in a university in Mexico, and thirty psychiatric outpatients. Analyses indicated that both verbal and figural TTCT scores of the participants were significantly correlated with novelty seeking, harm avoidance, persistence and self-directedness.

Thus, correlational studies indicate that creativity is related to a wide array of traits. Some are socially desirable and some undesirable. The direction of correlations is meaningful, the positive ones being indicative of traits that may support creativity, and the negative ones indicative of possible hindrances. Still, correlational research is not sufficient evidence of causality. Correlational findings should probably only be put into practice if they fit well with other quantitative research findings, such as those generated in experimental investigations.

Experimental research

Experimental research is characterized by manipulation and control. The overarching objective is to eliminate possible confounding variables in order to as clearly as possible identify actual causes (not just correlates). Unlike most other methodologies, experimental research concerns itself with 'induced changes in performance . . . [creativity is] something which can change or be changed within an individual rather than as something that varies among individuals' (Hyman, 1964, p. 70). This suggests a clear distinction from the psychometric view, explored later in this chapter, for unlike the experimental approach, psychometric research is intended to identify abilities and traits that vary in degree from individual to individual.

The primary strength of experimentation is that causality can be determined. (Indeed, unlike Gay and Anastasia, 2003, we are combining causal-comparative and experimental research.) One drawback is that whatever is uncovered in experimental research might not apply outside the experimental setting. A second drawback is that experimental research tends to concern itself with immediate influences. It rarely takes long-term or distant influences (e.g. family background, culture, values) into account. Later in this chapter, the historiometric approach is summarized. It is suited to culture and long-term influences. A related concern about experimental research is that only certain parts of the creativity syndrome can be studied experimentally. There may be critical components of creativity that cannot be brought into the laboratory. Keep in mind that creativity sometimes involves spontaneity and various forms of autonomy (e.g. freedom of thought), and these are lost with experimental control.

Still, the range of experimental foci is impressive. One comprehensive review (Runco & Sakamoto, 1996) of reviewed experimental studies on creativity found experimental support for the following:

- Creativity is often manipulated via information. That information is often intended to communicate as explicitly as possible something about creativity or about appropriate tactics for behaving in a creative manner. Experimental research since that review was completed supports this same conclusion (Runco, 2007).
- Reactions to experimental manipulations are moderated by individual differences in attitudes, personality and values.
- Creative solutions that depend on insight may be manipulated but do not support the Gestalt view that there is an all-at-once and sudden 'ah ha!'.
- Both *procedural* and *declarative* knowledge may contribute to creative work (the former manipulated via the presentation of tactics, the latter via factual information).
- The non-verbal aspects of creativity can be manipulated. This may help educators who have students with strengths outside the language arts. Imagery, for example, may be facilitated.
- Intuition has been manipulated in several experimental studies (Bowers, Regehr, Balthazard, & Parker, 1990; Jausovec, 1989; Metcalfe, 1986).
- Creative thinking seems to benefit from a broad attention.
- It is also related to certain kinds of affect. For some people, tension leads to creative thinking. Positive affect may also contribute to creative thinking, though here it depends on the kind of work or task at hand. It is also possible that there is a kind of emotional flexibility that is related to creativity. This would explain why creative individuals sometimes suffer from mood disorders, though the idea here is that it is the swing or shift of mood more than the mood itself.
- Although intrinsic motivation is clearly tied to originality, extrinsic factors sometimes assist creativity.

Quantitative research findings are the most convincing when there is triangulation. Findings from any one approach should fit with theoretical predictions, but it is also convincing if they fit with results from investigations using other methodologies.

There are a number of such bridges between the experimental and non-experimental research on creativity. One is that the influences on creativity that were manipulated and measured in experimental research tend to have optimal levels. More is not better. Optima have been reported in experimental, psychometric, cognitive, educational, developmental, and psycho-economic research on creativity (Runco & Sakamoto, 1995). One example of an optimum was given above: It is probably good to have a moderate amount of general intelligence, but a very high IQ is not necessary and may even indicate that the individual gives too much weight to conventional thinking and has difficulty with original thinking.

A second example, and one that can be easily applied to the classroom, involves autonomy. That is one of the core characteristics of creativity, and no wonder. It probably makes it easy to be original if a person is autonomous. But if the individual is too autonomous, he or she will probably not bother to take others into account, work with others and share ideas. This will create problems in the classroom and, in some ways, make it difficult to behave is a fashion that is creative in a way that others will appreciate.

Meta-analysis

Meta-analyses provide an overall picture of creativity by compiling what has been reported in previous studies. The data in a meta-analysis are the results of previous studies. The aim, then, is to summarize the findings of many research studies into a single statistic. Admittedly, statistics can appear to be impractical; and for that reason meta-analyses may seem to be least useful of the methodologies reviewed in this chapter. But there is a practical implication: meta-analyses provide highly reliable and trustworthy findings. If they are findings about practical principles or creative processes, they are useful. Think of it this way: they are statistics but may very well ensure that the best practical decisions are reached. This view about the practicality of meta-analytic results is supported by the fact that most meta-analyses in creativity studies have focused on enhancement and educational research. Before we summarize what the meta-analyses have concluded, a bit more about the standardization processes and generalizability should be presented.

Meta-analysis averages results of the previous studies on a particular topic. Results from each previous study are statistically standardized so they are comparable. Meta-analyses include as many previous studies as possible but the results will be influenced by the studies included and therefore by criteria used to select or omit previous research. Some meta-analyses exclude dissertation reports or unpublished studies (Gay & Airasian, 2003; Fagard, Staessen, & Thijs, 1996). Along the same lines, meta-analysis is possible only after a sufficient number of studies have been conducted in the field. It is therefore not helpful for a recently identified issue.

The most important characteristic of the meta-analysis is that results from each study are translated into an *effect size*, and these are then averaged (Gay & Airasian, 2003). There are different opinions, but according to Cohen (1969), 0.20 is a small effect size, 0.50 is medium and 0.80 is large.

Rose and Lin (1984) employed meta-analysis to examine the effectiveness of long-term creativity training programmes. The overall mean effect size for creative training on all components was only moderate (0.47) according to Cohen's standards. However, impact of training programmes was higher on verbal creativity (0.596) than on figural creativity (0.372). Training had the greatest impact on originality scores for both verbal and figural creativity (0.693 and 0.426, respectively). Rose and Lin pointed out that Creative Problem Solving (CPS) had the most consistent effect on TTCT scores (0.629). Twenty years later, Scott, Leritz, and Mumford (2004) examined seventy studies and reported an overall effect size of 0.68. The largest effect sizes obtained were for divergent thinking (0.75) and problem solving (0.84). When the effect size of the components of divergent thinking was examined, originality produced the largest effect size (0.81), and elaboration produced the smallest (0.54).

Ma (2009) described the effect size of different kinds of enhancement efforts. He was able to examine 2,013 effect sizes from 111 previous studies. The unweighted grand mean effect size of the 111 studies was 0.69 and the weighted grand mean effect size was 0.72. These are very close to the large effect size cut-off. The mean effect sizes on the four categories of creativity were 0.45 for non-verbal creativity, 0.79 for verbal creativity, 0.86 for problem solving and 0.34 for emotional creativity. These results are encouraging in that they imply that creativity is influenced by enhancement and education efforts. Other meta-analyses have examined the relationship of creativity to intelligence (Kim, 2008), mood (Davis, 2009), imagery (LeBoutillier & Marks, 2003) and environmental climate (Hunter, Bedell, & Mumford, 2007).

Historiometric studies

Historiometry has been defined as 'the application of quantitative methods to archival data about historic personalities and events to test *nomothetic* hypotheses about human thought, feeling, and action' (Simonton, 1999, p. 815). Nomothetic hypotheses focus on universals, or at least generalizations, across groups. They are in contrast to idiographic hypotheses, which apply to individuals. Practically speaking, both nomothetic and idiographic research findings can be useful for educators and others interested in understanding and perhaps enhancing creative talents.

Historiometric studies utilize various sources of data, including encyclopedias, biographical dictionaries and anthologies. Objective data are vital because the interest is in identifying nomothetic laws that are not dependent on any one particular place, person or era. A significant advantage of historiometric data is the reliance on unobtrusive measures that are not influenced by the controls of a laboratory or psychometric technique. Disadvantages include the use of historical records. If those contain objective and reliable data, meaningful analyses are possible. If not, nothing much can be done; more data cannot be collected. Additionally, there are questions that are not amenable to archival study. Consider the role of mood in creativity. What if definitions of mood or affective disorders have been developed after the historical data have been collected? Last is that historiometric research is laborious. The data are often scattered around the libraries, records, encyclopedias and selected books (Simonton, 1999).

One of the earliest historiometric studies was conducted by Cox (1926). She used biographical data to estimate the IQs of 301 individuals. The parents of the 301 individuals tended to be of above-average intelligence, so Cox inferred a strong hereditary impact on talent. She also concluded that talents might not be fulfilled without superior environmental advantages. Notably, her calculation of IQ was somewhat subjective: she estimated the IQ scores by comparing intellectual achievements to those of more typical peers, which is a common comparative method, but Cox had only biographical and not actual performance data.

Simonton (1976) reanalysed Cox's (1926) data, but looked to the relationship between ranked eminence of creators and leaders and developmental (father's status, intelligence and education) and productive (versatility, lifespan eminence and vocational choice) variables. Results indicated that ranked eminence had no relationship with father's status. Creators were more intelligent than leaders. Intriguingly, Simonton described how precocious geniuses might motivate others to keep records, in which case there are data about them that may not be available for persons who do not push to have their lives recorded. Also important was that, among creators, education was related to reputation, but only up to a point. Simonton described this as a curvilinear inverted-U function. The relationship was actually negative for the leaders.

Simonton (1991) also tested Galton's (1869) theory of genius. This holds that people vary in their natural intellectual ability (g) and that this ability determines eminence and social recognition. Simonton compared 28 presidents, 2,012 philosophers, 772 artists,

696 composers and a subset of 92 composers and concluded that the single-factor model, relying on g, provided a precise and parsimonious explanation and was superior to other theories and models.

Runco *et al.* (in press) focused on 1,004 eminent persons whose biographies had previously been examined by Ludwig (1995). They used a method that is regularly used in biographical studies to estimate reputation: they counted the number of sentences allocated to any one person in the *Encyclopaedia Britannica*. The 1891 and 2002 editions were compared using these counts. Most important was that there were differences between the two editions, indicating that reputations are not stable. Although this brings into question the stability, and therefore reliability, of reputation as a historiometric index, it does not mean that reputations (and historical data) are useless. In fact, a more recent study (Runco, Acar, & Kaufman, submitted for publication) reported that reputation in biographical sources is related to educational level, moodiness, presence of psychopathology, and various other qualities and attributes.

As an example of historiometric investigation of socio-cultural context, consider Simonton's (1975) study of creative role models, cultural diversity, political fragmentation, imperial instability, political instability, war and cultural persecution on eminence. He collected information concerning approximately 5,000 creative individuals from history texts, anthologies and biographical dictionaries. He divided creativity into two sorts: discursive creativity consisted of science, philosophy, literature and musical composition, and presentational creativity consisted of painting, sculpture and architecture. Time series and regression analyses showed that role-model availability was related to presentational creativity. Political fragmentation influenced both kinds of creativity. Imperial instability influenced discursive creativity.

Some historiometric investigations focus on products rather than on people. Martindale (1990), for example, examined American poetry from 1750 to 1950. He divided that period into twenty-year intervals and, using his own theory of the creative process, quantified patterns of arousal potential, primordial content and stylistic changes. Analyses indicated that the first of these showed a linear increase, while primordial content showed a significant but non-linear trend. Stylistic changes were very clear beginning at 1800 and continuing until 1890. Martindale also found that a consistently decreasing number of emotional words appeared in American poetry during this period.

One final example of historiometric work should be given. That is because it examined one particular work. Simonton (2007) examined Picasso's sketches for *Guernica* in order to test the idea that artistic work represents a Darwinian process or expertise-driven process. The former would imply that the sketches reflect a process of blind variation and selective retention, and are therefore non-monotonic. The latter contends that the sketches exhibit a systematic and monotonic improvement: each consecutive sketch is another step towards the goal and at each step, sketches indicate a sharpening of the idea. To compare the two views, one pro-Darwinian judge examined the sketches, along with two anti-Darwinian judges and two neutral raters. The ratings suggested a consensus among judges and indicated that the process was non-monotonic or Darwinian. Only one figure showed monotonic progress, while the others did not exhibit an upward trend. These findings suggested that sometimes creative work is blind rather than well planned and directed. Surely, additional research should be conducted to replicate the findings from the study of *Guernica*. As an aside, the products of students and children have also been studied in quantitative research. This is not historiometric, but the use of products makes it highly objective. It is interesting that in one of these investigations, judgements about the creativity of artwork given by professional artists seemed to be less useful than judgements about the same artwork given by students themselves (Runco, McCarthy, & Svenson, 1994).

Psychometric studies

Think for a moment how often paper-and-pencil tests are used in American schools. Those tests are useful only to the degree that they are psychometrically sound. Simply put, a good test is valid and reliable. That applies to all tests, including those used in the schools, as well as to creativity tests. Validity indicates that the test is measuring what you think it is measuring. Reliability indicates that it does so in a fair and consistent fashion.

Psychometrics has been labelled 'one of the few technological successes in psychology' (Kline, 1991, p. ix). It can be defined as 'the scientific study of patterns of correlations among various types of cognitive and biological measures and IQ' (Ceci, 1996, p. 403). Although use of psychometric methods in the literature goes back to the end of the nineteenth century (Barron & Harrington, 1981), it became dominant only with Guilford's (1950) presidential address to the American Psychological Association. Guilford's (1968) own work on the structure of the intellect (SOI) was especially influential. SOI theory was based on the factor-analytic conceptualization of human cognition and, of most relevance to the present discussion, the statistical separation of what Guilford called *divergent production* and *convergent production*.

The psychometric approach has several strengths. It is generally more objective than, say, self-reports or interviews. Those may be biased by verbal ability, memory or *socially desirable responding*. In fact, psychometric research is usually explicit about the *degree* of objectivity. This is supplied by reliability and validity coefficients. Also, the psychometric approach can be broadly applied. It can be used to study personality (e.g. Feist, 1999), creative cognition (e.g. Runco, 2007), social influences on creativity (e.g. Amabile, 1990), environmental correlates of creativity (Witt & Beorkrem, 1989), and so on. Drawbacks include the *criterion problem*. Put simply, there is no generally valid criterion against which creativity tests can be validated. In fact, for many purposes, if there were such a criterion, there would be no need for another test. A related concern is that creativity tests do not necessarily relate to creative behaviour as it actually occurs in the natural environment (Crockenberg, 1972; Gardner, 1983). The basis for this view is that true creativity may be intrinsically motivated and spontaneous, and neither of these things is possible when a person receives a test.

The most significant psychometric issue involves *discriminant validity* (Runco, 1999). The separation of creativity from general intelligence was frequently questioned twenty-five years ago, but the more recent issue of discrimination involves domain differences (Baer, 1994; Karmiloff-Smith, 1993; Plucker, 2004; Runco, 1987; Baer & Kaufman, 2005). A number of tests take task specificity into account, but some assume that there is a general creative talent.

The most commonly used test assesses divergent thinking (DT). DT tests are open-ended. They allow the examinee to produce a number of ideas; and these may be unique or unusual. Convergent thinking tests, in contrast, ask for conventional answers. Most academic tests are primarily convergent, which implies something about rewards opportunities for creativity in traditional classrooms.

DT tests allow fluency (numerous ideas), originality (unusual or unique ideas), flexibility (variety of ideas) and, sometimes, elaboration (extensions of one line of thought, or what

Guilford, 1967, p. 188 called 'added details to something already produced'). Fluency has been used by itself. Vosburg (1998), for example, used only fluency because it has high correlations with flexibility and originality (also see Hocevar, 1979). Yet originality is actually more important for creativity. Runco and Albert (1985) found that, in some samples, originality is reliable and offers unique information even when variance attributable to fluency has been statistically removed. It is not a good idea to use fluency alone.

Guilford (1967) described twenty-four distinct divergent production abilities, all with low correlations with IQ. Guilford did entertain the notion that some characteristics of IQ might be a prerequisite of divergent thinking. This would explain the 'threshold theory', which was mentioned earlier in the chapter (some general intelligence is necessary for high divergent thinking scores, but only up to a point, beyond which the two are unrelated).

Guilford's tests, including the Utility Tests (e.g. 'name as many uses as possible for a brick'), Consequences (e.g. 'What would be the consequences if none of us needed food any more?'), Sketches ('Draw as many objects as possible' using a basic figure, such as a circle), Name Grouping (e.g. number of syllables, starts with a vowel) and Figure Production (e.g. add a line to the figure to create a new one), were usually administered with time limits. This is another controversial point. Time may distract an examinee and keep him or her from fully exploiting an original line of thought. There are clear implications of this for the classroom.

Mednick (1962) developed the Remote Association Test (RAT) after going into detail about the role of associations in creative thinking. The basic idea is that when we think divergently, one idea leads to another, and another, and so on. Eventually a remote and original associate is found. The reliability of the RAT is more than adequate but its validity is inconclusive, and it is a highly verbal test. As such, it may have a verbal bias. Still, associative theory is useful, aside from the RAT. It even applies to DT. Wallach and Kogan (1965) cited Mednick, for example, in their work on the creativity of schoolchildren. They then modified Guilford's tests to facilitate associations. The DT scores were unrelated to intelligence and supported the idea that creative thinking is most likely when tests are presented without time limits and in a relaxed, game-like (rather than test-like) setting.

The Torrance Test of Creative Thinking (TTCT) is the most widely used and carefully studied DT test battery (Kaufman, Plucker, & Baer, 2008). This is in part a result of revisions of the test and longitudinal studies (summarized below). It is also helpful that the battery consists of Verbal and Figural sections and alternative forms. These allow comparative and pre-post treatment research.

There have been attempts to study DT using other kinds of measures. Auzmendi, Villa, and Abedi (1996), for example, developed a multiple-choice DT test 'to shorten the amount of time required for the administration and scoring' (Abedi, 2002, p. 267). Questions such as 'What would you do if you were solving a difficult problem?' are presented and examinees asked to choose from one of several options (e.g. ask the teacher or someone else for help; read a book on the subject; come up with my own answer). The multiple-choice format lends itself to standardized administration and makes scoring very straightforward, but validity is limited. That is no doubt because the multiple-choice format does not really allow ideation. Examinees do not really generate their own ideas.

Chand and Runco (1993) described realistic tests of DT, the idea being that examinees might put more effort into their ideas if the problems related to their experiences. One task read, 'It is a great day for sailing, and your friend, Kelly, asks you if you want to go sailing. Unfortunately, you have a big project due tomorrow, and it requires a full day to complete.

You would rather be sailing. What are you going to do? Think of as many ideas as you can.' It may be that realistic tests do interest examinees, but they also make it more likely that ideas will be drawn from memory and biased by experience, rather than spontaneous and truly original (Runco & Acar, 2010).

Williams's (1980) Creativity Assessment Package (CAP) also draws from theories of divergent thinking. It is scored for fluency, flexibility, originality, elaboration and titles. Examinees work on a series of frames in which they can draw. The CAP includes a test measuring Divergent Feeling as well as Divergent Thinking. The Williams Scale (also a part of the CAP) is intended to assess curiosity, complexity, imagination and flexibility. It allows ratings to be given by teachers and parents.

A key question for all of these tests is how well they relate to actual creative behaviour. One of the best ways to answer that question is to conduct a longitudinal study.

Longitudinal studies

Longitudinal studies are unique in that they collect data from the same individuals on several occasions in order to measure changes over time (Subotnik & Arnold, 1999). An advantage of longitudinal studies is that they provide a clear picture of development and change, and they may do so over a long period. The alternative method for addressing the same sorts of questions is cross-sectional (comparison of groups representing different ages, and therefore periods) and assumes that groups being compared are in fact comparable. This assumption is not necessary for longitudinal studies, though they are subject to attrition and require a tremendous investment on the part of both researcher and participant (Gay & Airasian, 2003).

Longitudinal studies are particularly useful for checking the predictive validity of a test or indicator: they can thus offer support for long-term predictions. A clear example of this is Torrance's longitudinal study, which began in the late 1950s. He collected data from approximately 400 children in two elementary schools in Minneapolis. The initial goal was to develop a test of creativity that is applicable to everyone from kindergarten to graduate school (Torrance, 1967). He probably did not know when he began, in 1958, that follow-up assessments would be reported fifty years later (Runco, Millar, Acar, & Cramond, in press).

TTCT scores were collected in 1958, along with a set of other indicators. In the first follow-up, Torrance (1969) reassessed the participants during high school. There were three criterion variables: creative quantity (the sum of weights assigned to the number of creative achievements), creative quality (rating of the originality of the creative achievements on a ten-point scale) and creative motivation (rating based on the student's vocational aspirations). The results showed that creative achievement was predicted by all four TTCT scores (for fluency, originality, flexibility and elaboration), though the elaboration index was not significantly related to creative quantity and creative motivation. Notably, other measures, including IQ tests, were not nearly as accurate as predictors as the TTCT.

A second follow-up was conducted twelve years after the first administration of the TTCT. Torrance (1972) used the same criteria but analysed the male and female data separately. Also, he used five scores, including both originality and inventive level. He found that all five scores were significantly correlated with all three criteria for both male and female participants. Oddly, the correlations were remarkably higher among males.

Torrance (1981) later asked whether scores from TTCT administered at the elementary school could predict actual creative achievement. This is an interesting question, with the recent separation of creative potential from creative performance (Runco, 2007). Torrance addressed it by collecting twenty-two years' follow-up data from 220 students. He again used the achievement measure, mentioned above. As predictor he focused on the Just Suppose Test. Results indicated that all five measures significantly correlated with TTCT scores for both males and females. IQ measures are correlated only with two or three of the criteria.

At odds with Torrance's longitudinal results, Kogan and Pankove (1974) reported negative evidence regarding predictive validity of divergent thinking tests. They did use a different test of DT (from Wallach and Kogan, 1965) but found that DT did not predict overall extra-curricular activities and accomplishments for fifth-grade students. There was a marginally significant correlation (and therefore prediction) for the tenth-grade students. There were also differences among schools. Kogan and Pankove (1972) revisited these data for a five-year follow-up and confirmed the differences among schools. Predictions were most accurate among small schools.

Howieson (1981) also examined predictions from the TTCT in an attempt to reconcile discrepant findings from Torrance's (1972) and Kogan and Pankove's (1974) longitudinal studies. Participants in Howieson's research were initially 12 years old, with the follow-up ten years later. Howieson used a self-report checklist as criterion of performance. Analyses showed that a creative group based on 1965 assessment showed a significantly higher performance than a non-creative group in art, writing, science, and generality of achievement, but not in music and leadership. Originality was isolated as the best single predictor of achievement. Looking just at the DT scores, fluency was more stable across the ten-year period for females, but for males it was originality. According to Howieson, the conflicting results from Torrance (1972) and Pankove and Kogan (1974) might be attributed to a sleeper effect whereby creativity potential is more clearly manifested later in life than earlier.

Cropley (1972), Cramond, Matthews-Morgan, Bandalos, and Zuo (2005), and Runco, Millar, Acar, and Cramond (in press) also reported longitudinal studies of DT. Cramond *et al.* (2005) used Torrance's data from the late 1950s in their forty-year follow-up. They were able to collect follow-up data from ninety-nine individuals. Along with the four predictor variables of creativity and IQ, presence of a mentor and the index of creativity consisting of the five indices in the previous studies were also included in the list of predictors. The criteria were quantity and quality of publicly recognized creative achievements. In this follow-up, they relied on a structural equation model. It provided a good fit with the data and supported the conclusion that the predictive validity of TTCT holds up even over a forty-year span.

Runco *et al.* (in press) recently extended this work by analysing the fifty-year follow-up data for TTCT from fifty-eight respondents. They found that TTCT scores were significantly correlated only with personal achievement, while an interaction of intelligence and creativity was significantly related only to public achievement. The composite of four DT indices showed a significant quadratic trend with the personal achievement criterion. When they examined data from Torrance's Beyonders Checklist, *love of work* and *tolerance of mistakes* were related to public achievement, and *minority of one* and *well-roundedness* were related with personal achievement. Men were significantly higher in public achieve-ment than women, but there was no significant gender difference in personal achievement.

Yamada and Tam (1996) and Plucker (1999) reported useful reanalyses of data from Torrance's longitudinal study.

It may come as a surprise that such a number of longitudinal studies of creativity have been completed. After all, they are time-consuming and can be expensive. Still, several very good longitudinal investigations have been reported, in addition to those just summarized. Milgram and Hong (1993) reported an eighteen-year follow-up of forty-eight individuals who had taken the Tel-Aviv Creativity Test, for example, and they found creativity test scores (but not intelligence) to be good predictions of leisure activity. Clapham, Cowdery, King, and Montang (2005) examined the predictive validity of the Owens Creativity Test (OCT) and the Structure of Intellect Learning Abilities Test (SOI-ELCT) with the criteria of creative self-assessment about work activities and patent submissions of engineering students fifteen years later. They found that the Owens Creativity Test was significantly correlated with both criteria while SOI-ELCT was not correlated. They explained the success of the OCT in that its items require the generating of ideas related to mechanics and including mechanical devices, whereas SOI-ELCT consisted of figural, semantic or symbolic ideas. Russ, Robins, and Christiano (1999) tested the theoretical link between pretend play and creativity with a four-year longitudinal study of thirty-one children. They measured pretend play at first and second grade, and divergent thinking and affect in fantasy four years later. They found that quality of fantasy and imagination exhibited at pretend play can predict future divergent thinking ability. Also, early DT scores predicted later DT scores. This provided some evidence for the stability of DT. However, affect in play did not predict creative activity.

Dollinger (2006) designed a seven-year longitudinal study about the use of photographic essays as an indicator of individualistic tendencies: a predictor of more creative lifestyles and placing a higher value on creativity. He found significant correlations between the ratings of photographic essays and creative achievements over the seven-year period. Stohs (1991) described an eighteen-year longitudinal study involving artists. She reported that artists with stable careers had more artistic endeavours and were paid much better that those with sporadic and disrupted careers. Also, they had more stable marriages. Interestingly, Stohs refuted the starving artists stereotype, concluding that at best it applied to one-third of the sample.

Getzels and Csikszentmihalyi (1976) followed thirty-one fine artists and discovered that various problem-finding actions (for artists, during a pre-drawing stage) were significantly related with success measured seven years later. This was a very important research finding, given what it says about problem finding (that which comes before problem solving, including problem identification and problem definition). It is also important that Getzels and Csikszentmihalyi worked with artists and artwork, not just divergent thinking of the solution of problems presented via paper and pencil.

Conclusions

Admittedly, several generalizations were made in this chapter. There is, for example, great variation among the different approaches, but also variation within each. Think back on all of the different ways that historiometric research was employed, for example, or how longitudinal studies were used to validate tests and examine predictive validity, to evaluate programmes and enhancement efforts, to examine changes in talent or its correlates that appear over time, and so on. It is often a generalization to describe any one quantitative method as if it includes only one kind of research or addresses only one question.

Creativity will probably never be fully understood if only quantitative research is conducted, but without a doubt the quantitative approach is useful. This is especially true if you stand back, as we have in this chapter, and consider what has been discovered with various methods, including experimental, correlational, longitudinal, and so on. Indeed, there is no one method that is most appropriate for understanding creativity. Each may offer something. Recall here that correlational research could be used to examine a large number of the components of the creativity complex, while experimental research offered information about actual causality. Longitudinal research addresses questions of development and maturation, and meta-analyses produce results that are based on all previous research rather than one sample of subjects. Each says something about creativity.

There is no one perfect method for the study of creativity. This is especially true given the need to define creativity as a complex; each facet of that complex (personality, cognitive skill, affect, motivation, meta-cognition) may each best be examined with a unique approach, an approach that is best suited for that particular facet of creativity. Also, creative performances are difficult to define. This has led to the criterion problem mentioned on p. 162 (Vernon, 1970; Runco, 2007).

One overarching problem is that creativity requires originality; and originality is by definition something new. The trick with research on creativity, then, is to use existing methods with something that may be entirely new! With this in mind, it is best to avoid debating the best approach, theory or method. It is best to recognize the challenge and complexity of creativity and to look to the various methods as complementary. Recall here the point about bridges among research findings and how many experimental results fit well with non-experimental findings.

Educators will most likely be as interested in the practical implications of the quantitative results as they are in the limitations and strengths of the methods. For this reason, practical implications were underscored throughout this chapter. Recall here (1) the possibility that expectations held by parents and teachers influence creative behaviour; (2) that creative thinking may be most likely in open-ended tests, while traditional academic tests tend to be closed rather than open; (3) that time may be necessary for finding remote associates, and remote associates tend to be original, so time is good for creativity and should be provided when teachers expect their students to think creatively; (4) that originality of thought seems to be separate from fluency of ideas and from productivity; (5) that creativity may vary from domain to domain, depending on how it is defined; and (6) that creative thinking seems to be distinct from general intelligence. This last point suggests that we will not understand creativity unless we look specifically for creativity. To really understand creativity, it can be enormously helpful to employ quantitative methods or to look to results from research using sound quantitative methods.

References

Abedi, E. (2002). A latent-variable modeling approach to assessing reliability and validity of a creativity instrument. *Creativity Research Journal, 14*, 267–276.

Aljughaiman, A., & Mowrer-Reynolds, E. (2005). Teachers' conceptions of creativity and creative students. *Journal of Creative Behavior, 39*, 17–34.

Amabile, T. M. (1990). Within you, without you: The social psychology of creativity and beyond. In M. A. Runco & R. S. Albert (Eds.), *Theories in creativity* (pp. 61–91). Newbury Park, CA: Sage.

Auzmendi, E., Villa, A., & Abedi, J. (1996). Reliability and validity of a newly-constructed multiple-choice creativity instrument. *Creativity Research Journal, 9*, 89–95.

Baer, J. (1994). Divergent thinking is not a general trait: A multi-domain training experiment. *Creativity Research Journal, 7*, 35–46.

Baer, J., & Kaufman, J. C. (2005). Bridging generality and specificity: The amusement park theoretical (APT) model of creativity. *Roeper Review, 27*, 158–164.

Barron, F. (1969). *Creative person and creative process.* New York: Holt, Rinehart & Winston.

Barron, F., & Harrington, D. (1981). Creativity, intelligence, and personality. *Annual Review of Psychology, 32*, 439–476.

Boersma, F. J., & O'Bryan, K. (1968). An investigation of the relationship between creativity and intelligence under two conditions of testing. *Journal of Personality, 36*, 341–348.

Bowers, K. S., Regehr, G., Balthazard, C., & Parker, K. (1990). Intuition in the context of discovery. *Cognitive Psychology, 22*, 72–110.

Ceci, S. J. (1996). General intelligence and life success: An introduction to special themes. *Psychology, Public Policy, and Law, 2*, 403–417.

Chand, I., & Runco, M. A. (1993). Problem finding skills as components in the creative process. *Personality and Individual Differences, 14*, 155–162.

Chavez-Eakle, R. A., Lara, M. C., & Cruz-Fuentes, C. (2006). Personality: A possible bridge between creativity and psychopathology? *Creativity Research Journal, 18*, 27–38.

Clapham, M. M., Cowdery, E. M., King, K. E., & Montang, M. A. (2005). Predicting work activities with divergent thinking tests: A longitudinal study. *Journal of Creative Behavior, 39*, 149–167.

Cohen, J. (1969). *Statistical power analysis for the behavioral sciences.* New York: Academic Press.

Cox, C. M. (1926). *The early mental traits of three hundred geniuses.* Stanford, CA: Stanford University Press.

Cramond, B., Matthews-Morgan, J., Bandalos, D., & Zuo, L. (2005). A report on the 40-year follow-up of the Torrance Tests of Creative Thinking: Alive and well in the new millennium. *Gifted Child Quarterly, 49*, 283–291.

Creswell, J. W. (2005). *Educational research: Planning, conducting, and evaluating quantitative and qualitative research* (2nd ed.). Berkeley, CA: Courier/Kendallville.

Crockenberg, S. B. (1972). Creativity tests: A boon or boondoggle for education? *Review of Educational Research, 42*, 27–45.

Cropley, A. J. (1972). A five-year longitudinal study of the validity of creativity tests. *Developmental Psychology, 6*, 119–124.

Davis, M. A. (2009). Understanding the relationship between mood and creativity. *Organizational Behavior and Human Decision Processes, 108*, 25–38.

Dollinger, S. J. (2006). Autophotographic individuality predicts creativity: A seven-year follow-up. *Journal of Creative Behavior, 40*, 111–124.

Fagard, R. H., Staessen, J. A., & Thijs, L. (1996). Advantages and disadvantages of the meta-analysis approach. *Journal of Hypertension, 14*, 9–13.

Feist, G. J. (1999). Personality in scientific and artistic creativity. In R. J. Sternberg (Ed.), *Handbook of human creativity* (pp. 273–296). Cambridge: Cambridge University Press.

Feist, G. J., & Runco, M. A. (1993). Trends in the creative literature: an analysis of research in the *Journal of Creative Behavior* (1967–1989). *Creativity Research Journal, 6*, 271–286.

Fernald, L. W., & Solomon, G. T. (1987). Value profiles of male and female entrepreneurs. *Journal of Creative Behavior, 21*, 234–247.

Firestien, R. L., & Lunken, H. P. (1993). Assessment of the long term effects of the Master of Science Degree in Creative Studies on its graduates. *Journal of Creative Behavior, 27*, 188–199.

Fryer, M., & Collings, J. A. (1991). British teachers' views of creativity. *Journal of Creative Behavior, 25*, 75–81.

Galton, F. (1869). *Hereditary genius: An inquiry into its laws and consequences.* London: Macmillan/Fontana.

Gardner, H. (1983). *Frames of mind: The theory of multiple intelligences.* New York: Basic Books.

Gay, L. R., & Airasian, P. (2003). *Educational research: Competencies for analysis and applications* (7th ed.). Berkeley, CA: Carlisle Communications.

Getzels, J. W., & Csikszentmihalyi, M. (1976). *The creative vision: A longitudinal study of problem finding in art.* New York: Wiley.

Griffin, M., & McDermott, M. R. (1998). Exploring a tripartite relationship between rebelliousness, openness to experience and creativity. *Social Behavior and Personality, 26,* 347–356.

Guilford, J. (1950). Presidential address to the American Psychological Association. *American Psychologist, 5,* 444–454.

Guilford, J. P. (1967). *The nature of human intelligence.* New York: McGraw-Hill.

Guilford, J. P. (1968). *Intelligence, creativity and their educational implications.* San Diego, CA: Robert Knapp.

Guilford, J. P., & Christensen, P. R. (1973). The one-way relation between creative potential and IQ. *Journal of Creative Behavior, 7,* 247–252.

Helson, R. (1971). Women mathematicians and the creative personality. *Journal of Consulting and Clinical Psychology, 36,* 210–220.

Hocevar, D. (1979). Ideational fluency as a confounding factor in the measurement of originality. *Journal of Educational Psychology, 71,* 191–196.

Hocevar, D. (1980). Intelligence, divergent thinking, and creativity. *Intelligence, 4,* 25–40.

Howieson, N. A. (1981). Longitudinal study of creativity: 1965–1975. *Journal of Creative Behavior, 15,* 117–135.

Hunter, S. T., Bedell, K. E., & Mumford, M. D. (2007). Climate for creativity: A quantitative review. *Creativity Research Journal, 19,* 69–90.

Hyman, R. (1964). Creativity and the prepared mind: The role of information and induced attitudes. In C. W. Taylor (Ed.), *Widening horizons in creativity* (pp. 69–79). New York: Wiley.

Jausovec, N. (1989). Affect in analogical transfer. *Creativity Research Journal, 2,* 255–266.

Joy, S. P. (2008). Personality and creativity in art and writing: Innovation, motivation, psychoticism, and (mal)adjustment. *Creativity Research Journal, 20,* 262–277.

Karmiloff-Smith, A. (1993). Is creativity domain-specific or domain-general? Clues from normal and abnormal development. *AISB Quarterly on Artificial Intelligence and Creativity, 85,* 26–31.

Kaufman, J. C., Plucker, J. A., & Baer, J. (2008). *Essentials of creativity assessment.* New York: Wiley.

Kim, K. H. (2008). Meta-analyses of the relationship of creative achievement to both IQ and divergent thinking test scores. *Journal of Creative Behavior, 42,* 106–130.

Kline, P. (1991). *Intelligence: A psychometric view.* London: Routledge.

Kogan, N., & Pankove, E. (1972). Creative ability over a five-year span. *Child Development, 43,* 427–442.

Kogan, N., & Pankove, E. (1974). Long-term predictive validity of divergent thinking tests. *Journal of Educational Psychology, 66,* 802–810.

LeBoutillier, N., & Marks, D. F. (2003). Mental imagery and creativity: A meta-analytic review study. *British Journal of Psychology, 94,* 29–44.

Ludwig, A. M. (1995). *The price of greatness.* New York: Guilford Press.

Ma, H. H. (2009). The effect size of variables associated with creativity: A meta-analysis. *Creativity Research Journal, 21,* 30–42.

MacKinnon, D. (1965). Personality and the realization of creative potential. *American Psychologist, 20,* 273–281.

Martindale, C. (1990). *The clockwork muse: The predictability of artistic change.* New York: Basic Books.

Mednick, S. A. (1962). The associative basis of the creative process. *Psychological Review, 69,* 220–232.

Metcalfe, J. (1986). Feeling of knowing in memory and problem solving. *Journal of Experimental Psychology: Learning, Memory, and Cognition, 12,* 288–294.

Milgram, R. M., & Hong, E. (1993). Creative thinking and creative performance in adolescents as predictors of creative attainments in adults: A follow-up study after 18 years. *Roeper Review, 15*, 135–139.

Mohan, M. (1973). Is there a need for a course in creativity in teacher education? *Journal of Creative Behavior, 7*, 175–186.

Plucker, J. (1999). Is the proof in the pudding? Reanalyses of Torrance's (1958 to present) longitudinal data. *Creativity Research Journal, 12*, 103–114.

Plucker, J. (2004). Generalization of creativity across domains: Examination of the method effect hypothesis. *Journal of Creative Behavior, 38*, 1–12.

Prabhu, V., Sutton, C., & Sauser, W. (2008). Creativity and certain personality traits: Understanding the mediating effect of intrinsic motivation. *Creativity Research Journal, 20*, 53–66.

Preckel, F., Holling, H., & Wiese, M. (2006). Relationship of intelligence and creativity in gifted and non-gifted students: An investigation of threshold theory. *Personality and Individual Differences, 40*, 159–170.

Rose, L. H., & Lin, H. (1984). A meta-analysis of long-term creativity training programs. *Journal of Creative Behavior, 18*, 11–22.

Runco, M. A. (1987). The generality of creative performance in gifted and nongifted children. *Gifted Child Quarterly, 31*, 121–125.

Runco, M. A. (1999). A longitudinal study of exceptional giftedness and creativity. *Creativity Research Journal, 12*, 161–164.

Runco, M. A. (2007). *Creativity theories and themes: Research, development, and practice.* Burlington, MA: Elsevier Academic Press.

Runco, M. A., & Acar, S. (2010). Do tests of divergent thinking have an experiential bias? *Psychology of Aesthetics, Creativity, and the Arts, 4*, 144–148.

Runco, M. A., Acar, S. & Kaufman, J. C. (2010). *Changes in reputation and relationships with game and biographical data.* Manuscript submitted for publication.

Runco, M. A., & Albert, R. S. (1985). The reliability and validity of ideational originality in the divergent thinking of academically gifted and nongifted children. *Educational and Psychological Measurement, 45*, 483–501.

Runco, M. A., & Albert, R. S. (1986). The threshold theory regarding creativity and intelligence: An empirical test with gifted and nongifted children. *Creative Child and Adult Quarterly, 11*, 212–218.

Runco, M. A., Kaufman, J. C., Halladay, L. R., & Cole, J. C. (in press). Change in reputation as index of genius and eminence. *Historical Methods.*

Runco, M. A., McCarthy, K. A., & Svenson, E. (1994). Judgments of the creativity of artwork from students and professional artists. *Journal of Psychology, 128*, 23–31.

Runco, M. A., Millar, G., Acar, S., & Cramond, B. (in press). Torrance tests of creative thinking as predictors of personal and public achievement: A fifty year follow-up. *Creativity Research Journal.*

Runco, M. A., & Okuda Sakamoto, S. (1995). Reaching creatively gifted children through their learning styles. In R. M. Milgram, R. Dunn, & G. E. Price (Eds.), *Teaching and counseling gifted and talented adolescents: An international learning style perspective* (pp. 103–115). New York: Praeger.

Russ, S. W., Robins, A. L., and Christiano, B. A. (1999). Pretend play: Longitudinal prediction of creativity and affect in fantasy in children. *Creativity Research Journal, 12*, 129–139.

Runco, M. A., & Sakamoto, S. O. (1996). Optimization as a guiding principle in research on creative problem solving. In T. Helstrup, G. Kaufmann, & K. H. Teigen (Eds.), *Problem solving and cognitive processes: Essays in honour of Kjell Raaheim* (pp. 119–144). Bergen: Fagbokforlaget Vigmostad & Bjorke.

Scott, G., Leritz, L. E., & Mumford, M. D. (2004). The effectiveness of creativity training: A quantitative review. *Creativity Research Journal, 16*, 361–388.

Sheldon, K. (1995). Creativity and goal conflict. *Creativity Research Journal, 8*, 299–306.

Simonton, D. K. (1975). Sociocultural context of individual creativity: A transhistorical time-series analysis. *Journal of Personality and Social Psychology, 32*, 1119–1133.

Simonton, D. K. (1976). Biographical determinants of achieved eminence: A multivariate approach to the Cox data. *Journal of Personality and Social Psychology, 33*, 218–226.

Simonton, D. K. (1990). History, chemistry, psychology, and genius: An intellectual autobiography of historiometry. In M. A. Runco & R. S. Albert (Eds.), *Theories of creativity* (pp. 92–115). Newbury Park, CA: Sage.

Simonton, D. K. (1991). Latent-variable models of posthumous reputation: A quest for Galton's *G. Journal of Personality and Social Psychology, 60*, 607–619.

Simonton, D. K. (1995). Exceptional personal influence: An integrative paradigm. *Creativity Research Journal, 8*, 371–376.

Simonton, D. K. (1999). Historiometry. In M. A. Runco & S. Pritzker (Eds.), *Encyclopedia of creativity* (Vol. 1, pp. 815–822). San Diego, CA: Academic Press.

Simonton, D. K. (2007). The creative process in Picasso's *Guernica* sketches: Monotonic improvements versus nonmonotonic variants. *Creativity Research Journal, 19*, 329–344.

Stohs, J. M. (1991). Young adult predictors and midlife outcomes of 'starving artists' careers: A longitudinal study of male fine artists. *Journal of Creative Behavior, 25*, 92–105.

Subotnik, R. E., & Arnold, K. D. (1999). Longitudinal studies of creativity. In M. A. Runco & S. Pritzker (Eds.). *Encyclopedia of creativity* (Vol. 2, pp. 163–168). San Diego, CA: Academic Press.

Torrance, E. P. (1962). *Guiding creative talent.* Englewood Cliffs, NJ: Prentice-Hall.

Torrance, E. P. (1967). The Minnesota studies of creative behavior: National and international extensions. *Journal of Creative Behavior, 1*, 137–154.

Torrance, E. P. (1969). Prediction of adult creative achievement among high school seniors. *Gifted Child Quarterly, 13*, 223–229.

Torrance, E. P. (1972). Predictive validity of the Torrance Tests of Creative Thinking. *Journal of Creative Behavior, 6*, 236–252.

Torrance, E. P. (1981). Predicting the creativity of elementary school children (1958–80) – and the teacher who 'made a difference.' *Gifted Child Quarterly, 25*, 55–62.

Vernon, P. E. (1970). *Creativity: Selected readings.* Harmondsworth, UK: Penguin Books.

Vosburg, S. K. (1998). The effects of positive and negative mood on divergent thinking performance. *Creativity Research Journal, 11*, 165–172.

Wallach, M. A., & Kogan, N. (1965). *Modes of thinking in young children: A study of the creativity–intelligence distinction.* New York: Holt, Rinehart & Winston.

West, D. (1993). Restricted creativity: Advertising agency work practices in the US, Canada and the UK. *Journal of Creative Behavior, 27*, 200–213.

Williams, F. (1980). *Creativity Assessment Packet.* Buffalo, NY: DOK.

Williams, S. D. (2004). Personality, attitude, and leader influences on divergent thinking and creative organizations. *European Journal of Innovation Management, 7*, 187–204.

Witt, L. A., & Beorkrem, M. (1989). Climate for creative productivity as a predictor of research usefulness and organizational effectiveness in an R&D organization. *Creativity Research Journal, 2*, 30–40.

Yamada, H., & Tam, A. Y. (1996). Prediction study of adult creative achievement: Torrance's longitudinal study of creativity revisited. *Journal of Creative Behavior, 30*, 144–149.

Chapter 15

From voice to choice

Evaluation and action research into creativity

Tony Cotton

Introduction

It is becoming relatively common for teachers to undertake action research as a way of changing their practice. It is also common for researchers to be asked to evaluate such action research programmes. The result is that researchers often find themselves trying to sort out whether they are researching the teacher learning that took place in and through the action research, or the changes that the teachers made as a result of that learning. Funders often want to hear about the latter, while researchers generally hold that the process that has produced this learning is at least as important, because it is teacher learning that leads to sustained change. Finding a way of reconciling these dilemmas can be challenging.

This chapter looks at one such case: the evaluation of a project called 'Voice to Choice', which aimed to re-engage disaffected learners across four community colleges through their involvement in opera workshops. The evaluation was commissioned by a local authority interested in the impact on student achievement of a series of creative workshops led by an opera company. Initially, a simplistic correlation between creative activity, engagement of previously disaffected students, and their achievements in school was posited. The chapter challenges this simplistic view and illustrates how the use of teacher action research can tell the story of 'what it is like to be here' from the young people's point of view and lead to a challenge to the way that schools are structured, rather than seeing creativity as an easy route to success. The evaluation employed collaborative, participatory and self-study methods that brought together evaluation, creativity and a form of action research.

Evaluation and democratic practices

Elliot Eisner (2005, p. 7) suggests that the conception of creativity has changed from its being seen as a 'mystical' talent shared by a few to being conceived as a capacity that can be developed in everyone and that can underpin every kind of human activity. His early life as a painter led him into developing the notion of research as connoisseurship and critique. His description of educational connoisseurship involves asking, and rigorously exploring, the question 'What is it like to be here?'

So for Eisner, creativity is not an optional extra, or a way of enhancing people's life experience. It is a fundamental part of human existence. This would suggest that the twin activities of teaching and research should also engage with the notion of creativity in terms of the experiences offered to our learners and the ways in which we research their experiences. If the research process itself is to be creative, it is likely to empower those engaged in the research. They will develop the skills of 'educational connoisseurship', leading them to come to understand the difference they are making through the decisions they take as teachers.

Eisner (1991, p. 72) suggests that the question 'What is it like to be here?' is non-trivial and that such a question can only be answered by researchers taking a careful and rigorous approach to qualitative research, an approach that takes the issue of 'voice' as primary. Schratz and Walker (1995, p. 14) argue that such democratizing of research challenges traditional relationships between researcher and researched: 'If we are to find ways to make research democratic then we have to find ways to break the mould that confines research to a highly selected group of specialists.' Eisner also argued for a democratic approach to research:

> The growing desire to engage teachers in the change process has led to the notion of 'teacher empowerment'. In general, the idea is that, as important stakeholders in what schools do, teachers need to have the authority to plan and monitor the quality of the educational process in their schools. The effort, in a sense is to democratize educational reform by giving teachers a say-so in what happens.
>
> (2005, p. 141)

This can be interpreted as a call for participatory action research.

In the 'Voice to Choice' evaluation, the research was conducted by the participants themselves – teachers in collaboration with each other – supported and mentored by a team from Nottingham Trent University in the UK, with the academic team being responsible for both conducting parallel research and synthesizing the research into a single report. Teachers were encouraged to work collaboratively with other staff and their students. In a sense, teachers carried out a piece of 'self-study' (see Loughran & Russell, 2002) in that they investigated their own practice and its effects, investigating themselves as, in Jack Whitehead's useful phrase, 'living contradictions, living out one's values' (Whitehead, 1989).

Self-study has evolved methods that enable it to be used by busy, initially untrained practitioners who learn to research 'on the job', continually refining their understanding and skills during the process. Particularly relevant to this project, such methods included creative processes in data collection, analysis and presentation. But this project involved not only self-study but also action research. Action research is a cyclical process of problem formulation, evidence collection, analysis and reformulation. The whole cycle is characterized by a critical reflectivity about the meaning of the data and about the possibilities for improving the particular lived situation. Since the researcher is the practitioner, the precise formulation of the problem to be investigated depends on the individual. This form of research is a very powerful means of engaging practitioners in change, including self-change. However, this aspect of the research was less visible in the evaluation, and thus teachers' learning appears in some aspects of the evaluation and not others.

In this evaluation, the research data included anecdotal records, field notes, descriptions, logs, questionnaires, interviews, tape recordings and still photographs (see Kemmis & McTaggart, 1988; Altrichter, Posch, & Somekh, 1993; Mitchell, Weber, & O'Reilly-Scanlan, 2005). Although the evaluation was based in part in the action research paradigm, the methods employed also showed an awareness of the creative process, and the writing offers creative nuance aiming to develop questions about the way the world *might be* rather than offer simplistic views of the way the world 'is'.

However, it was an evaluation. Drawing on the work of Tony Brown and Liz Jones, who explored action research through the lens of postmodernism, I would argue that

> research becomes the instrument through which we build and understand our practice, not to reach some higher plane of perfection, nor to be in touch with where we are in life, but rather to make explicit a reflective/constructive narrative layer that feeds, whilst growing alongside the life it seeks to portray.
>
> (Brown & Jones, 2001, p. 69)

The dilemma for an evaluator/researcher is thus how to (re)present the research/evaluation. How can we capture the creative process and comment on its 'effectiveness' against an unproblematized view that student engagement in creative projects leads to motivation and academic success? And this was the view that was held strongly by the commissioning group, the local education authority, and by senior members of staff in the schools. John Schostak (2002, p. 2) describes this paradox aptly when he suggests that 'the lived always seeks to be represented in some way and thus sacrifices the sense of life for the sense of meanings in order to relive'. We attempted to limit this sacrifice in reporting the evaluation through the use of exemplification through 'little stories' (Cotton & Griffiths, 2007), graphics to replicate the photographs selected by the participants to 'represent' the project, and an extended narrative.

The evaluation: flexibility and pragmatism

The Voice to Choice project took place in the context of an increasing influence of creativity within educational settings. Anna Reid and Peter Petocz (2004, p. 45) have suggested that creative teaching can be seen as a way of encouraging students 'to see the essence as well as the detail of the subject, to formulate and solve problems, to see the connectedness between diverse areas, to take in and react to new ideas'. This was largely the view that was taken within this project. The evaluation thus focused on three themes. These themes were developed in collaboration with the teachers and took as their starting point the aims of the project:

1   The project wished to explore the impact of creative learning on 'disaffected' learners' achievement. The teachers were interested in how this group of young people defined personal success and achievement. Data that were collected to explore this theme included questionnaire data from all the learners engaged in the workshop, data from focus-group interviews carried out by teachers, and individual interviews carried out by teachers.
2   The teachers also wanted to explore how the same learners defined effective teaching and learning; data from the same individual interviews and questionnaires supported this analysis.
3   Finally, we agreed it was important to explore the impact of the workshops on the students.

The process began with an evening session at which representatives from each college were introduced to the philosophy and practice of action research. This session also engaged the teachers in beginning to explore what creativity meant for them in terms of learning and teaching, and how they might measure success in the 'Voice to Choice' project. After this joint session, the teacher-researchers followed different paths. Two of the schools carried out pre and post interviews with a focus group of students. The pre interviews focused on students' definitions of success in school and their expectations of the project. The post workshop interviews revisited student perceptions of success and then focused on the student perceptions of the learning that had taken place in the workshops and how this had affected them in terms of their wider experience within school. One of the schools asked the students to keep a journal throughout the workshop experience.

At two of the colleges, the teachers supporting the workshops carried out case studies of six children. The members of this case-study group were observed by the teachers and interviewed before the workshops. They were also interviewed by the researcher after the workshops. An initial visit by the evaluation team supported the teachers in putting together interview schedules that focused on times when the children had felt successful in their learning, asking them to outline the characteristics of successful teachers. Although these learners had been characterized as 'disaffected' within school, the team felt it was important to explore how the school could support these learners in engaging with learning. This then allowed the evaluation to explore the characteristics of the opera workshop which met these learners' needs, as described by the learners themselves. These teachers also carried out pre and post workshop interviews as well as engaging in the photo-analysis described in a later section.

The teachers' reports showed that they valued both the process and the outcomes of these interviews. One teacher told me, 'It is a luxury to have thirty minutes to have a detailed conversation with the students. We don't normally have time to do this and it really makes you think about your own practice.' We can hear echoes of the underpinning philosophy of action research here – a genuine sense of having time and space to understand the impact of actions on individual learners.

In the third school, the teachers were unable to commit to supporting the evaluation process at all. The pragmatic solution for the evaluation team was to engage themselves as non-participant observers during the workshops. Detailed narrative observations were carried out. As these workshops took place after the process of analysis in the other two schools, the observation was a space both to take notice of the process of the workshop and to reflect on how this process met the stated needs of the students.

Measuring success

Funders expected that the project would produce measures of success for students. The evaluation team and the teacher-researchers were able to draw the criteria for measurement from the views and voices of the students involved in the project rather than by using a predetermined template.

The initial questionnaires, which were conducted only in the two colleges able to fully commit to the evaluation process, asked the students to identify someone they knew who was a successful learner and then describe the characteristics of this person and explore what it was that exemplified successful learning. They were also asked to describe a time when they themselves had been successful. These questions were then explored in more detail in individual interviews with a focus group of students. It was then possible to find common themes in students' measures of personal success, even if this success was exhibited by others in their schools.

The external evaluation team and the teachers then used the analysed data and the post-workshop interviews to explore the ways in which the opera workshop had met the students' definitions of successful learning and successful teaching. These themes were as follows:

I feel successful when I overcome a perceived weakness or a barrier to learning is removed

This criterion originated in students noticing their achievements in areas that they had assumed they would not be successful in. One student suggested that they remembered a time when they were successful in an information technology (IT) lesson. They said it made them 'feel proper', in contrast to their perceived view of themselves as a failure in IT. Similarly, another student described mathematics as an area that they had felt 'rubbish' about, but when they moved to a new teacher, 'it was great 'cause we, like, all worked together as group and I learned loads'.

Opera Trust met this criterion for the young people. One described the change in her view: 'When I first thought of opera, I thought of OLD movies . . . I never expected it to be as good as it was.' Another suggested, 'I thought opera was just for posh people but this is a life-changing experience.' By the end of the workshops, many students were excited by the new skills they had learned. Students described how they had learned 'new ways of singing' and said, 'I'm loads more confident in my singing now.' They could also describe the skills they had learned in some detail: 'I can get my pitch right now and my breathing helps me sing louder.'

Opera Trust also allowed many students to notice how they were developing, and how previous barriers to learning were coming down. For example, one student said, 'I have never sung in a performance, and this activity has helped me a lot to overcome my fear of singing in front of audiences.' Another suggested, 'When I first joined I was quiet and shy but on the second day I got more confident and joined in more.' Finally, one student who had been described as very shy and timid by his teacher said that by the end of the workshops he felt, in his own words, 'really loud and strong of myself.'

I feel successful when I can draw on personal experience to support learning, or when I can apply my learning outside school

This success criterion operated in two ways. First, students described feeling successful in school when they had been able to draw on their own experience in the classroom. For example, in a drama lesson, 'I acted out this part, which had a lot in common with my own family circumstances.' This was seen as success as it meant 'I could just let everything go and make the performance realistic'. Opera Trust was seen as supporting this as it allowed the students to devise scenes around their own interests and ideas. One of the students said, 'It was great because we could write our own songs and words.'

Second, students remembered successes or described success when remembering times at which learning had had a direct impact on their experiences and opportunities outside school. Successful students are those who 'can communicate with people; if she needed money to start a business she could get it', or the friend who 'did plumbing, and that will really help him in the future'. This image of success was not reflected in students' view of the Opera Trust workshops. In fact, the only students who were critical of the experience saw the process as irrelevant to their needs. This was particularly the case with the students at one school, who were described as being identified as 'gifted and talented'. These students were clear about what they needed from school: 'I'm going to be an art teacher so I need to do art A level and then go to university'; 'I'm going to open my own hairdressing salon so I need to get good GCSEs so I can go to college and get business training'. These students had opted out of the Opera Trust workshop after one or two sessions, as they saw it as irrelevant to their needs.

The following extract from my research journal exemplifies this:

> Julie only attended the first workshop. She had a very practical approach to school. She was very clear about her future too. She wants to go onto a hairdressing course – then go to University to study 'business' in order to set up her own salon. She couldn't see the point of the Opera Trust workshop. 'I suppose that if I was going to be a drama teacher it would have been worth going, or if I was going to be an actor but I'm not going to be a drama teacher so it was a bit pointless.' She was also very pragmatic about learning – 'If you want to learn you listen, if you don't you don't listen. It's your choice.' She also saw subjects in a hierarchy, describing Maths, English and Science as the most important subjects for getting on in life and getting a good career.
>
> (Personal research journal)

I feel successful when I can measure my achievement

Instant feedback and self-assessment were clear measures of success for the students. Examples of this would be gaining a swimming badge. 'I couldn't swim before I came to Southern and now I can.' Other examples were awards such as Duke of Edinburgh awards, or even attendance awards. All of these gave the students tangible rewards.

The Opera Trust workshop was deemed as successful measured against this criterion by the students, as the final production was a fixed endpoint in the process. They could measure the success of the final production by audience feedback which made it clear to them that they were indeed successful and had achieved. Their comments on the final performance suggest tangible feelings of pride: 'It was brilliant and came together really well.' 'The performance was great and I felt privileged to be involved.'

I feel successful when I am given responsibility

The final theme that came through in students' descriptions of success was the times when they felt as though they had been given personal responsibility. This might be for other people, for example 'I felt really good the day the Year 6 came down and I had to look after them', or responsibility for tasks, for example 'I'm really good in maths and get given loads of important jobs to do.'

The students suggested that the responsibility for coming up with ideas for the final production contributed to their feelings of success. They told me that they felt 'really proud' because 'I actually contributed to the final performance'. Another student said, 'I enjoyed coming up with our own songs which we sang in front of everybody else at the performance.'

Effective teaching and learning: what was learned from the Opera Trust workshop?

One of the aims for the project was to construct and implement a model of creative learning in informal and formal contexts to support student learning and professional development.

One student, Helen, had very clear views about the difference between teachers who supported her learning and those whom she didn't see as effective. My research journal describes our conversation:

> Helen spoke entirely in one-word answers. She couldn't look me in the eye. The most important thing for her had been that she had been allowed to work with her friends. Teachers don't normally let her work with her mates because they are disruptive. She particularly enjoyed picking one friend and being asked to work in a four with two people you did not know as well. She talked at most length about 'safe' and 'bait' teachers. She defined safe teachers as 'Safe teachers are those that you can talk to.' She described one safe teacher who did not even teach her. She only knew her because she taught next to a classroom that she was always sent out of.
>
> She chose to go to the sessions because all her friends had been asked to go and she wanted to be with her friends. She appeared very proud that she had attended all the sessions, even those that were held after school. She felt as though the sessions had made her more confident. She thought that teachers would say she was more confident in lessons now.
>
> (Personal research journal)

Thus, for Helen, teachers fell into two groups: 'safe' and 'bait'. The difference between the two groups was simple. Her safe teachers connected to her as an individual; she felt as though they trusted her and she would confide in them. She described this in detail although she didn't want the detail including in the report. She described the Opera Trust team as 'safe' teachers. This was supported by several other students, who described effective teachers as those who 'take care of you.'

This may seem an obvious point to make in terms of effective teaching. We clearly cannot learn if we do not feel 'cared for'; however, in terms of creativity, such 'care' may be seen as vital, as many of the students suggested that they felt quite nervous in the early stages of the process. Here personal support is important to allow learners to engage with the creative process. This care was also exhibited in understanding students at an individual level. One student described this when they said that the Opera Trust teachers were 'good because they get to know what you are like and give you the right work'. For this student, this contrasted with lessons in school when everybody 'is given the same stuff and just told to get on with it'. Similarly, students described lessons in which they felt as though they were not successful as those in which teachers did not seem to exhibit caring behaviours. For example, they felt they did not learn in lessons when teachers 'just shout at you and put you down', or when teachers 'just tell you what to do and then say, "Get on with it"'.

The interview data also suggested that teachers who showed themselves to be experts in their field and shared this expertise through an apprenticeship approach are valued by their learners. One of the teachers described a key moment in the workshops for him: 'The performers made the children stand very close to them. They then sang the "Hallelujah Chorus" at full volume and in close harmony. This blew the kids away.' Here teaching can be seen as a modelling process. The students are apprentices who are gradually inducted into a new community in which they too can become expert. This apprenticeship approach may be seen in contrast to a culture of facilitation or support in which teachers and children explore new areas of learning together, or alternatively a view of knowledge as something simply to be passed on to learners.

The same teacher described how the time constraints in the school timetable did not allow him to follow this model:

> The kids are always asking me to bring my trumpet in. I'm always saying 'yes' and I'm always forgetting. Well, I bring it in for the GCSE group. I suppose I think for the kids in the other groups – well, you don't want to show them Everest.

It may be an area for development to explore how such an apprenticeship might be developed in areas not traditionally seen as creative. How might students in a mathematics classroom experience teacher expertise and come to explore mathematics through the teacher modelling their known mathematical skills, for example? There is also the challenge for teachers who are engaged in teaching a wide range of students all day every day. As one teacher said, 'You couldn't work like that all the time. You would burn yourself out.'

Finally, the students also valued the collaborative approach to the project and described their most effective teachers in school as those who developed collaborative activity. One student described what was positive for her about Opera Trust in the following way: 'It's like a big conversation and you get involved. If you say something you can't really be wrong – you can argue.'

It is worth noting that the Opera Trust teaching process was seen by all students as positive and that students could all describe teachers in their formal schooling who operated in the same way. What is also interesting is that the positive practices were seen within individual teachers rather than attributed to particular subjects. So, mathematics was simultaneously 'bait' and 'safe', depending on which teacher was being described.

So, in summary, effective teaching as demonstrated within the Opera project can be seen as:

- offering care and personal support to learners;
- understanding and responding to learners as individuals;
- modelling skills and expertise and developing this in learners through an apprenticeship approach;
- developing and supporting collaborative activity in the classroom.

Exemplification through 'little stories'

The evaluation also needed to capture the ways in which both students and teachers learnt from the Opera experience. This section exemplifies the students' experience, using images from one of the workshops and the stories behind the images as told by the teachers. The workshops in one of the schools were documented by one of the teachers, who took over 150 digital images of the sessions. The students who attended the workshops were also given disposable cameras and asked to document the process for themselves. Both students and teachers were then taken through an analytical process by a researcher from Nottingham

Trent University. This process 'winnowed' the images until the single image which for the teacher and the students most powerfully described 'what it was like' to engage with the process was found.

The teachers were also interviewed by the evaluation team to get beneath these images and to find the stories that represented the successes of the workshop for them. In this chapter, these photographic images are replaced by graphical representations of the photograph. Using these representations serves two purposes. First, it anonymizes the photographs without losing the power held within the image. Second, it serves to generalize; the photograph ceases to represent a single moment in time and offers itself as an image that we can interrogate for ourselves. We may think, 'This reminds me of a time when . . . '

The image that was most powerful for the *students*, 'Three girls walking', is shown below. The students selected this one as for them it represented their memories of 'working all together' and 'making up our own song and learning to sing it'. These comments support the evidence from the interviews and the questionnaires that the students valued the chance to collaborate, to learn new skills and the way in which they were expected to take responsibility for the process. It also mirrors the view mentioned earlier that the students valued being able to draw on their own experience to devise and perform songs.

This is also a powerful image of ownership. The three young women stride confidently down the corridor in their school. The space is theirs; they are comfortable within the space and within themselves.

The following images were selected by the *teachers* through a careful selection process as representative of the success of the programme. All the images were given to the teachers from the school, who were then asked to select any images which for them resonated with the themes outlined earlier. Once we had a selection of images, they were then asked to work as a group to select the single image that 'best' described the project viewed through the lens of a specific aim. Once the image had been selected, the teachers offered a rationale for the choice in terms of the story behind the image. The following 'little stories' can be seen as representing the memories that remain at the end of such a creative project. These memories are often retold after such creative projects and become the living evaluations of success.

The first is 'Simeon and his dog':

Simeon never made the final production but he did get really heavily involved. It is a really interesting case. He doesn't usually get involved in this sort of thing but I think he came this time because I'm his tutor. He got really heavily involved with Tim because Tim had a dog and Simeon is really into his dog. He often sits separately in school and he still sits reasonably separately; he wasn't always included but he doesn't look like a victim. He looks confident, not like some kids do when they are separate. He's still not part of a team, though. He came in with his dog later to show Tim; it was hugely important to him. He'd never done anything like that before. It was a real social experience for him. And then he didn't get to the final performance because he forgot. It didn't seem to bother him, though.

This image was selected to exemplify the promotion of social inclusion. The story tells of a young man who is on the edges of inclusion in school and although not entirely included within the creative process, used the process to develop relationships with other adults that became very important to him. This relationship with one of the Opera Trust workers has continued by email. For Simeon, the process supported him in learning how to build on positive relationships he already has, in this case with his form tutor, and to use this confidence to make important connections with new people. It is the story of a small success, one which might go unnoticed, but an experience that may be formative for the young man involved.

The next images may be called 'Finding voice':

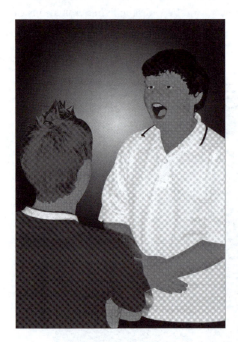 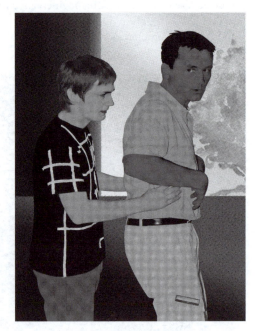

It was amazing to see the boys singing to each other, opening their mouths, not being embarrassed; it's brilliant. There is Antony who is normally dead quiet. He doesn't have much confidence and he messes around a bit and there he is, holding his diaphragm and singing his socks off. All the others were really proud of him, especially Ashley in the other photo. Ashley was really proud of Antony; he kept saying how good he'd been. And that's Ashley, who is essentially withdrawn. He won't look at you usually; his eyes kind of go to the side if you talk to him; he is stunned and amazed at things around him all the time. He blushes really easily and there he is hanging on to Guy and actually engaging. He's lost all that embarrassment and history. He's never been tactile, even though I think he wants to be, that's why he loves drama. He told me he wouldn't come to the workshops if he had to sing, and there he is. It's lovely – there's a real physical thing there. He is so engrossed in wanting to get better at singing, in learning how to do it, that he has forgotten himself, he's forgotten that he is physically shy – and that is finding your voice.

These two images show how the project raised self-esteem and aspirations through the creative process. The 'little story' eloquently describes the transformation in two young men through the creative process. There is a shift in self-esteem in terms of movement from one self, 'shy, quiet, embarrassed', to an alternative sense of self, one that is confident and engaged. And it is through discovering this alternative self that these two young men have come to voice.

Closing reflection

I have suggested that the task of researching creativity should, in itself, be creative. As researchers, we should work hard to answer the question 'What is it like to be here?' and should engage those who are living and working within the situation we are examining, in sharing and analysing their experiences creatively.

It soon became clear that this evaluation would not tell simple truths about the world; it would not offer a tool kit by which creative projects could transform learning in school and enhance pupil engagement. Doris Lessing (2002, p. 13) reminds us that describing 'truth' is elusive: 'How little I have managed to say of the truth, how little I have caught of all that complexity; how can this small neat thing be true when what I experienced was so rough and apparently formless and unshaped.' I faced an additional problem in trying to (re)present the stories describing 'what it is like to be here'. The Foucauldian notion of archaeology helped me. Foucault describes 'archaeology' as

> an attempt to describe discourses. Not books (in relation to their authors), not theories (with their structures and coherences), but those familiar yet enigmatic groups of statements that are known as medicine, political economy, and biology. I would like to show that these unities form a number of autonomous, but not independent, domains, governed by rules, but in perpetual transformation, anonymous and without a subject, but imbuing a great many individual works.
>
> (Foucault, 1972, back cover)

He goes on to describe a notion of 'things said'. This revisits immediately the question of 'What can we say?' Archaeology explores how 'things said' come into being, how they are interpreted, transformed and articulated.

One result of the research was to expose the ideology present within current practice and through this description offer a view of possible futures. It was clear to the evaluation team from the project results that we could not simply ascribe terms such as 'disaffected' to large groups of young people. They were not 'disaffected'; they had a clear view of what constitutes effective teaching and learning, and were engaged and motivated when these needs were met. This and other creative projects such as the one I have described meet these needs. They allow learners to succeed in new and challenging areas; they allow learners to draw on their individual experiences outside school for inspiration; they give constant positive feedback and they ask learners to take on responsibility.

This is what I hoped the colleges would take away from the evaluation. Unfortunately, this was not a simple answer; the evaluation did not give a model of a creative project that could be imported into colleges to re-engage learners. Rather, it found that if a college wishes to engage all learners, it must revisit its assessment, learning and teaching practices so that these are built around:

- offering care and personal support to all learners;
- understanding and responding to all learners as individuals;
- modelling skills and expertise and developing these in learners through an apprenticeship approach;
- developing and supporting collaborative activity in the classroom and in the college.

This was not an easy answer, but is one that is more likely to build sustainable, engaged learning communities within schools and colleges.

Acknowledgement

I wish to acknowledge the contribution of Morwenna Griffiths to this chapter. She put together the initial bid for the project and sections of the chapter draw on this bid. I would also like to thank Adam Knowles for transforming the photographs into the images presented here.

References

Altrichter, H., Posch, P., and Somekh, B. (1993). *Teachers investigate their work: An introduction to the methods of action research*. London: RoutledgeFalmer.

Brown, T., and Jones, L. (2001). *Action research and postmodernism: Congruence and critique*. Buckingham, UK: Open University Press.

Cotton, T., and Griffiths, M. (2007). Action research, stories and practical philosophy. *Educational Action Research*, *15*(4), 545–560.

Eisner, E. W. (1991). *The enlightened eye: Qualitative inquiry and the enhancement of educational practice*. New York: Macmillan.

Eisner, E. W. (2005). *Reimagining schools: The selected works of Elliot W. Eisner*. London: Routledge.

Foucault, M. (1972). *The archaeology of knowledge*. London: RoutledgeFalmer.

Kemmis, S., and McTaggart, R. (1988). *The action research planner*. Geelong, Victoria: Deakin University Press.

Lessing, D. (2002). *The golden notebook*. London: Flamingo Press.

Loughran, J., and Russell, T. (Eds.) (2002). *Reframing teacher education practices: Exploring meaning through self-study*. London: Falmer Press.

Mitchell, C., Weber, S., and O'Reilly-Scanlan, K. (2005) *Just who do we think we are? Methodologies for self-study in teaching*. London: RoutledgeFalmer.

Reid, A., and Petocz, P. (2004). Learning domains and the process of creativity. *Australian Educational Researcher*, *31*(2), 45–62.

Schostak, J. (2002). *Understanding and conducting qualitative research in education: Framing the project*. Buckingham, UK: Open University Press.

Schratz, M., & Walker, R. (1995). *Research as social change*. London: Routledge.

Whitehead, J. (1989). Creating a living educational theory from questions of the kind, 'How do I improve my practice?'. *Cambridge Journal of Education*, *19*(1), 41–52.

Chapter 16

Research methods for Web Two dot whoah

Elisabeth Soep

As a researcher working at the intersection of youth, learning, and media culture, I probably should have seen it coming. I'm talking about the full extent to which digital innovations have redefined our fields of study, research relationships and methods for carrying out and 'writing up' analysis.

But evidence of this shift took me by surprise more than a year ago, when I was doing some online research for a forthcoming book on youth media and learning (Soep & Chávez, 2010). My ethnographic site for the book was Youth Radio, an organization where I play a dual role, as both participant – Senior Producer in the youth-driven newsroom – and researcher. I'd been associated with Youth Radio, in one form or another, for eight or so years. At the time, I was reworking a chapter called 'Converged literacy' in which I was forming an argument about the new learning demands and opportunities created when young people produce media reaching massive audiences (Jenkins, 2006). In this particular section of the chapter, I was focusing on a radio story that a teenaged Youth Radio reporter, Finnegan Hamill, had produced called *Emails from Kosovo*, which excerpted his correspondence with a girl living in Kosovo just as war was breaking out in that region. The story turned out to be huge. It ran as an eight-part series on National Public Radio, was quoted verbatim by then-president Bill Clinton, and went on to win the prestigious Alfred I. DuPont award for journalistic excellence. All this attention and impact turned Finnegan into a public figure. He'd been reporting the news and then he became the news – making appearances on CNN, *The Today Show*, even *People* magazine.

Using *Emails from Kosovo* as a shining example, I was on a roll with the chapter, writing up the sophisticated literacy practices collaborative media projects can foster in young producers. And then, double-checking the spelling of his name, I came across a blog post Finnegan himself had written years after the series ran. It was called 'My year as Kosovo Boy', and in it Finnegan shared some harsh reflections on what the experience had been like for him. At one point, he described what happened when *Today Show* host Katie Couric asked him what he had learned from working on the series. Finnegan confessed to his blog readers, 'I couldn't think of a damn thing.'

It was a humbling moment, to say the least. Here I'd been developing an argument about all that Finny, and others like him, can learn by producing high-impact media content. And then, through an internet search I accidentally discovered some crucial data I hadn't known existed. This unexpected information was directly relevant to – and to a certain extent undermined – my research-based conclusions. Who was the observer here, and who the observed, I had to ask, as I read Finnegan's blog, since I was both a researcher and a producer at Youth Radio, and therefore both analysing and implicated in his critique.

I don't want to overstate the case. Youth media research has a tendency to assign a kind of automatic 'authenticity' to expressions of youth voice (Fleetwood, 2005) – as if hearing directly from young people is all we need to do to understand the complex and sometimes fraught meanings attached to youth media projects and products. First off, Finnegan was already in his twenties by the time he wrote the post. Second, his reflections raised some important questions about the relationship between media production and learning, which contributed significantly to but did not trump the varied interpretations others, including his editors and peers at the time, the story's audiences, and I, could legitimately put forth with respect to the creative process behind the *Emails from Kosovo* series. But his account, and the fact that it, like my own, would be permanently available to anyone, anywhere, at any time who had access to an online search engine profoundly unsettled the conventional research dynamic. No longer can researchers who study youth media production single-handedly demarcate the beginnings, middles and ends of the processes we examine. The making and remaking continue long after we leave our field sites, beyond the superimposed and arbitrary boundaries we erect to wall off our units of analysis. Nor can researchers assume that it will be our academic peers, for the most part, who hold us accountable – in documented, public, retrievable ways – for our arguments and conclusions. Youth media producers themselves, as research 'subjects', have always formed their own interpretations and accounts of the experiences we analyse. What's different now is that they're publishing their assessments alongside our own.

In this chapter, I examine the afterlife of youth-produced content: what happens in the comments sections and link-rich online conversations that take place after the 'completion' of a given media project. This phase of participation is governed by a different set of players, agendas, stakes, consequences, and rules of engagement as compared with those associated with the original media production process, especially in the case of media projects originating from community-based organizations. Youth media organizations typically aim to promote youth development and literacy as well as positive outcomes for communities, media audiences and even job markets.[1] The participants who join the production process after the fact – bloggers and commenters in particular – do not necessarily share those orientations or pro-social goals. Nor are they beholden to funders or non-profit norms, which always operate somewhere behind the products these organizations release to the world, as evidence of both mission-driven achievements and grant-driven compliance. Researchers know little about the creative work that takes place inside the new digital 'architectures' for co-creation, or what these practices mean for the original authors and their varied literacies (Karaganis & Jeremijenko, 2007; Sefton-Green, 2005). Of particular interest to me here are implications of these changes in digital culture for research methods.

Ethnographers are always creating and negotiating boundaries. What information do we consider? What do we leave out of data collection and analysis? When do we start looking? When do we stop? These matters of site (the what questions) and time (the when questions) are less straightforward than ever for creativity researchers who focus on digital media production. We investigate processes and products that by definition spread, via links, uploads and downloads, and remixes, and that have the potential to be never-ending and ever-extending, as a result of the proliferation of platforms that invite authors and users to keep on making and engaging, long after the original work has been published. In a sense, even the absence of 'conversation' below a youth-produced media post is its own kind of statement, to the extent that an empty comment field, often marked as such with a bleak, 'comments (0)' at the bottom of the post, can permanently and publicly brand the product as failing to engage its audience.

In light of these and other developments in digital culture, I use this chapter to examine the meanings and politics of researchers' protocols for 'bounding' our sites and times of study, arguing in the end for appropriating the anthropological framework of 'multi-sited ethnography' (Marcus, 1998) even within single sites of study. The research site I focus on here is Youth Radio-Youth Media International, a hybrid youth development organization and professional production company with its headquarters in Oakland, California, with bureaux and correspondents across the US and reporting from around the world. Founded in 1992 by Ellin O'Leary with San Francisco Bay Area high school students Deverol Ross, Chano Soccarras, Ayoka Medlock, Noah Nelson and Jacinda Abcarian, the organization serves primarily low-income youths and young people of colour, recruiting for its free programmes from local under-resourced, re-segregating public schools. Serving approximately 300 young people per year, students can move from introductory to advanced after-school converged media classes into paid internships as peer educators, facility administrators, reporters, producers and engineers (approximately fifty young people annually are on payroll at any given time). The organization's production company, Youth Media International, generates content for its own website, youthradio.org; outlets include National Public Radio, the BBC, The Huffington Post, the *San Francisco Chronicle* and MTV News, as well as niche blogs, YouTube, and the internet's varied social media sites. Having won US broadcast journalism's most prestigious honours, including the George Foster Peabody and Edward R. Murrow Awards in addition to the DuPont for *Emails from Kosovo*, the organization is unusual. And yet Youth Radio's engagement with young people as media producers, and its work across formats (audio, video, photography, print) and platforms (online, broadcast, mobile), provide a rich context for analysing dynamics affecting both makers and researchers at a contradictory moment of promise and challenge (Soep, 2007b).

My own perspective on Youth Radio and the youth media field encompasses both of these points of view. I work as a maker alongside young people within a model I have characterized elsewhere as 'collegial pedagogy',[2] and I also research our own work and related projects across the US, with a focus on implications for learning and literacy. This double perspective is not always comfortable, and certainly there are things I can't (or don't want to) see because I am 'in' the work and not standing outside. But, indebted to traditions of community-based participatory research and participant action research (Minkler & Wallerstein, 2003; Morrell, 2004; Torre & Fine, 2006), I believe that there are also special affordances that come with this unorthodox research position. Perhaps most relevant here is a capacity to watch what happens to individual media projects long after an outside researcher would most likely have moved on to other questions or sites, and to participate with young people in navigating how that afterlife unfolds.

Youth media examined

Youth media researchers have bound their units of analysis and sites of study in various ways. There are surveys of the field that seek trends and patterns evident across practice and scholarship – for example, studies that identify the range of organizational goals espoused, media genres taught, and populations served, or those pinpointing the tendency for researchers to advocate for youth media's benefits rather than deeply explore its contradictions and limitations (Buckingham, Burn, & Willett, 2005; Campbell, Hoey, & Perlman, 2001). There are regularly released reports, including those by the Pew Research Center, the Kaiser Family Foundation and Harvard University's Berkman Center for Internet and Society, tracking rapidly changing habits in media and technology usage and spotlighting hot-button issues ranging from cyber-safety to social media's role in domestic and global conflict. Qualitative research tends to deploy case-study and ethnographic methods to examine implications of media practices within and beyond schools for key dimensions of youth development, social organization and the formation of multiliteracies, sometimes grounding analysis in up-close study of individual organizations and projects within which researchers play various roles (e.g. Chávez & Soep, 2005; Fine, Roberts & Bloom, 2004; Fleetwood, 2005; Goodman, 2003; Hull, 2003).

The most recent wave of research on digital media and learning emanating largely from researchers affiliated with the MacArthur Foundation's Digital Media and Learning initiative offers the category of 'genres of participation' as one way to organize research data and locate young people's everyday media practices within broader social and cultural 'ecologies' that have significant implications for learning and the production of both opportunity and inequality, even when these activities take place outside environments centred on explicit instruction (Davidson & Goldberg, 2009; Ito et al., 2010; Seiter, 2008). Overall, it's a growing body of work that creates a foundation for further efforts to apply the very insights that have emerged from analysis of our research subjects' media ecologies – for example, the implications of the internet's permanent, searchable digital archive for youth identity and literacy – to understanding our own methods for gathering data and generating knowledge.

Production cycle remixed

With creativity studies, especially those centred on media-making, researchers often calibrate both fieldwork and analysis to a four-part production process. Typically it starts with pre-production, a period of research, preparation and planning. Next comes production, when participants collect the materials they need to tell their stories. And then there's post-production, the time for organizing, editing, crafting and polishing the finished product. Finally, data collection will sometimes extend to a phase of distribution, tracking how media products circulate among audiences, whether goals were met and desired impacts achieved.

Innovations in digital technology and media culture have already reconfigured the order, pacing and gatekeeping mechanisms that have traditionally governed these four production phases. These changes convert the production process from a predictable sequence of steps into a cycle without a given starting or stopping point, or fixed pathway from start to finish.

For example, because of the proliferation of user-generated and -curated media outlets, a producer might start with the fourth phase, distribution, by grabbing existing digital content and making a case for why that story belongs on a website's front page – turning dissemination into an act of creation. A video-game player or writer of 'fan fiction' might start at number three, essentially post-producing someone else's media by hacking into an existing game's code, or retooling another author's narrative, thus transforming the media experience into something new. The widespread availability of 'everyday media' (e.g. home videos and digital photos, archived voicemail recordings) can launch a creative project at number two, mid-production, with recordings in hand, around which the maker only later frames a narrative. These and other examples show that media production doesn't necessarily start at the beginning, if we imagine the beginning as a process of pulling an original idea out of the air, or from the inner resources of an individual's mind. Rarely does the process march forward without lots of stopping short, reversing course and circling back to start again.

These shifts in the production cycle have serious implications for how we frame and thus study creativity as a social practice. By now, it is commonplace to argue against a view of creativity as a property of any one individual's imagination. We know that creativity, like literacy, is lodged inside social contexts (Gee, 2000; Street, 1984). Though one person might get the signature or byline for a given finished work, be it a painting or a poem or a radio story, there is a whole crowd of hidden collaborators behind that product, who've co-created it through practices including mentoring and modelling, giving and receiving critique, and leveraging influence and opportunity within sociologically complex art worlds (Becker, 1982; Bourdieu, 1984).

The advent of social media, which brought us blogs like Finnegan's, takes the inter-activity behind creative production to a whole new level – and pulls that participatory dimension to the front and centre. Now it's not just the author, delivering a fixed and polished message. Rather, expressing oneself through social media means launching and sustaining a conversation with various 'networked publics', members of which the originator of the work may know and even admire, but never control (Ito, 2008). danah boyd (2007) has argued that young people use social media platforms to write themselves and their communities into being. They are doing more than authoring their own lives and identities. They are creating contexts in which others can respond to, repurpose and sometimes subvert their messages. That online community can take the original creative content in entirely new directions, whether the 'first author' likes it or not. This has always been the case for artists and producers who send their work into the world and surrender control over its interpretation and use. What's different as a result of social media is that the feedback loops are coded directly into the original product, through comment streams and search engine algorithms. The boundary between the creator's expression and the public's uptake is disappearing.

Recycling research

This view of creativity as a socially and technologically mediated practice, in turn, trans-forms the practice of research. Ethnographic methods have always heavily invested in the demarcation of proper research sites, so much so that tales of entering and exiting 'the field' are a full-blown subgenre within ethnographic writing (Pratt, 1986). 'Stories of entry and exit usually appear on the margins of texts,' according to Gupta and Ferguson (1997, p. 12), 'providing the narrative with uncertainty and expectation at the beginning and closure at the end'. Entry and exit stories imbue ethnographic texts with an aura of authenticity – an 'I was there' quality. These rhetorical devices also bestow authority, by highlighting the difference and distance between researcher and researched – a distinction considered necessary for the ethnographer to maintain analytical perspective. He or she typically 'writes up' the study after separating from the field, and '[t]emporal succession therefore traces the natural sequence of sites that completes a spatial journey into Otherness' (Gupta & Ferguson, 1997, p. 12).

Gupta and Ferguson's emphasis on temporality is especially germane to the ways in which digital culture interrupts research protocols. Time in ethnography is never neutral, argues

Johannes Fabian (1983), who views time as an instrument to impose order that can deny 'coevalness' between the researcher and the researched. Fabian bases his argument on a critique of traditional ethnographies, wherein anthropologists live with their research subjects for an extended but finite period of time: 'the ethnographer will be an ethnographer only if he outlives them, i.e., if he moves *through* the Time he may have shared with them into a level on which he finds anthropology' (Fabian, 1983, p. 61).

'Finding anthropology' is, in Fabian's sense, about enclosing research subjects in their own time-frame, using ethnographic writing and analysis as a way to rise above the everyday rhythms, clocks and calendars of the people who animate our research. The concept of 'rising above' is key here, pointing to the implicit (though unsubtle) hierarchy that sets in when research relationships are so fundamentally out of sync, as if time stands still for research subjects, who are caught in an everlasting present, while researchers move forward, marking progress even in the act of taking leave. With these critiques in mind, I want to apply Fabian's argument to contemporary ethnographies of digital culture, which likewise can be faulted for containing our subjects in time-frames of their own. If my initial characterization of *Emails from Kosovo* depended on a separation between the time of Finnegan's production and my own analysis, his blog post pulled the two of us face to face within the same temporality. This kind of activity will happen more and more in youth media research as 'subjects' publicly author their own accounts of the very same experiences we describe, and as they find themselves engaged and sometimes embroiled in conversations with online interlocutors long after they thought they'd moved on – even 'aged out' – of their media production assignments. It behoves us as researchers not to wait for individual young people to pull us back into 'coevalness,' but to craft methods and strategies of analysis that follow projects across digital space and time.

Web Two dot whoah?

Fast-forward exactly ten years from the time when the *Emails from Kosovo* series hit big, and Youth Radio once again was at work on a story touching on transnational themes of war. This time, a reporter from the newsroom, Pendarvis Harshaw, travelled with Youth Radio's News Director, Nishat Kurwa, to Ireland for a reporting trip. Pendarvis, an Oakland native, produced a story for National Public Radio's *All Things Considered* that explored the status of relations between young Catholics and Protestants living on either side of the 'peace wall' that runs through western Belfast. The story opened like this:

Pendarvis Harshaw: Inside a Belfast classroom, a group of girls giggles and paints pictures of American celebrities. It feels like a teenager's bedroom.
Unidentified girl 1: I want to be a lawyer when I grow up, and I want to go to Harvard University.
Unidentified girl 2: I just want to be a pop star.
Harshaw: This working-class part of Belfast has the same problems as any inner city: a high rate of teen pregnancy, and young people at the risk of drug abuse. The classroom windows are covered by bomb-proof bars. They're left over from the constant violence in this area only ten years ago, Catholic–Protestant violence known as The Troubles. Murals are painted on almost every corner building. The murals show war heroes and battle slogans, telling the story of why west Belfast is divided by what's called the Peace Wall.

Girl 3: It took really long to build it and it would take really long to knock it down because it's really, really big and really, really long.

Harshaw: That's L—— H——. She's 11 years old. She goes to the Clubhouse Community Centre in Belfast. It has two branches open for kids here, one on the Catholic side of the Peace Wall and one on the Protestant side. That's where Leigh lives.

Girl 3: There's a Peace Wall, and there shouldn't really be one because even though it does help separate the Catholics and Protestants and stop them from fighting, no other place really has one. So it's a bit not normal.

Pendarvis's story goes on to explore the enduring effects of The Troubles in this region for a generation whose parents rioted in the streets, and now send their offspring to programmes aimed at Catholic–Protestant reconciliation. The story closes on an image reflecting how things have changed:

Harshaw: Our guide stopped at a red light and pointed out a fully armoured Range Rover. He said, 'Ten years ago, this was the only kind of police car in the city.' We only saw one bulletproof SUV our entire trip. For NPR News, I'm Pendarvis Harshaw.

And yet, it seems, some things never change – that is, tensions among US citizens surrounding what constitutes 'proper English' and who deserves a prominent place in the national media. These tensions surfaced hours after Pendarvis's broadcast, in the first two comments that appeared on National Public Radio's website. The first comment read:

I don't mind the 'youth' part of youth radio . . . today's story on Belfast had interesting information, and the reporter sounded engaged in the subject. . . . HOWEVER I cringed each time he said 'belfass' 'behrum' (bedroom) ETC. ETC. PLEASE! PLEASE! Standard American English for ALL American reporters!

March 6, 2009 7:04:30 PM PST

Recommend (1)

Report abuse

The second comment read:

Four things make me change stations: (1) Pledge breaks. (2) This I believe. (3) Story Corps. and (4) Youth Radio.[3] Sorry, but I tune to NPR for reports from professional adult journalists. But NPR seems to want to keep reverting to amateur hour. Maybe these kids would be better off spending their time on real academic subjects. . . .

March 6, 2009 6:16:52 PM PST

Recommend (5)

Report abuse

The comments deride Pendarvis's reporting as 'amateur', his pronunciation as 'cringe'-inducing and his time spent preparing the story as misguided – on the grounds that he should be pursuing 'real academic subjects'. The assumptions implicit in these criticisms say more, of course, about US linguistic, racial and academic ideologies than they do about Pendarvis's actual story, but I asked him what went through his head when he read these comments. Seven months had passed, and he laughed, 'What is the "standard English" between an African American man and a group of Irish people? No one speaks the Queen's English in that conversation!' But still, at the time of the broadcast, he was discouraged. He had a long talk with Youth Radio's News Director, Nishat Kurwa, who'd been with him in Ireland, about his frustration. What was the point, he wondered, of doing journalism if this was the reaction he was going to get? It was further evidence of something he already knew. When he was reporting for public broadcasting audiences, he wasn't reaching 'his demographic': 'I'm not talking to an audience I care about.'

After that conversation, Nishat sent out an email to the newsroom's adult production team with the subject line 'Web 2.0 – when it's personal'. She pasted the two comments on Pendarvis's story into the message and noted that the 'personal' nature of these kinds of unregulated responses is part of what Youth Radio has to wrestle with more than other production companies, given the organization's positive youth development goals, in its efforts to engage online audiences.

There was some email back-and-forth after Nishat's note went out, discussing whether Youth Radio should intervene in some way in the comment stream, or whether Pendarvis himself should respond. It's an increasingly common conversation media producers need to have, in a social media context that promotes belief in letting 'the community regulate itself'. One of the defining principles of what is known as 'Web 2.0' is the idea that you need to trust your users. Rather than censor problematic comments or other forms of user participation, a tenet of Web 2.0 is for website publishers to create the space for members of the community to bury or argue down the comments they disagree with, and to reinforce the material that resonates.

The problem with this logic, as appealing as it is to democratic ideals, is what happens when there's a significant gap between the author's social values and identities (what Pendarvis calls 'my demographic') and the 'community' he or she reaches through any given media outlet. I don't mean this in a reductive sense: that communities, whether online, in real life or criss-crossing between, are defined in any predictable way by categories of race, class or gender. And of course in vibrant communities there are opportunities for nuanced discourse across difference. The question is whether that kind of rich conversation, or 'self-regulation', in Web 2.0 terminology, will happen automatically or requires intentional intervention.

Two days after Nishat sent out that email, three more comments showed up on the site, in reverse chronological order:

> First and foremost, I would like to acknowledge that Mr. Harshaw did an incredible job on his report. If I recall correctly any individual could contribute to National Public Radio, not just professional adult journalist. Perhaps, if listeners spent more time listening to the content of his report, as opposed to trying to create alleged word mis-pronounciations, they would have grasped the effectiveness of the story.
> March 9, 2009 2:11:43 AM PDT
> Recommend (5)
> Report abuse

The second comment read:

> 'Maybe these kids would be better off spending their time on real academic subjects'
> . . . Do you honestly mean to tell me that learning about world history and current
> events is not a 'real' academic subject?!?!?! In an age where the youth would rather be
> watching MTV and playing video games 'you want to cut down a young man who is
> trying to expand his boundaries' . . . I have had the blessing to meet Mr. Harshaw and
> he is THE MOST knowledgeable and insightful people I have met on Howard's
> campus. Keep up the good work Pen :)
> March 9, 2009 2:07:46 AM PDT
> Recommend (8)
> Report abuse

And a third read:

> I feel compelled to question the narrow-mindedness of the comments I've read here.
> Bigotry with the tagline 'Standard American English for ALL American Reporters!' is
> a shameful slogan designed by someone with a blind spot about who creates the
> 'standard' American English in our country. And if someone does not care for the first
> person narratives of This I Believe, Story Corps and Youth Radio, why not just move
> along? Why be so bitter about it? The advice that 'maybe these kids would be better off
> spending their time . . . ' says more about how narrowly the listener defines his world
> and his idea of what is worthwhile than it does about people who listen or contribute
> to these marvelous programs. Thank you, Mr. Harshaw. I for one loved your piece on
> Belfast.
> March 9, 2009 1:55:15 AM PDT
> Recommend (4)
> Report abuse

When the adult production staff saw these comments show up, we were pleased. Look, the
community regulated itself! The Web 2.0 logic worked. Except, it turns out there was more
to the story than we initially realized. Pendarvis had taken matters into his own hands.

'Why are they coming at my neck on NPR?' is a paraphrase of the status update Pendarvis
remembers posting on his Facebook profile after his Ireland story aired, alerting them to
what was happening with a link to the piece. 'My friends don't listen to NPR,' he explains,
'but depending on how busy they are, I put up something with an interesting, juicy heading,
they'll click on it, and if they feel so inclined, they'll respond to it. I have a nice little social
network following.' Pendarvis has more than 2,000 Facebook friends. He got lots of
support, he says, from that network, mostly telling him to 'keep doing your work' and not
to 'trip off the haters'. This kind of response, Pendarvis says, reversed the crushing feeling
he initially experienced reading the negative comments on his story. And there's an added
benefit, in his view: 'It's a tremendous feeling that you can connect your friends, knowing
their habits, they receive their news from TMZ or allhiphop.com, and I can connect them
to a story on National Public Radio.' Crucially, he's making that connection via content he
had created, highlighting the importance of enabling young people who've otherwise been
marginalized from digital and media privilege to participate as producers in these contexts,
and not just audiences, no matter how active and vocal those audiences can now be.

A case for multi-sitedness

What's striking, in this account of the production process behind one youth media story, is that so much of the action took place after the piece was technically finished. Researchers who study creativity and literacy have a strong set of tools to draw from in our efforts to analyse the work involved in making a story like Pendarvis's dispatch from Ireland. We need to build up new repertoires for examining the digital afterlives of these stories, methods that help us investigate how these 'post-post-production' activities relate both to the original production process and to larger questions about imagination as a social achievement. There are new literacy demands involved in creating work that generates 'participation' among audiences and online communities, as evident in Pendarvis's move to leverage his own social media network to reshape the conversation ensuing about his work. There are new political, organizational and even legal considerations as well. How do youth media producers and their collaborators monitor, navigate and create momentum behind the content they generate, even when comments get ugly? Even when organizational missions are at stake? Even when laws protecting intellectual property, privacy and safety are violated through digital manifestations of everything from content appropriation to hate speech?

To address these and other questions through research, one needs 'a mode of study that cares about, and pays attention to, the interlocking of multiple social-political sites and locations' (Gupta & Ferguson, 1997, p. 37). This kind of research requires strategies that can sense movements and ripple effects across on- and offline activities and can notice creative and cultural practices that defy that dichotomization. The methods we need must acknowledge that the connections that interlock our varied research 'sites and locations' can be built into the architectures of these environments or forged by young people who migrate across them like it's nothing, over the course of their daily lives.

One resource for developing that mode of study can be found in the methodological approach of 'multi-sited ethnography'. It's an approach that rejects the still dominant (though widely critiqued) conception of culture as a phenomenon contained within a single place, as if culture were a kind of inherited membership possessed by a defined group of people.[4] Ethnography practised the old-fashioned way has been governed by a principle of immersion. It 'dwells' inside one culture, until the ethnographer leaves and writes it up. While 'we learn a great deal from such studies', argue Dimitriadis and Weis (2006, p. 478), 'what we do not know is what happens to them after they leave these specific locations.' Multi-sited ethnography, as characterized by Marcus (1998), answers that question by operating on a principle of migration. It 'follows' people, objects, metaphors, conflicts, tensions, plotlines, across time and space.

And so we have a real methodological opportunity, to treat even our studies of individual field sites or circumscribed media projects as 'multi-sited' investigations. The site of Pendarvis's original production of the Ireland story was in Belfast itself. A second site was Youth Radio's newsroom, where he collaborated with Nishat and others to craft the story's script and audio mix. A third site could be defined transactionally, via the editorial process between Youth Radio and National Public Radio. And then there is the site of the online conversation I have described here, the afterlife of his broadcast that constituted its own context for creative expression and contestation deploying digital tools. Each of these sites is driven by its own histories, cognitive and aesthetic demands, politics, and opportunities for hope and disappointment. The timeline that runs through these varied sites is considerably more prolonged than a conventional framing of creative production as all the work that goes into generating a piece of media in the first place. And crucially, it's a timeline that never truly ends, even after the comments stop and Pendarvis has moved on, because the material is permanently available as part of a digital culture and infrastructure that never stands still. And once this chapter is published, or if I decide to blog about it myself, the conversation will start up again.

Notes

1 For example, Buckingham (2003); Campbell, Huey, and Perlman (2001); Goldfarb (2002); Goodman (2003); Herr-Stephenson, Rhoten, Perkel, and Sims (forthcoming); Kinkade and Macy (2003); Kirwan, Learmonth, Sayer, and Williams (2003).
2 In Chávez and Soep (2005).
3 'Pledge drives' are the periods of time public broadcasting stations set aside by interrupting programming to solicit donations from audiences. 'This I Believe' and 'Story Corps' are both independent public radio projects that invite listeners to submit content for radio broadcast.
4 See, for example, Varenne and McDermott (1998); Pratt (1986).

References

Becker, H. (1982). *Art worlds*. Berkeley: University of California Press.

Bourdieu, P. (1984). *Distinction: A social critique of the judgement of taste*. Cambridge, MA: Harvard University Press.

boyd, d. (2007). Friends, friendsters, and top 8: Writing community into being on social networking sites. *First Monday*. Retrieved on 15 January 2007 from www.firstmonday.org/issues/issue11_12/boyd/

Buckingham, D. (2003). *Media education: Literacy, learning and contemporary culture*. Cambridge: Polity Press.

Buckingham, D., Burn, A., & Willett, R. (2005). *The media literacy of children and young people*. London: Centre for the Study of Children, Youth and Media.

Campbell, P., Hoey, L., & Perlman, L. (2001). *Sticking with my dreams: Defining and refining youth media in the 21st century*. Groton, MA: Campbell-Kibler Associates. Retrieved on 18 January 2008 from www.campbell-kibler.com/youth_media.html

Chávez, V., & Soep, E. (2005). Youth Radio and the pedagogy of collegiality. *Harvard Educational Review, 75*(4), 409–434.

Davidson, C., & Goldberg, D. (2009). *The future of learning institutions in a digital age*. Cambridge, MA: MIT Press.

Dimitriadis, G., & Weis, L. (2006). Multisited ethnographic approaches in urban education today. In J. L. Kincheloe, k. hayes, K. Rose, & P. M. Anderson (Eds.), *The Praeger handbook of urban education* (Vol. 2, pp. 470–481). Westport, CT: Greenwood Press.

Fabian, J. (1983). *Time and the Other: How anthropology makes its object*. New York: Columbia University Press.

Fine, M., Roberts, R., & Bloom, J. (2004). *Echoes of Brown: Youth documenting and performing the legacy of Brown v. Board of Education*. New York: Teachers College Press.

Fleetwood, N. (2005). Authenticating practices: Producing realness, performing youth. In S. Maira & E. Soep (Eds.), *Youthscapes: The popular, the national, the global* (pp. 155–172). Philadelphia: University of Pennsylvania Press.

Gee, J. (2000). The new literacy studies: From 'socially situated' to the work of the social. In D. Barton & M. Hamilton (Eds.), *Situated literacies* (pp. 180–196). London: Routledge.

Goldfarb, B. (2002). *Visual pedagogy: Media cultures in and beyond the classroom*. Durham, NC: Duke University Press.

Goodman, S. (2003). *Teaching youth media: A critical guide to literacy, video production, and social change*. New York: Teachers College Press.

Gupta, A., and Ferguson, J. (1997). Discipline and practice: 'The field' as site, method, and location in anthropology. In A. Gupta & J. Ferguson (Eds.), *Anthropological locations: Boundaries and grounds of a field science* (pp. 1–46). Berkeley: University of California Press.

Herr-Stephenson, B., Rhoten, D., Perkel, D., & Sims, C. (paper in progress). Learning with and about digital media and technology in afterschool programs, libraries, and museums.

Hull, G. (2003). Youth culture and digital media: New literacies for new times. *Research in the Teaching of English*, *38*(2), 229–233.

Ito, M. (2008). Participatory learning in a networked society: Lessons from the digital youth project. Paper presented at the annual meetings of the American Educational Research Association, New York City.

Ito, M., Baumer, S., Bittanti, M., boyd, d., Herr-Stephenson, B., Horst, H., Lange, P., Mahendran, D., Martinez, K., Pascoe, C., Perkel, D., Robinson, L., Sims, C., & Tripp, L. (2010). *Hanging out, messing around, geeking out: Kids living and learning with new media.* Cambridge, MA: MIT Press.

Jenkins, H. (2006). *Convergence culture: Where old and new media collide.* New York: NYU Press.

Karaganis J., & Jeremijenko, N. (Eds.). (2007). *Structures of participation in digital culture.* Durham, NC: Duke University Press

Kinkade, S., & Macy, C. (2003). What works in youth media: Case studies from around the world. International Youth Foundation. Retrieved on January 17, 2008 from www.nokia.com/NOKIA_COM_1/Corporate_Responsibility/Society_/Youth_development/Life_skills/Publications/WW-youth_Led_Media.pdf

Kirwan, T., Learmonth, J., Sayer, M. & Williams, R. (2003). *Mapping media literacy.* London: British Film Institute, Broadcasting Standards Commission, Independent Television Commission. Retrieved on 17 January 2007 from www.ofcom.org.uk/static/archive/bsc/pdfs/research/litmap.pdf.

Marcus, G. (1998). *Ethnography through thick and thin.* Princeton, NJ: Princeton University Press.

Minkler, M., & Wallerstein, N. (2003). *Community-based participatory research for health.* San Francisco: Jossey-Bass.

Morrell, E. (2004). *Becoming critical researchers: Literacy and empowerment for urban youth.* New York: Peter Lang.

Pratt, M. L. (1986). Linguistic utopias. In N. Fabb, D. Attridge, A. Durant, & C. McCabe (Eds.), *The linguistics of writing* (pp. 48–66). New York: Methuen.

Sefton-Green, J. (2005). Timelines, timeframes, and special effects: Software and creative media production. *Education, Communication, and Information*, *4*(1), 99–110.

Seiter, E. (2008). Revisiting 'old' media: Learning from media histories. In T. McPherson (Ed.), *Digital youth, innovation, and the unexpected* (pp. 27–52). Cambridge, MA: MIT Press.

Soep, E. (2007). Jumping for joy, wracking our brains, searching our souls: Youth media and its digital contradictions. *Youth Media Reporter*, November, 102–109.

Soep, E., & Chávez, V. (2010). *Drop that knowledge. Youth radio stories.* Berkeley: University of California Press.

Street, B. (1984). *Literacy in theory and practice.* Cambridge: Cambridge University Press.

Torre, M., & Fine, M. (2006). Researching and resisting: Democratic policy research by and for youth. In S. Ginwright, P. Noguera, & J. Cammarota (Eds.), *Beyond resistance! Youth activism and community change* (pp. 269–286). New York: Routledge.

Varenne, H., & McDermott, R. (1998). *Successful failure: The school America builds.* Boulder, CO: Westview Press.

Chapter 17

Baselines and mosaics

The challenges of researching a flagship national programme

David Parker and Naranee Ruthra-Rajan

Introduction

In this chapter, we will summarize the development of approaches to national evaluation and research undertaken in England by Creative Partnerships (CP) over the period 2002–2009. In our capacity as the Creative Partnerships national research team (from 2004 onwards), we have been challenged by the interrelationships and tensions between open-ended inquiry and the need to account, often in quite specific ways, for the programme's impact. While these two aspects often seem to contain irreducibly complex and competing aims, we will describe approaches that have made it possible, in our view, to create a blend of investigations covering a range of themes.

We will set out a number of challenges, each with a particular inflection (policy, methodology and operational issues), and illustrate how a nationally driven approach to research and evaluation attempted to embrace variation across the programme while providing a common framework of themes and evaluative practice that helped create a rigorous national evidence base.

Context

We joined Arts Council England (ACE) in 2004 to form a small research unit in the Creative Partnerships team. At that time, CP was a department within Arts Council England. Until then, there had been no discrete research support within the Creative Partnerships national team, although there had been some commissioning of evaluative work from the Arts Council's research department. While we had been recruited to Creative Partnerships in order to build an evidence base and to test the range and depth of impacts across the intervention more objectively, we were also very much part of the ongoing drive to 'make the case' for the benefits of the work, and to find ways of expressing those benefits in ways that could be readily understood by a wide range of stakeholders, including our funders.

Creative Partnerships is the Labour government's flagship creative learning programme for schools.[1] At the time of writing, it has been in operation for almost eight years, but the idea for the programme is at least a decade old. It came into being during the early years of Blair's New Labour government and was part of a series of forward-looking ideas that to an extent captured a pre-millennial response to a somewhat amorphous set of challenges. There seemed to be at that time an imperative to hypothesize sets of future education and employment needs and to consider in general terms how fit for purpose systems and structures were to meet those predicted needs. This included debates around education

(DCMS, 2001; NACCCE, 1999). One of the key terms used to catch the mood for what needed to change, and what seemed to be missing from young people's educational experiences, was 'creativity'. Of course, in many respects this was not new at all; the general idea of a child-centred, creative and play-focused approach to pedagogy has a long history in progressive educational movements (Abbs, 2003: see also Chapter 1, the introduction to this collection). However, with the emphasis on creativity the Creative Partnerships initiative became an important part of the Labour government's emerging sense of what it meant to meet a rapidly changing set of wider social needs.

The National Advisory Committee on Creative and Cultural Education (NACCCE), chaired by Sir Ken Robinson, played a key part in defining these pressing educational challenges. The report emerged as a way of more sharply defining what had already been hinted at in the government's Education White Paper *Excellence in schools* in 1997, which, while laying considerable emphasis on literacy and numeracy (and eventually giving rise to the national strategies for both), also acknowledged that

> [i]f we are to prepare successfully for the twenty-first century we will have to do more than just improve literacy and numeracy skills. We need a broad, flexible and motivating education that recognises the different talents of all children and delivers excellence for everyone.
>
> (cited in NACCCE, 1999, p. 5)

While the national literacy and numeracy strategies were essentially offering new and more structured ways to enable better transfer of existing knowledge and curricula, this third aim of flexible, motivated and talented learners was something new and suggested the creation of a more systemic approach to culture and creativity within the curriculum. NACCCE focused on this challenge and came to suggest that

> [t]he key message of this report is the need for a new balance in education: in setting national priorities; in the structure and organisation of the school curriculum; in methods of teaching and assessment; in relationships between schools and other agencies. . . . There has been a tendency for the national debate on education to be expressed as a series of exclusive alternatives, even dichotomies: for example, as a choice between the arts or the sciences; the core curriculum or the broad curriculum; between academic standards or creativity; freedom or authority in teaching methods. We argue that these dichotomies are unhelpful. Realising the potential of young people, and raising standards of achievement and motivation includes all of these elements.
>
> (NACCCE, 1999, p. 9)

As a direct result of NACCCE, Creative Partnerships was proposed as a potential solution to some of these challenges. This was an innovative idea, not least because it brought together two government departments: the DCMS (Department for Culture, Media and Sport) and the (then) DfES (Department for Education and Skills). Although the DCMS was investing most of the funding for Creative Partnerships (in the first year, for example, the DCMS invested £20 million while the DfES invested £2.5 million),[2] it was always clear that schools were going to be the mainstay of the initiative, serving as units of change within the programme and as the meeting ground for key participants: artists and other creative practitioners, young people and teachers.

At the time Creative Partnerships first piloted work, in 2002, there were quite different types and levels of interest from the two funding departments, based on some implicit assumptions and values. These departmental interests were synthesized in a Policy Framework that was circulated to Creative Partnerships staff in August of 2002. It was signed by Secretary of State for Culture, Media and Sport, the Secretary of State for Education and Skills, and the chairman of the Arts Council.

It is worth laying out the aims and objectives of the initiative as it was seen at that time.

The aim of Creative Partnerships is to:

Identify effective, sustainable partnerships between schools and arts, cultural and creative organisations and individuals, leading to the development of a national strategy.

The Objectives of Creative Partnerships are to:

- Pilot 16 models for sustainable Creative Partnerships between schools and arts, cultural and creative organisations and individuals, to provide enhanced and enriched opportunities for young people to develop skills, knowledge and critical appreciation of the arts, culture and creativity; and to
- Provide opportunities for teachers to enhance their creative teaching skills, knowledge and critical appreciation, and for increased family and community involvement with the arts, cultural and creative bodies;
- Build the capacity of the cultural and creative sectors to be able to work effectively with schools in developing creativity in the process of learning;
- Seek to build on and consolidate connections between other relevant government programmes, which are sustainable, replicable, and can be disseminated; and
- Undertake independent evaluation of the Partnership models to identify effective practice, which is sustainable, replicable and can be disseminated; and
- Provide rigorous evidence of the effects of engagement with the programme, which can be used for further policy development.

(Creative Partnerships, 2002)

In section 4 of the same document, which deals with expected outcomes, the Policy Framework sets out seven areas of impact:

1   enhanced perception of the importance of culture and creativity in education;
2   enhanced understanding of the importance of culture and creativity in education and how these can contribute to the raising of standards;
3   improved learning outcomes for pupils actively involved in creative projects in the creative partnerships;
4   increased participation in cultural and creative activities;
5   producing creative learners and the skills needed for the new economy;
6   increased job satisfaction among teachers;
7   increased participation of cultural and creative organizations and schools in joint projects.

It is clear from these aims, objectives and outcomes that the twin ambitions to increase cultural participation and raise standards come to the fore. Consequently, during the time of the programme's early operation (between 2001 and 2004), what exactly was meant by 'creativity', and where the implied priority order lay in the outcomes listed above, depended very much on both departmental and sectoral agendas and the prior histories and ambitions of those delivering the programme. These complex definitional and motivational issues speak directly to any research or evaluation attempting to capture the impact of the programme. For the purposes of this chapter, it is not possible to outline all of the key drivers, but, as we will mention below, there was a significant reprioritizing from a broad interest in access to arts and culture to deeper concerns with whole-school change and school improvement.

What this meant on the ground, certainly in the years 2002–2004, was that the debates and definitions between the main stakeholders – funders, deliverers, local authorities, head-teachers – gave rise to a programme architecture that was as liberating as it was confusing. The Policy Framework quoted from above can be read as a broad, ambitious and com-plementary set of objectives, or as the fusion of sets of fundamentally opposed aims, each with their own competing histories. The virtue of this was that as a process that was about piloting practice and learning lessons for roll-out, there was a flexibility that allowed the local creative directors a degree of inventiveness, and they could begin to grow the programme in ways that felt relevant to local people.[3] As the sixteen pilot areas developed a series of openly different, pluralistic approaches to delivery and staff deployment, so they began to illustrate some of the best ways for Creative Partnerships to roll out to a further nine, and then eleven, areas between 2004 and 2006. It was this mixed picture of a 'national pilot with local variation' that the research team effectively inherited in the summer of 2004, when it was required to build a case around impact and effect.

In basic terms, Creative Partnerships was a nationally driven initiative that operated through local delivery organizations. Each of the nine Arts Council English regions (South West, East, South East, London, West Midlands, East Midlands, Yorkshire, North East and North West) had, initially, one or two local Creative Partnerships offices, but with expansion of the programme in 2004 and 2005 the local offices in each region totalled four. Each office began by setting up partnerships with between fifteen and twenty-five schools, sometimes but not always in partnership with local authority staff. By the time all thirty-six local offices were operating, in April 2006, we had worked with over 285,000 young people and over 24,000 teachers across the country.

First steps: identifying the research and evaluation challenges

As we've seen from the early Policy Framework, Creative Partnerships was under a great deal of scrutiny from the outset, and with good reason. The initial budget of £49.3 million over two years was the largest single investment in arts and cultural education for many decades, and there was an understandable eagerness to have a national means of evaluation in place to capture a baseline and track schools and pupils going forward. However, there were operational and historical tensions in the first evaluation brief, and these relate strongly to deep-rooted debates on the primary purpose of engaging young people in culture and art.

Beneath the emerging consensus interventions related to the arts and young people were a series of quite fundamental differences about how this group might expect to benefit from such activities. Was the main purpose to increase participation in and understanding of the arts and culture, was it to promote and develop a new and urgently needed set of 'creative skills', or perhaps to bolster the National Curriculum and help contribute to a rise in standards? Examples of these tensions came to the fore in early meetings and communications between ministerial departments and the Arts Council England, and the need for both advocacy case studies, to give a flavour and feel for effects of the programme, and more quantitative findings to inform strategies for roll-out nationwide, was at the heart of many exchanges.[4]

In addition, there are some fundamental issues around baselining within schools, particularly the question of how relevant the process is when each school must appropriate and make sense of the 'offer' made by the programme. Every school is in a unique position, each making differentiated use of other government and local initiatives. Additionally, the local area and, to some extent, the school-by-school variations in programme delivery meant that a standard baseline survey of pupils, staff and achievement rates had the potential to miss other important variables that inevitably feed into any account of impact. During the first two or three years of the programme, most complications around evaluation stemmed from both the lack of homogeneity in offer across local Creative Partnerships area offices, and schools having to essentially appropriate the intervention and 'make it their own'.

Despite these challenges, a large-scale national evaluation by the National Foundation for Educational Research (NFER) was commissioned by Arts Council England's Research Department in 2002. They were working on the basis that a national programme would have a series of organizing principles that united inevitable local variety into a measurable 'common' intervention. In reality, there was greater freedom and variation within the piloting process than had perhaps originally been envisaged. These two key issues – the varied starting points of schools and the varied Creative Partnerships 'offers' made locally by area offices in those piloting years of 2002–2004 – placed considerable strain on the baselining approach.

The NFER undertook a survey of schools (n = 259). A further survey of young people was undertaken; it was sent to 10,300 of them (with a 63 per cent response rate). These surveys were augmented by qualitative interviews with a range of stakeholders including creative directors, programmers and brokers, creatives and a range of local authority partners. And while large studies are certainly well suited to capturing large-scale data sets, they are less able to refine their information gathering and their analytical lens part-way through the process. Consequently, as the Creative Partnerships initiative itself developed in ways that varied considerably from an initial policy idea, it became clear that it was very difficult for the evaluation to keep pace with those developments. The NFER quite properly continued to capture data in accordance with its research design, but to those staff managing the delivering of the programme these were data that increasingly felt less in step with the inputs and outcomes that were actually occurring as a result of the initiative. For example, as part of the baselining exercise, the NFER sought to establish levels of participation among Creative Partnerships schools with the arts and cultural sector, and when it was discovered that there was already a high degree of engagement, it became difficult to attribute the level of value added by Creative Partnerships (Sharp et al., 2006, p. 13). Meanwhile, the deliverers of Creative Partnerships suggested in national team meetings that while existing levels of visits to museums and galleries, to cite just one example, were indeed a measure of a school's connectedness to the sector, such measures did little to explore the qualitative shifts in the nature, type and effects of those relationships brought about by Creative Partnerships' activities. Quantitative measures of growth were not effective ways of charting deeper shifts in the nature of cultural and creative provision to schools.

So, while some rich and revealing case studies were added by the NFER to complement the survey design, the questionnaire element seemed to reflect an abstract conception of the programme that had already, by early 2005, been superseded on the ground (Sharp *et al.*, 2006).

A meta-analysis of commissioned research

With the national evaluation of the pilot years of Creative Partnerships giving us back only a partial account of impact, we turned our attention to those smaller studies that had been commissioned locally by area office staff. In 2005, we surveyed all existing local research through a meta-analysis (Sefton-Green, 2005) and found that the programme had again been evaluated somewhat unevenly in terms of the impacts it might have had. Many of the approaches to local research exhibited a series of polarities that neatly described the history underpinning research in this sector – from story-based advocacy studies that placed a premium on the development of individual self-expression through to more functionalist accounts of small groups of young people acquiring 'core curricula' skills (such as literacy and numeracy) as a result of engaging in a programme of creative learning.

The research reviewed as part of the meta-analysis comprised sixty locally commissioned reports. An analysis of these reports suggested a categorization of findings in terms of scope (the size and duration of the activity being reported on) and kind (the methodological and theoretical perspective behind the research), as well as the style, address and implied readership of the report or research. The typology pointed to where Creative Partnerships had located its research and evaluation energies to date and where there may have been high degrees of overlap and repetition. Our aim was for this categorization and possible aggregation of accounts of effect to help define the next phase of nationally driven research and evaluation activities. In summary, we found, broadly speaking, that four types of local research had been undertaken: area evaluations, accounts of practice, accounts of process, and emergent or related issues.

Area evaluations

There were four local areas covered by the area evaluations. Although different in ambition and style, these evaluations tended to offer accounts of practice and process on the basis of interview and observation. They relied on self-reporting and they did not offer wholesale statistical summaries of operations, taking instead as their focus the description and labelling of the distinctiveness of Creative Partnerships' activity. This was undertaken as a form of *capturing achievement*. Their credibility arose substantially from their use of universities and academics to validate achievement.

Accounts of practice

Around half of the reports surveyed fell into this category. They ranged from full book-length reports (e.g. Brice Heath, Paul-Boehncke, & Wolf, 2005) to small-scale, single-classroom, single-project accounts (e.g. Robey, 2004). The use of methods to analyse practice was diverse and the use of reporting techniques equally wide-ranging. Some accounts of practice were merely publications describing events or activities (e.g. the descriptions of conferences and events held in Birmingham, such as 'The Creative City').

On the other hand, some attempted complex analyses of learning (e.g. Miles, 2004), drawing on explicit theoretical understanding and/or grounded in a variety of conceptual affiliations.

The style of presentation and choice of research methods varied here too. There was a continuum of styles, with an emphasis on layout and visual imagery on the one hand (e.g. Anon., 2004) and on tightly argued study on the other. Most accounts in this category tended to be loose kinds of 'case study'. Some of these were elaborate (e.g. Miles, 2004; Applied Ethnographics, 2005), others more superficial (e.g. Nicol, 2005), and/or very small-scale (e.g. Jukes, 2004). While scale is not always an indicator of depth or reach, many studies in this category did slip between anecdote and case study, and are basically *advocacy and argument* forms of research (e.g. Brice Heath & Wolf, 2004, 2005; Brice Heath *et al.*, 2005). The absence of peer review and strict academic lenses to regulate these approaches meant on the one hand that such styles remain more accessible and useful for practitioners, but on the other that they can lack robustness and validity.

Accounts of process

Nearly a third of the research fell into the category of accounts of process. Here the commissioning agency, usually a local Creative Partnerships office, was keen to validate how it had worked during an initial or pilot phase. The emphasis was on describing processes and procedures. The main topic of study was frequently partnerships and the relationship of artist to curriculum. In some cases, the processes were analysed from comparative perspectives across Creative Partnerships area offices (e.g. Best, Craft & Jeffrey, 2004) but were mainly within a single Creative Partnerships (e.g. Haines, 2004). Most of these kinds of reports rely on self-reporting and are concerned to validate Creative Partnerships' approaches, and/or at best make recommendations for processes or procedures to be developed or changed (e.g. Woolf *et al.*, 2004). Most of these reports use a case-study approach.

Emergent or related issues

Studies were also organized around thematic issues and attempted to map out issues (e.g. governance, parents, young people at risk) and then show how such issues related to Creative Partnerships' activity. Where this was done, the exemplification from Creative Partnerships was necessarily slight. Studies of how Creative Partnerships might have been addressing broader capacity-building issues (initial teacher training, continuous professional development) fitted in here and followed standard evaluation models (e.g. Wood, 2005). This category of studies explored more of the indirect and wider effects and impacts of Creative Partnerships.

In general, *locally commissioned* research had usually been designed in isolation from other studies occurring in other Creative Partnerships areas at the same time, and with the following aims in mind:

- to reflect on delivery processes with (in some cases) the aim of changing and improving these;
- to describe and analyse impact, both in terms of quality and quantity;
- as illustrative and advocacy material for local stakeholders;

- to establish and develop theoretical and conceptual understandings of creative learning;
- to meet the differing interests and needs of different audiences in terms of its focus on particular topics (e.g. built environment or emotional literacy).

Also, it used a range of different metrics and methodologies, thus seeking to produce evidence based on a variety of values and framed in different languages.

Although this created difficulties inasmuch as the separate research projects, often just focusing on one Creative Partnerships area, were extremely difficult to aggregate into a coherent national 'whole', it was also the case that during the earliest stages of delivering the initiative there were pluralistic interests in the work, stemming from a range of stake-holder perspectives. These included headteachers, local authorities, parents, young people, artists and others. Reflecting on these often competing needs, we realized that as a national research team we would need to construct ways of admitting plurality while injecting the missing elements, namely cross-area comparisons, commonality of method and approach, and a more consistent way of monitoring the programme nationally, while encouraging more sharing of data between different commissioned researchers and teams.

Some simple first steps to introduce greater consistency were gradually introduced throughout 2005. These took a number of forms but essentially comprised the following:

- bringing to an end the direct local commissioning of work (this helped avoid dupli-cation and repetition);
- opening a nationally moderated peer-reviewed 'call for research' (this helped promote variety but enabled us to insist on elements of cross-comparison, thus avoiding a focus on just one Creative Partnerships area and opening us up to agendas outside of the need to commission research looking at impact solely for the purposes of accountability);
- gathering all extant researchers then currently engaged in work for day seminars to help make the act of synthesizing findings and locating common themes an integral part of collaborative reflection (this helped us to share data and emergent knowledge across active research projects);
- producing synthesizing texts in the form of literature reviews that made shorter work of key studies across many disciplines (this helped fill some of the perceived 'knowledge gap' left by the cessation of locally commissioned research).

In conjunction with this new research programme, there were two important developments in monitoring and evaluation which proved to be significant first steps in the process of establishing Creative Partnerships in its current formulation:[5] a creative learning programme organized into three main school strands. The following sections will deal with each of these changes in turn.

Programme development: a focus on schools and a move to self-evaluation

We have already mentioned the decision taken by DCMS and DfES in June 2003 to roll out the Creative Partnerships programme to twenty-five new areas in two phases. This meant it also became necessary to renegotiate the policy framework. At this stage, the high-level focus was still very much on access to culture rather than foregrounding 'creative learning', as shown by the first few lines of the new Policy and Delivery Agreement (PDA) 2004–2006, which positioned Creative Partnerships as '[e]nhancing access to a fuller cultural and sporting life for children and young people and giving them the opportunity to develop their talents to the full' (Creative Partnerships, 2004, p. 5).

But our observations of practice in schools, combined with the emergent findings, began to reveal a process of educational change and creative learning that was understood by each school very much on its own terms. Consequently, the detail of the PDA as it went through a process of negotiated revision with the DCMS and DfES began to reflect this: the focus started to shift much more to educational priorities. The overall DCMS priority then translated into the overall aim of Creative Partnerships, namely to 'foster effective, sustainable partnerships' between schools and the cultural sector to enable 'young people to develop their learning, both across and beyond the formal curriculum'. And although, as described earlier in the chapter, the DfES contribution to Creative Partnerships (£2.5 million) was covered by a separate financial memorandum, the objectives described in the DCMS Policy and Delivery Agreement also began to reference 'whole school improvement and personalised learning' (DCMS, 2004, p. 8). Finally, the only two targets that were numerically defined related to student attendances and how many teachers had received further professional development, rather than any impact Creative Partnerships was having on 'enhancing access' to cultural opportunities.

So, from an initial strong emphasis on cultural access there emerged a stronger theme around school change and improvement. The Creative Partnerships research team was left to resolve how best to make sense of this new focus.

At the same time, from 2005, a self-evaluation model that had been developed by one of the original sixteen areas (Kent) was rolled out across the country on a pilot basis. The model had been developed by Creative Director Anna Cutler and her team, based on literature about creativity and the team's own experience and observations of the Creative Partnerships programme in Kent. It took as its basic structure nine elements of creativity (Cropley, 2001) and divided participants into three groups (young people, teachers and creative practitioners) to ensure that all views were captured and that observations were triangulated. Each group was asked about its members' learning in relation to these nine elements, and then about the learning of the other two groups. In addition to that, all groups were asked to consider a number of inputs, including what language, skills, values and qualities were brought to the project by the creative practitioner. For the first time, participants in Creative Partnerships projects, including area office staff, were being asked explicitly to consider the rationale for the choices made at key stages of their programme management. This had the double effect of promoting a new common discourse to describe valued outcomes and of serving as an instrument for ongoing management of individual projects by the area offices. A key aspect of this model was that what might count as evidence of impact was negotiated and understood on participants' own terms, so while there were common categories broadly describing effect, there was room for each participant to describe in his or her own terms the ways in which change might be said to have occurred. We also decided, with a view to ensuring appropriate levels of rigour, to include an externally led annual audit of this process.

Our decision to roll out this model of self-evaluation using a common national framework was informed by work undertaken by Earl and Katz (2006), which suggested that

> [t]he notion of using external auditors for self-evaluation is gaining recognition within the evaluation community. This process fuses the power of self-evaluation for focusing

reflection by the key decision-makers and building organizational capacity for change with the rigour and credibility of external evaluation experts who undertake routine audits.

(p. 4)

The introduction of this self-evaluation model was intended to replace the varied approaches to externally led evaluation happening locally, as described earlier, and also to identify what was common across all area programmes.

A mosaic approach to accounts of impact and effect

So far, we have described a process that married up an inherited body of previously commissioned local research and evaluation from the early years of Creative Partnerships (2002–2005) with a refocused need to make some high-level sense of the programme across the country during the latter period of Creative Partnerships (2006–2009). In this section, we want to consider the particular value this research and evaluation 'mosaic' might offer.

We have already spoken of the instrumentalist approach that at first underpinned the government response to the NACCCE report: the need to meet economic and educational demands, most of which were by their very nature unforeseeable and underdefined. We have also referred to the history of arts education and its evaluation. The Creative Partnerships research and evaluation programme needed to traverse this terrain and provide evidence that could attest to the programme's impact in relation to all of the agendas we have so far described: accounts of pupil attainment, development of new skills, and broader shifts in educational systems and pedagogy.

This gradual shift in focus, privileging the needs of schools and harnessing the potential benefits of cultural and creative practice in relation to an improvement agenda, was also an indication of how important educational impacts were politically. As well as reflecting the learning we were accumulating about the effectiveness of Creative Partnerships, it was important also to make a strong political case for the continuation and expansion of the work. In 2007, during the build-up to the government's allocation of public funds through the Comprehensive Spending Review process, we needed to build evidence that clearly demonstrated the value and impact of Creative Partnerships within the education sector.

It is clear that the research and evaluation programme Creative Partnerships developed came to define to some extent both its purpose and its achievements. The changes grew initially out of the policy discourse that framed the whole initiative in 2002, but as the pace and coverage of programme delivery grew and as findings emerged from research Creative Partnerships had commissioned, it became necessary to refine the programme and the systems underpinning it. As we came to understand the way Creative Partnerships was being used within a school improvement context, we responded by investigating that issue in more depth. In turn, this contributed to changes in policy and a refinement of our core purpose. Whether Creative Partnerships would have been able to gain as deep an understanding if we had maintained a single, overarching national evaluation rather than a series of studies that emerged from reflections on delivery of the programme is debatable. However, we would contend that this thematic approach allowed us to play to the strengths of research and evaluation in this sector and to create narratives of effect that drew on the strongest possible evidence. The range of research we commissioned was an exploration of key elements of the Creative Partnerships initiative, focusing variously on school change, youth voice, parental engagement, impacts on pupil attainment and behaviour, the contribution to the creative and cultural economy, and also the development of a national self-evaluation model.[6]

At the heart of this process, and through our own journey depicting impacts of a national initiative, there may be joint lessons in the construction of value and the understanding of effect, in terms both of cultural work with young people and the systemic effects on schools as organisations. It is a paradox of creative work that often the most profound and lasting impacts can happen unexpectedly and in unintended ways. Additionally, the changes happen incrementally over time, becoming absorbed in ways that make them almost impossible to differentiate from what appear to be new norms and habits. The link between intention and result is often unforeseen or, when intended, part of a complex mix of factors, and so can only be rationalized *post hoc*. This is a major challenge for funders, who want to have outputs and outcomes that can be agreed up front for significant spans of time and that imply (even if they do not state) basic definitions of the core purposes of large-scale interventions or national programmes. While this is responsible and ethical, particularly when we consider that this work is publicly funded, it also needs to incorporate measures of flexibility and adaptability. Programmes seeking to explore or develop skills associated with arts, culture and creativity need to be able to accommodate the fundamental principle that creative endeavour is itself an outcome, not solely the vehicle for a series of other agendas.

In the Ofsted (Office for Standards in Education) report *Learning: Creative approaches that raise standards* (2010), we begin to see evidence that these changes in our approach to project evaluation are taking effect:

> Effective steps have been taken to:
>
> - improve clarity, rigour and coherence in selecting schools to participate
> - use local knowledge to direct resources and to challenge specific schools, for example ones where the local authority has pointed to dull learning and hard-to-shift underachievement
> - monitor systematically, tracing the impact of targeted intervention
> - clarify roles, linked to planning and evaluation, to ensure that interventions are realistically aligned to pupils' starting points and meet the needs of specific groups.
> (Ofsted, 2010, p. 41)

With Ofsted beginning to value explicitly the role of Creative Partnerships in school change and with a degree of fit between our approach to self-evaluation and broader systems of charting educational development (such as the widely used School Improvement Plan), it is increasingly possible to find a common thread running through the language of creative education and the discourse of school improvement.

When we have been thinking of our national studies exploring the nature and effect of the Creative Partnerships initiative from an assessment of the links with attainment and attendance, through to more elusive concepts of ethos and 'youth voice',[7] down to evaluations of individual projects, the underlying research and evaluation principles have been the same. We have created parameters and frameworks, we have provided principles and themes, we have given shape and definition to the possible start points for all this work – but thereafter the key has been to let the participants find their own way, articulating accounts of impact for themselves, and for us to remain responsive and to make changes of our own where necessary.

In setting out in broad terms the key developments of our approach to research, we wanted primarily to suggest the importance of coordinating a national overview through a 'mosaic' approach – a way of cross-comparing across locations and themes, remaining sensitive to local difference, and using metrics and analytical tools that afforded us opportunities to 'aggregate' key findings. Even where locality and specific school needs are the key principles underpinning programme delivery, there are strong reasons to ally a centrally driven research strategy to this grounded approach. We feel that our way of coming at these challenges has helped the programme navigate the important learning spaces between policy and delivery, and to have the time to reflect and redefine itself. Throughout this process of understanding, the key elements of the Creative Partnerships offer have been scaffolded by a theoretically driven account of impact that we hope will contain lessons for large-scale educational interventions beyond the life of the current initiative.

Notes

1 www.creative-partnerships.com.
2 Over the period Creative Partnerships has been running (from 2002 to date), annual funding from government has been as follows: 20002/03, £22.5m; 2003/04, £26.8m; 20004/05, £27.8m; 2005/06, £34.9m; 2006/07, £36.5m; 2007/08, £37.5m; 2008/09, £38.3m; but in each of these years, the only rise came from the DCMS, with the Education Department funding remaining at £2.5m per annum.
3 Each local Creative Partnerships team usually comprised four full-time staff members: a Creative Director, an Operations Manager, a Creative Programmer and a Team Assistant.
4 Letter from Mela Watts, Divisional Manager, Department of Education and Skills, to Peter Hewitt, Chief Executive of the Arts Council, February 2004.
5 In 2009, the Creative Partnerships programme and team were transferred from Arts Council England to a new organization, Creativity, Culture & Education (CCE), an independent charity set up in 2008. See www.creativitycultureeducation.org.
6 See the research pages of the CCE website, www.creativitycultureeducation.org.
7 See www.creativitycultureeducation.org/research-impact/currentresearchprojects.

References

Abbs, P. (2003) *Against the flow: Education, the arts and postmodern culture.* London: RoutledgeFalmer.

Anon. (2004). *Dancing, learning, dancing, learning.* Report for Creative Partnerships Slough.

Applied Ethnographics. (2005). *Boyz2Men.* Report for Creative Partnerships Nottingham.

Best, P., Craft, A., & Jeffrey, B. (2004). *Creative Friends model within Creative Partnerships Black Country.* Report for Creative Partnerships. Wolverhampton: Black Country Creative Partnerships.

Brice Heath, S., & Wolf, S. (2004). *Visual learning in the community school.* Kent: Creative Partnerships.

Brice Heath, S., & Wolf, S. (2005). *Dramatic learning in the primary school.* Durham/Sunderland: Creative Partnerships.

Brice Heath, S., Paul-Boehncke, E., and Wolf, S. (2005). *Made for each other: Creative sciences and arts in the secondary school.* London: Creative Partnerships, Arts Council England.

Creative Partnerships. (2002). Creative Partnerships Policy Framework. Internal document.

Creative Partnerships. (2004). Creative Partnerships Policy and Delivery Agreement. Internal document.

Cropley, A. J. (2001). *Creativity in education and learning: A guide for teachers and educators.* London: RoutledgeFalmer.

DCMS (Department for Culture, Media and Sport). (2001). *Culture and creativity: The next ten years.* Retrieved on 20 November 2009 from www.culture.gov.uk/images/publications/Culture_creative_next10.pdf

DCMS. (2004). Creative Partnerships: Policy and Delivery Agreement. Internal document.

Earl, L. M., & Katz, S. (2006). Review of Creative Partnerships Evaluation Plan. Internal report for Creative Partnerships, Arts Council England.

Haines, L. (2004). *The lead artist in Nottingham schools.* Report for Creative Partnerships Nottingham.

Jukes, A. (2004). *Developing creativity for learning in Caldmore Primary School.* Report for Creative Partnerships Black Country.

Miles, S. (2004). *Learning creativity through young people's lives.* Report for Creative Partnerships Durham and Sunderland.

NACCCE (National Advisory Committee on Creative and Cultural Education). (1999). *All our futures.* Department for Education and Employment and Department for Culture, Media and Sport. London: DfEE.

Nicol, G. (2005). *Evaluation of Excite.* Report for Creative Partnerships Black Country.

Ofsted. (2010). *Learning: Creative approaches that raise standards.* London: The Stationery Office.

Robey, N. (2004). How did The Emerald Cave provide opportunities for play with young children? School's internal report. Birmingham.

Sefton-Green, J. (2005). A 'meta-level' study of Creative Partnerships evaluation and research. Internal Report. London: Creative Partnerships, Arts Council England.

Sharp, C., Pye, D., Blackmore, J., Brown, E., Eames, A., Easton, C., Filmer-Sankey, C., Tabary, A., Whitby, K., Wilson, R., & Benton, T. (2006). *National evaluation of Creative Partnerships.* Slough, UK: NFER.

Wood, D. (2005). *Evaluation of Creative Partnerships CPD.* London: Arts Council England, Creative Partnerships.

Woolf, F. *et al.* (2004). *Training and development needs of artists working in participatory settings in the West Midlands.* Report for Creative Partnerships Black Country.

Index

Page numbers in *italics* refer to tables; *n* indicates endnote.